The Case for Marriage

THE CASE FOR
Marriage

Why Married People

Are Happier, Healthier,

and Better Off Financially

Linda J. Waite

Maggie Gallagher

BROADWAY BOOKS

New York

To Rafe

Visit our website at www.broadwaybooks.com

First Broadway Books trade paperback edition published November 2001

Designed by Carla Bolte

The Library of Congress has cataloged the hardcover as follows:

Waite, Linda J.
The case for marriage/Linda J. Waite and Maggie Gallagher.—1st ed.
p.   cm.
Includes bibliographical references and index.
1. Married couples—United States—Psychology.   2. Man-woman relationships—United States.   3. Single people—United States—Psychology.   I. Gallagher, Maggie.   II. Title.
HQ536.W33 2000
360.81´0973—dc21   00-022672

ISBN 0-7679-0632-2

1   3   5   7   9   10   8   6   4   2

Contents

A Note on Research Sources

This book is based on original research by Linda Waite and on her synthesis of hundreds of cross-disciplinary scientific studies (most based on large, nationally representative samples) in sociology, economics, medicine, psychology, sexology, and law. Together, these studies investigate the effects of marriage on virtually all demographic groups: young, middle-aged, and old; Anglo and African-American; the well-to-do and the poor; men and women.

The specific couples described in this book are taken from a variety of sources, including The American Family Panel, a joint qualitative research project of the Institute for American Values; Rutgers University; and the Religion, Culture, and Family Project of the University of Chicago Divinity School. The research was carried out under the direction of Norval Glenn of the University of Texas and Benjamin Zablocki of Rutgers University, and funded in part by the Lily Endowment. Names of these couples and others interviewed by Maggie Gallagher have been changed. Quotations from interviews done by other researchers are identified by author, title, and page number of the published source. Anecdotes about married and cohabiting couples drawn from this and other qualitative research projects are used for illustrative purposes only. Their inclusion here does not imply that the researchers who conducted these interviews endorse all our conclusions.

The Vow

I take thee to have and to hold, from this day forward, for better for worse, for richer for poorer, in sickness and in health, to love and to cherish, till death do us part, according to God's holy ordinance and thereto I give thee my troth.

With this ring, I thee wed, with my body I thee worship, and with all my worldly goods I thee endow.

—The Book of Common Prayer, 1552

Duly conscious of the solemn obligations of marriage, the bride-groom made the following declaration to his bride: "Be conse-crated unto me as my wife according to the laws of Moses and Israel. I will love, honor, and cherish you; I will protect and support you, and I will faithfully care for your needs, as prescribed by Jewish law and tradition." And the bride made the following declaration to the groom: "In accepting the wedding ring, I pledge you all my love and devotion, and I take upon myself the fulfillment of all the duties incumbent upon a Jewish wife."

—From the *Ketubah,* the Jewish marriage contract

1

THE MARRIAGE WARS:

Five Myths of the Postmarriage Culture

In America over the last thirty years, we've done something unprecedented. We have managed to transform marriage, the most basic and universal of human institutions, into something controversial.

For perhaps the first time in human history, marriage as an ideal is under a sustained and surprisingly successful attack. Sometimes the attack is direct and ideological, made by "experts" who believe a lifelong vow of fidelity is unrealistic or oppressive, especially to women.

"Even in the early 1960s," sum up social historians Steven Mintz and Susan Kellogg, "marriage and family ties were regarded by the 'human potential movement' as potential threats to individual fulfillment as a man or a woman. The highest forms of human needs, contended proponents of the new psychologies, were autonomy, independence, growth, and creativity," which marriage often thwarted. The search for autonomy and independence as the highest human good blossomed with the women's movement into a critique of marriage per se, which the more flamboyant feminists denounced as "slavery," "legalized rape," and worst of all, "tied up with a sense of dependency."

"From this vantage point," Mintz and Kellogg note, "marriage increasingly came to be described as a trap, circumscribing a woman's social and intellectual horizons and lowering her sense of self-esteem."[1]

Even today scholars warn, as one 1995 college textbook put it, "[M]arriage has an adverse effect on women's mental health."[2] Reflecting both these broader trends and this expert consensus, the proportion of high-school-senior girls who agreed that most people will have fuller and happier lives if they choose legal marriage rather than staying single or just living with someone dropped about one-fourth (or ten percentage points) between 1976 and 1992, while the opinion of boys remained unchanged.[3] Indeed, a journalist recounts the time she congratulated a twenty-four-year-old woman on her impending nuptials. "She grabbed my hand, held it, and said with emotion, 'Thank you!' As it turns out, I'd been the only woman to offer her congratulations without immediately expressing worry that she'd done the wrong thing." Her friends "simply couldn't fathom why she'd tossed away her freedom."[4]

But for the most part, the war on marriage is not a frontal assault from outside enemies but a sideways tug-of-war inside each of us between competing values: between rights and needs, between individualism and community, between fear and hope, between freedom and love. On the one hand, we cherish marriage as the repository of our deepest hopes and wishes to forge stable families, to find lasting love. On the other hand, we fear being "tied down" or "trapped" and jealously guard our right to redefine ourselves and our lives, with or without our partners' consent.

Mel Harris (the actress who played Hope on *thirtysomething*), a twice-divorced mother who understands "the logistical problems that can only arise when dealing with three kids and six sets of parents," captures something of the ambivalence toward marriage all Americans share in varying degrees: "The other day [my son] Byron asked me if I was ever going to marry again, and I told him the truth: I don't know. . . . Some people might think I perceive marriage in a flippant way because I have been divorced twice. I'm not proud of the divorces. I feel marriage is a serious, sacred thing."[5]

Despite the startling rise in divorce, cohabitation, and unwed parenthood, marriage remains a core value and aspiration of many Americans. One might imagine that, as Professor Norval Glenn puts it, "Americans are marrying less and succeeding less often at marriage because alternatives have become more attractive, relative to marriage, than they once were." But, Glenn continues, survey data on attitudes toward marriage provide "scant evidence for it."

We aren't as certain anymore about whether marriage is good for other people, but when it comes to their own life goals, Americans put marriage at the top of the list. Ninety-three percent of Americans rate "having a happy marriage" as either one of the most important, or very important objectives. Asked to select their top two goals, a majority of Americans included a happy marriage as one of the choices, far outpacing such other life goals as "being in good health" (35 percent) or even having "a good family life" (36 percent). In 1992 the number-one aspiration of high-school seniors was "having a good marriage and family life," and the proportion of seniors calling that goal "extremely important" has actually risen over the last two decades.[6] Only 8 percent of American women consider remaining single an ideal, a proportion that has not changed over the last generation.[7]

The paradox, as Glenn writes, is that "marriage remains very important to adult Americans—probably as important as it has ever been—while the proportion of Americans married has declined and the proportion successfully married has declined even more."[8]

Americans are still the marrying kind. But our ideas about what marriage means have changed in subtle ways that undermine our ability—as individuals or as a society—to achieve the goals of wedlock, creating a lasting love between a man and a woman, and a firm bond of mutual support between a mother and a father.

When it comes to marriage, Americans have both high hopes and debilitating fears. As two scholars put it after an exhaustive study of the attitudes of today's college students, "They are desperate to have only one marriage, and they want it to be happy. They don't know whether this is possible anymore."[9]

But the dreams and hopes of young Americans to forge more perfect unions are hampered by five myths that, despite the recent revival of interest in marriage, remain powerfully, if thoughtlessly entrenched in the conventional wisdom. For although marriage as an ideal still holds a firm fascination in Americans' minds, we believe that it is fair to describe America as a society on the verge of becoming a postmarriage culture. A postmarriage culture is not one in which nobody ever makes it to the altar. Rather, it is a culture in which marriage is viewed as unnecessary, or, strictly speaking, optional—a private taste rather than a matter of urgent shared concern.

Five Myths of the Postmarriage Culture

Postmarriage Myth 1: "Divorce is usually the best answer for kids when a marriage becomes unhappy."

Whether or not parents are married, many experts believe, is not what really counts. What matters is the quality of relationship between parents and between parent and child. Staying married "for the sake of the kids" thus doesn't make sense, because if you are in an unhappy marriage, your children will probably be better off if you divorce anyway.

"Many parents may indeed stay together because they believe divorce will harm their children," warn therapists Mel and Pat Krantzler in the new 1998 edition of their best-seller *Creative Divorce*. "What they fail to realize is that . . . more harm will result from 'staying together' than divorcing."[10]

This perspective is what most experts teach and what most Americans believe these days. It is certainly true that an abundance of evidence confirms that parents who fight a lot damage their kids. But is divorce always the better answer? In chapter 9 we'll tell you what the latest research shows about the circumstances under which divorce may be better for kids than continuing a marriage. And in chapter 10 we reveal new findings about what actually happens to very unhappily married couples who decide to stick it out rather than divorce. The results will surprise you.

Postmarriage Myth 2: "Marriage is mostly about children; if you don't have kids, it doesn't matter whether you cohabit or marry or stay single."

Staying in an unsatisfying marriage is pure "self-sacrifice" that we say unhappy adults should, or, more often these days, should not make on their children's behalf. In chapters 4 through 9, we look at the surprising new data documenting the powerful effect getting and staying married has on the well-being of adults. We will show you how, in some cases, for some people, marriage can literally make the difference between life or death.

Postmarriage Myth 3: "Marriage may be good for men, but it is bad for women, damaging their health and self-esteem and limiting their opportunities."

This is one of the most powerful and widespread of postmarriage myths. Experts and ordinary women alike tend to agree these days that for women, wedlock is risky business. "[Engels's] ideas have been criticized by radical, socialist and Marxist feminists," says a 1994 textbook, "but the central argument he makes about the connection of marriage and the oppression of women is one upon which they agree."[11] Professor Scott Coltrane of the University of California at Riverside applauds an author for "trying to figure out what good the institution of marriage is" because, he explains, "historically, marriage has been used (mostly by men) to regulate women's sexuality, control wealth, and exploit the labor of others."[12] "Marriage protects men from depression and makes women more vulnerable," says University of Washington psychologist Neil Jacobson in *USA Today*. "It is the best evidence that marriage is an institution that primarily benefits men."[13]

Ideas like these are now generally accepted, at least by educated women. But are they true? In chapter 12 we examine what the latest scientific evidence can tell us about the widespread belief that "his" marriage is far, far better than "hers." Does marriage affect men and women differently? And if so, is it really true that when it comes to wedded bliss, men grab all the goodies and women are left holding an empty bag? Who is really happier in a marriage? Here are the facts any mother advising a daughter, or any woman contemplating marriage—or divorce—needs to know.

Postmarriage Myth 4: "Promoting marriage and marital obligation put women at risk for violence."

The prevailing wisdom about the relationship between marriage and domestic violence goes something like this: Getting married puts women at risk for domestic violence because men often view their wives as property. The increasing rates of divorce are good because they show women can escape from domestic violence more easily now. Thus, efforts to enforce the marriage vow—to limit or delay divorce—literally threaten women's lives.

Does the scientific evidence support this bleak view of marriage? In chapter 11 we take a look at how marriage affects rates of domestic violence and stand the conventional wisdom on its head. You'll find out what kind of relationship really does put women (and their children) at special risk for violence and abuse, and why.

These four myths represent some of the fears and anxieties standing in the way of rebuilding stronger marriages. But the most powerful and dangerous myth is also the easiest to miss—because it goes to the heart of changes in our understanding of what the marriage relation is. The biggest change is the most subtle: Increasingly we tend to view marriage not as an objective fact but a subjective emotion—an inner feeling rather than an outer relation. The single most dangerous myth of the postmarriage culture is the idea that marriage—or divorce—is, can be, or should be, just another lifestyle choice, a purely personal relation created by the couple, for the couple.

Postmarriage Myth 5: "Marriage is essentially a private matter, an affair of the heart between two adults, in which no outsider, not even the children of the marriage, should be allowed to interfere."
In 1972 when Nena and George O'Neill penned their best-seller *Open Marriage,* Myth 5 was a revolutionary idea: "The meaning in marriage today must be independently forged by a man and a woman who have the freedom to find their own reasons for being and being together. . . . Only by writing their own open contract can couples achieve the flexibility they need to grow."[14] But the revolutionary slogan of yesteryear quickly becomes the cliché of tomorrow.

As sociologist Andrew Cherlin put it, married folks "are more likely today than in the past to evaluate their marriage primarily according to how well it satisfies their individual emotional needs. If their evaluation on these terms is unfavorable, they are likely to turn to divorce."[15]

Psychologists, in particular, have played a key role in persuading Americans that marriage is primarily for and about adult happiness. Deconstructing the idea that marriage has other stakeholders besides the spouses, many argued instead that it is the parents who fail to divorce who are derelict in their duties to their kids. Couples who stay together for the kids, as one licensed marriage therapist in Florida warned newspaper readers, "teach children to be extremely insecure and lacking in the skills to be intimate and caring."[16]

"[S]tudies suggest that there is less psychiatric disturbance in children from broken homes than in those from intact but unhappy homes," advises Dr. Richard Gardner in his influential guide *Psychotherapy with Children of Divorce*. "My own belief is that the effects on the children should be one of the considerations, albeit minor. The major determinants should be whether or not the parents feel there is enough pain in their relationship to warrant its being broken."[17]

Once again, public opinion shifted along with expert advice. In 1962, 51 percent of young mothers interviewed disagreed with the notion that parents who don't get along should stay together. Reinterviewed in 1985, 82 percent of these same women disapproved of staying together for the sake of the children. "It is my fundamental belief that anyone has a right to divorce rather than stay in a loveless marriage," Albuquerque family lawyer (and divorcée) Kathleen Robertson told *USA Today* confidently in 1998. "Staying is counterproductive. If you do not have a functional relationship, what sort of role model for marriage are you? If you are not happy, how will your child benefit?"[18]

Once this basic conception of marriage as an adult affair took hold, other cultural changes soon followed. As marriage ceases to be viewed as vital to children, single motherhood is elevated in status, no longer a family tragedy but just another personal option in a freedom-loving world. "If a woman can't find Prince Charming and wants a baby and is ready, society should not dictate what is acceptable," one pastor told the *Los Angeles Times*.[19] In 1994, when American teenage girls (the future mothers of America) were asked whether or not they personally would consider having a child out of wedlock, only half answered with a firm no.[20] A majority of all Americans and 70 percent of young adults agree that women should have the right to bear a child out of wedlock without reproach.[21]

Many say this new ideal represents a promotion in the status of marriage: we have higher expectations for it. No longer are people set-tling for Mr. or Mrs. O. K. Now, it's Prince Charming or nobody. But as marriage comes to be viewed as primarily a subjective, emotional rela-tion between two adults, the marriage bond begins to be described as just one of many equally valid lifestyle choices. Marriage is demoted from a uniquely honored relation to just another relationship.

Even our language reflects this shift. In many venues, from couples counseling to women's magazines, even using the word *marriage* seems to devalue respect for family and emotional diversity. New inclusive lan-guage has emerged, with *couples therapy* replacing *marriage counseling*.

A strange embarrassment or reluctance to use the word *marriage* is visible all over the Western world. The Marriage Guidance Council of Australia recently changed its name to Relationships Australia; Britain's Marriage Guidance Council metamorphosed into Relate.

A popular children's book about sex, pregnancy, and childbearing doesn't even mention the word *marriage*. The closest reference to it is in this vague phrase: "There are kids whose mothers and fathers live to-gether."[22] A U.S. textbook salesman, explaining why *marriage* seldom ap-pears anymore in the titles of college textbooks on marriage and the family, said, the word sounds too "old-fashioned" and "preachy" to stu-dents.[23]

Or more likely to the professors. Surveying the academic literature, Barbara Dafoe Whitehead observes, "[O]ne can't help but note the dwindling use of the word 'marriage.' Marriage becomes just one form of 'coupling and uncoupling' or one possible 'intimate lifestyle.' Even the words 'husband' and 'wife' are not used as routinely as one might expect. Instead, 'domestic partners,' 'pair-bonds,' or simply 'relationship' begin to denote the conjugal roles." Indeed, Whitehead continues, "a foreign vis-itor to almost any college campus in America might well conclude, after scanning course offerings, reading lists, and announcements of campus lectures, that marriage is some cultic practice, quite remote from the mainstream American experience."[24]

"There is little concern now that our society would 'disappear' if peo-ple stopped marrying . . . ," write the authors of a 1991 college textbook, shrugging off the idea that the wider society has any stake in the success of marriage, because after all, "the wife and husband team is not the only pattern for rearing children." Beautifully capturing and recapitulating the demotion of marriage into the "M-word," the textbook authors note, "Some researchers suggest that we will eventually stop thinking of marriage and lifestyle alternatives to it and develop a view of sexually based primary relationships that are expressed in a variety of forms."[25]

The subject guide for the fifty-first annual conference of the American Association for Marriage and Family Therapy in 1993 listed 277 topics and subtopics. Not once in all these subjects for conversation did the word *marriage* appear. "Odd as it may seem," David Blankenhorn points out, "the American Association for Marriage and Family Therapy has excised the word *marriage* from its basic vocabulary."[26]

Even those who believe that children are better off with two married parents fear that a renewed emphasis on the M-word may harm the many children now being raised in other situations. "The increasing diversity and turnover in family life, which largely emanates from partnership changes," one scholar argued in 1998, "makes policy built on marriage increasingly problematic and suggest that parenthood rather than marriage should be the primary policy focus, and that parenthood rather than marriage contracts should underpin family relations."[27] Similarly in the *Chronicle of Higher Education,* a Stanford professor warns against "trying to protect children by imposing a particular family pattern" on adults and instead recommends that society "draw on whatever parental and social resources are available to help children."[28]

Even lawmakers, judges, and policy analysts have begun to view marriage as part of a continuum of commitment rather than a distinct and distinctive relationship. Cities, courts, and corporations have begun to extend the benefits of marriage to other kinds of couples deemed the "functional equivalent" of marriage, and even to describe special supports for marriage as a form of "discrimination" against the unmarried. In a series of U.S. Supreme Court cases covering a variety of specific issues, the Court ruled that laws that take marital status into account violate the equal protection clause. "Employment policies that provide family health care . . . and other benefits only to married employees," proclaims Paula Ettlebrick in a January 4, 1995, letter to the *New York*

Times, ". . . constitute blatant employment discrimination." When Democratic Mayor David Dinkins first created a domestic-partnership policy in New York City, he hailed it as "a major step" in granting "close and committed relationships" the same rights as those given to "individuals bonded through the traditional concept of the family."[29]

His Republican successor, Rudy Giuliani, took the privatization of marriage one step further. In an exchange with the mayor over the further expansion of domestic-partnership benefits, John Cardinal O'Connor argued against extending marital benefits to unmarried couples because "[m]arriage matters supremely to every person and every institution in our society." The mayor responded by saying that restricting benefits to married couples violates a "healthy" division of church and state. "We're all here because people left other places because someone wanted to enforce their religious viewpoint as the view of the state."[30]

"The state should have no right to privilege or impose one form of family structure or sexuality over another," agrees Rutgers University law professor Drucilla Cornell. Taking this idea to its logical conclusion, she argues that there should be "no state-enforced single relationship— not monogamy, heterosexuality, polygamy, or polyandry." For, she continues, ". . . If we seek to repopulate the world with lasting love, it can be only on the basis of freely formed union." By which she seems to mean marriage contracts with no set duration, shape, form, or content.[31]

Because we view marriage as an inner emotion rather than an outer reality, we have a hard time conceiving that the state of being married, in and of itself, could enhance people's lives. Marriage is a piece of paper—a marker perhaps for things that matter, such as more money or better education, but in and of itself neutral in its effects. So for many years, family scholars tried to pierce the veil of marital status to uncover the "true" explanations for why married people, and children raised by married parents, seemed so much better off and why, in particular, children raised outside of marriage faced so many additional burdens and struggles. It's not marriage that matters it's—fill in the blank—race, poverty, money, education, quality of parenting that truly improves the quality of real people's lives.

As recently as the late '80s, for example, the Centers for Disease Control, in reporting higher rates of infant mortality among unmarried mothers, stated baldly that "the marital status of the mother confers neither risk nor protection to the infant; rather, the principal benefits of marriage to infant survival are economic and social support."[32] A nationally syndicated columnist could likewise confidently assert, "The children of affluent single mothers are not likely to concern us . . . they are not any more likely to become criminals than other children are."[33] As Carolyn P. Cowan, a member of the Council on Contemporary Families, recently put it, "It's not the family structure per se, it's the quality of the relationships between adults and children."[34]

Of course things such as race, income, and quality of relationships count, in the sense that all affect how well we live our lives and how our children fare. But in chapters 4 through 9, we will show you that marriage is not just a marker for these other more powerful social forces, whether it's enough money or true love as so many experts argue and so many Americans believe. We'll try to unlock the secret mechanism at work in the marital vow, to show you how and why marriage itself makes a difference. Equally important, we'll show how marriage can work its miracles only if it is supported by the whole society. Marriage cannot thrive, and may not even survive, in a culture that views it as just another lifestyle option.

So when people become afraid or reluctant to use the M-word or to base public or social support on the status of being married, marriage is indeed in trouble. In chapter 14, we'll tell you some of the steps individuals, government, faith groups, and community leaders can and must take to rebuild the marriage culture.

Most of all we hope to persuade you that privatizing marriage is profoundly counterproductive. For at the heart of the unacknowledged war on marriage is the attempt to demote marriage from a unique public commitment—supported by law, society, and custom—to a private relationship, terminable at will, which is nobody else's business. This demotion is done in the name of choice, but as we shall see in the next chapter, reimagining marriage as a purely private relation doesn't expand anyone's choices. For what it ultimately takes away from individuals is marriage itself, the choice to enter that uniquely powerful and life-enhancing bond that is larger and more durable than the immediate, shifting feelings of two individuals.

What you lose, you'll understand after reading this book, in thinking about marriage in this newly privatized way, is no less than the marriage bargain itself.

2

THE MARRIAGE BARGAIN

Is marriage merely a private, emotional relationship built by two individuals for their own private satisfaction, in which the larger society has no stake and no role?

Ask Matt and Dina, a Manhattan couple in their late thirties with a newborn baby, Mike. Both spouses took part in a pilot study on family life that was conducted in the early nineties by the Institute for American Values.

Matt runs a graphic-design business, while Dina designs theatrical costumes for a living. Matt, a funny iconoclast of a man who describes himself as "deeply, absolutely, fabulously" in love with his wife of fifteen years, describes marital love this way: "It means that I never have to worry about it or think about it or have any concern about who she is or how she will feel about me. If she came home and told me she killed somebody, I would say, 'What did he do?' I don't have any doubts about Dina."

But their relationship wasn't always like that. Over the last fifteen years, Dina and Matt have gone through a lot of the stages that contemporary couples go through: living together, marriage, divorce, and remarriage. Only unlike most couples, they married, divorced, cohabited with, and remarried each other.

Perhaps as a result of these experiences, Matt and Dina are more acutely aware of how marriage as a public act shaped their intimate relationship with each other, for good and for ill. They married for the first time "on a lark," says Matt. "She proposed to me in Bullock's."

"We were in the housewares department," confirms Dina, "and I looked around at everything—the dishes and stuff—because we had nothing. And I said to Matt, 'All this can be yours; all you've got to do is marry me.' And he said, 'Okay.' Because it was clear we weren't going anywhere. So it seemed reasonable that we should get a set of matched silverware."

But they discovered, as many cohabiting couples who marry do, that marriage is not just a ceremony. Getting married changed the way they thought about each other. And changed the way others treated them. For Matt, at twenty, the change was disorienting: "Marriage means something particular in our society," he says, "but we weren't as committed to one another as marriage actually means in this culture." They were young, far from settled down, partying with the rest of their crowd who were all still unmarried. After two years of marriage, they decided to divorce, he says, "to readjust our statutory relationship to mirror our actual relationship. We were out of sync. We weren't married, we were living together."

"It was such a disaster," says Dina, meaning the divorce, not the marriage. The problem was that if marriage didn't seem to describe their relationship properly, divorce created an even greater gap between internal and external reality: "We got divorced because we weren't getting along, not because we didn't intend to stay together," says Dina. "It was almost like we were punishing each other."

What draws couples such as Matt and Dina toward or away from this thing called marriage? What gives a piece of paper—whether a marriage license or a divorce decree—the power to transform our most intimate relationships? To answer questions such as these, we have to understand first what marriage is, what makes the marriage bargain unique. This is not as obvious as it once was.

For most of this century, our ideas about marriage were so deeply rooted, so widely accepted, as to become practically invisible. Nearly everyone got and stayed married. Married couples had kids; husbands supported wives; and wives subordinated their careers to their family's needs—working, if necessary, at the kinds of jobs that could be combined with the demanding task of making a home in the days before birth control, washing machines, and sliced bread.[1] Having children outside of wedlock was rare and obviously disreputable: not only because such children were apt to live in abject poverty but because sex outside of marriage was in itself disreputable. Unmarried pregnancy made sin visible.

Over the last two generations, this once unquestioned package of assumptions about marriage has come under a wide and varied array of cultural attacks: from feminists seeking better career opportunities for women, from welfare advocates seeking help for single-parent families, from playboy (and playgirl) philosophers discontent with restrictions on desire, and from psychologists and marriage therapists hoping to craft more emotionally satisfying relationships between men and women.

Not only the roles of men and women within marriage, but the role of marriage itself in society has become blurred. What do we mean by *marriage*? Is there a profound difference between "holy wedlock" and cohabitation? Is marriage fundamentally a social institution that must be socially constructed and supported? Or is it, as Americans increasingly tend to describe it, a private, personal, intimate, and emotional relationship built entirely by two people for their own personal happiness?

Our answers to questions such as these shape how we treat marriage, as scientists interested in studying social arrangements, as citizens crafting social policy, and as husbands and wives, mothers and fathers, friends and neighbors struggling to build lasting love.

If you feel that marriage is a purely private relationship, you will tend to believe, for example, that government has no business "privileging" marriage in any way. Policies or social attitudes favoring marriage constitute a form of discrimination against alternative sorts of relationships. No official benefits should be attached to the act of getting married. The tax code should treat your income the same whether you are married or single. Employers who provide insurance benefits for married couples shouldn't "discriminate" against unmarried couples. Ditto landlords and banks. Whether you are married or just living together, friends and relatives should treat you just the same. And if you are unhappy, it doesn't matter whether you are legally married or just romantically involved, you should decide to stay or go based on what will make you happy and fulfilled.

In this way of looking at the world, one increasingly popular in the West, marriage is essentially a vestigial personal ceremony, an external rite that is fine for the couple who wants to honor it but to which no-body else should pay any attention and upon which no important public respect or benefit should hang. If you accept this worldview, even your language will change, you will tend to refer to people as "partners" rather than spouses, to "relationships" rather than marriages. You will find yourself, almost inevitably, urging divorce when married people seem unhappy, for, to you, external structure and labels are irrelevant. If the inner relationship is not there, why keep up the façade?

If you believe that marriage is a public act and a social institution, on the other hand, the label matters very much. You see marriage as an act that changes the social world. Marriage creates obligations: between partners but also between others and the couple. You will tend to be-lieve, for example, that it is wrong to have an affair with a married per-son, even though you yourself aren't married, because it is wrong to participate in the breaking of a marriage vow, even if it is not your own. You will treat the spouses of family members differently than girlfriends or boyfriends simply because marriage makes them "part of the family" in a way that even the most intense passion between lovers does not. When other institutions—companies, government, businesses—treat married couples differently, that won't strike you as an injustice but as simple common sense: Married couples should be treated differently, be-cause marriage does make a difference. And perhaps sometimes a divorce will seem to you to be necessary, but you will always see it as a tragic event, the breaking of something sacred that should be done, if at all, only with the utmost reluctance, for truly serious reasons after all possible alternatives are exhausted.

Of course when it comes to marriage, most Americans at this point in history speak both languages. Sometimes we talk about it as a sacred covenant, bigger than the couple. And sometimes we privatize it com-pletely, agreeing as Hillary Clinton put it, "I learned a long time ago that the only two people who count in any marriage are the two who are in it."[2]

If we could persuade you, with this book, after a decade of research, of just one important new idea, it would be that this latter view of mar-riage is objectively wrong. Wrong in the sense that deep down, it is not the way, despite how we sometimes talk, most of us in America really look at marriage. And wrong in the sense that if we did adopt this view of marriage, marriage would lose its unique power. Agree to privatize marriage, in other words, and you do not expand people's choices—you effectively eliminate the choice to marry, for marriage means the purely voluntary option to raise your commitment to each other out of the purely private emotional realm.

So when we say marriage is not just a personal relationship, we are arguing both that it is not and ought not to be. Our own conclusion, drawn from the immense body of new research outlined in chapters 4 through 13, is that marriage is a social institution, not just a private relationship: Getting married doesn't merely certify a preexisting love relationship. Marriage actually changes people's goals and behavior in ways that are profoundly and powerfully life enhancing.

When Dina, for example, was asked what she had given up to get and stay married, the idea startled her. "Wow," she replied, "I don't think I gave up and I don't think that he did either. I think it was quite the opposite. As a result of being married, we were both able to do a lot more and achieve a lot more than we could alone."

While Americans do not ordinarily think about marriage in this way, Dina is right. Marriage creates not just a new unit of consumption but a new unit of production: Getting and staying married produces goods for the partners, for their children, and for the rest of society. Marriage is thus a creative act. It creates a new relation between spouses that changes the way they behave toward each other, toward their children, and toward the future.

Marriage is not only a private vow, it is a public act, a contract, taken in full public view, enforceable by law and in the equally powerful court of public opinion. When you marry, the public commitment you make changes the way you think about yourself and your beloved; it changes the way you act and think about the future; and it changes how other people and other institutions treat you as well.

The Public Side of Marriage

Americans think about marriage as an intimate, deeply personal relationship. And of course it is. But marriage, unlike other sorts of personal relationships, has an inherently public side. Marriage is what lovers do when they want to bring their love out of the merely private, internal realm of emotion and make it a social fact, something visible to and acknowledged by everybody from parents to bank clerks.

Marriage is thus not just a personal vow, it is a legally binding contract between two individuals. To be legal, a marriage must be performed by someone authorized by the state to do so, such as a judge, or a member of the clergy.

And what the law has joined, only the law can put asunder. Friends can dissolve their friendship by themselves, but it takes a judge to grant a divorce. Laws regulating divorce carry with them an implicit understanding of what marital obligations are.[3]

Marriage is also an agreement between the partners and society. This agreement, while less formal, is quite real. As sociologists know well, the force of social expectations can be as powerful as law. Married couples are expected to behave in certain ways, and most do.

Matt and Dina found out about the power of social expectations early in their marriage when they tried to reinvent the marital contract in two key areas: money and sex. Dina recalls the early years, when money was a big issue. "He always believed that you spent what you had to spend and you dealt with the consequences, and I tended to worry about it before the fact."

"How did you deal with that?" Maggie asked her, no doubt expecting some miraculous example of healthy marital communication.

"He did what he wanted to until he spent all our money, and then I said, 'Fuck you, I told you so,'" Dina replied. "I remember being so pissed with him about the money that I didn't want to sleep with him. I just thought—you're messing up my life, you're messing up my head, you're spending my money, we're broke all the time . . . you ain't getting any."

With this much turmoil over this much difference, Matt and Dina decided the practical thing to do was just to deal with money as if they were not married—to each his or her own. But because marriage is not just a private relationship, they couldn't always get others, like the IRS, for example, to agree.

"We tried to keep our finances separate," recalls Dina, "we tried desperately, because we thought that was one of the solutions that would work. But the thing is that legally you are contractually obligated in the same way. One of the things that we learned when we were married is that you can go in with ideas about how it should work, but you're bucking a major social trend. You can only change it so far. There are legal precedents you can't change; there [are] social attitudes you can't change. In the eyes of the law, we were a unit, so if he got into debt, I got into debt."

Matt and Dina ran into a similar trouble when they decided to relax the rules about marital fidelity—or at least Matt did. "One of the things that we found out also was that it didn't matter what freedom you allowed each other, no one else was going to permit that," recalls Dina. "Nobody would touch you with a ten foot pole." That is, no acquaintance of Dina's would touch Matt with a ten foot pole. "I'd go to a party, and—guys are dogs, they don't care if you're married at all," she chortles ruefully. "But the girls would not touch Matt because we were married."

After a while, they came to see those social pressures and expectations not as infringements on their freedom but simply as part of the deal, part of what they chose in freely choosing marriage. "I don't feel cheated, because that's what marriage is, and if you don't have your eyes open when you enter into it, then you shouldn't enter into it," says Dina. "Actually we run this marriage close to the letter of the law. We respect the contract that we know we signed legally."

"What is that?" Maggie asked.

"That we are responsible for each other," Dina replied without hesitation. "For each other's health, each other's well-being, mental health, financial stability. In fact, that we are each other's keepers. That, in fact, we have a responsibility to go to a fair amount of trouble in order to make sure that we stay together and we continue to be responsible for each other."

As Matt and Dina discovered to their immediate chagrin but their long-term gain, the marriage contract is really a very public package of expectations about how two people should behave and about the benefits that help them fulfill these obligations: A wife should spend weekends with the family, not friends; a husband can give his pregnant wife (but not his pregnant sister) his insurance benefits; a man or a woman should put his spouse first before the demands of parents, friends, or other family members; married people should support each other financially as well as emotionally.

Outsiders also recognize these new roles. The terms *husband* and *wife* carry with them a recognition of the legal, moral, and emotional relationship between the partners. Ask any executive secretary—If you want to get an answer for your boss over the phone out of an insurance company, a bank, or a doctor, pretend to be his wife or her husband.

Some of these privileges are accorded through social custom rather than law, which makes them all the more important. A wife can act as the agent for her husband, signing and cashing his checks, changing his plane reservations, making financial and medical decisions in his name. A husband can do the same in the name of his wife. Most husbands and wives manage their finances jointly, though there is no legal requirement that they do so.

Recent attempts by gay and lesbian couples to wed underline the reality that marriage is a social relationship, not a merely private one. Weddings cannot take place without witnesses. These ceremonies mark the passage of the partners from one status with its set of expectations to another. This passage is instantly recognizable not only to friends and family but to any stranger who glimpses a wedding band.

Gay couples can, with the help of a knowledgeable attorney, set up almost all the legal rights for their partnership that married couples get automatically at the wedding. They can have a big party for their family and friends to celebrate their "union." What gay couples cannot get is legal and social recognition of their relationship. For married couples, one's status as a member of a permanent, sexually-bonded married couple is obvious to others, even casual acquaintances; for gays, this recognition is absent and their relationship often hidden or ignored.

Ratifying the Vow

Marriage changes not only the couple's relation to each other, it changes the couple's relationship to the outside world. By choosing to marry, couples are entering a social institution that changes the way they will be treated by others, including, in many cases, the government, businesses, and religious communities.

Married individuals face different tax rates than they would if they were not married.[4] Widows can receive Social Security payments based on their husbands' earning records but only if the couples were legally married. In most companies, insurance benefits will be paid for an employee's husband but not for an employee's boyfriend.

Similarly, most religious organizations typically make sharp distinctions between married and unmarried couples, viewing marriage as, at the very least, the form of sexual relationship most pleasing to God.

Ted and Kay, another married couple interviewed for the American Family Panel, live just a few miles away from Matt and Dina, across the East River in Brooklyn. In certain respects, at least, the couples might as well be living in different universes. Ted and Kay are devout Jehovah's Witnesses, and their religion plays a powerful role in supporting marital norms, as Kay, a convert, is particularly aware.

Their religion, for example, had a profound influence on whether, when, and how they eventually married. Ted, a tall, handsome African-American who works for Con Edison, was separated from both his faith and first wife when he first met Kay, the rebel daughter of a middle-class Long Island Catholic family. They had a fling that turned into a love affair, and Kay found herself pregnant, out of wedlock, by a married man. The situation was not what she dreamed of as a girl.

For Kay and Ted, the road to marriage wasn't simple. For one thing, Jehovah's Witnesses don't permit no-fault divorce.

"The only grounds for a scriptural divorce is if someone [commits adultery]," Kay explains. "In other words, if you have two people who just weren't getting along and they got a divorce, they couldn't remarry." So Ted's first wife may have had grounds for divorce, but Ted did not. And when a divorced person wants to remarry, the Elders of the church make sure both partners understand the religious obligations they are assuming.

"That's one of the reasons that it took us so long to get married," said Kay. "You just can't get divorced—even if you get a scriptural divorce, which [Ted and his first wife] did—you just can't, like tomorrow, say I'm marrying this person now. They want you to wait. They want to make sure that you've given it thought. They talk to you. Because this was my first time getting married. They just wanted to make sure that I knew what I was doing."

Jehovah's Witnesses may take a more active role in marriage counseling than many other faiths, but most Americans define themselves as members of a religious denomination, and the vast majority say that they believe in God.[5] For people of faith, the act of getting married affects how a couple is perceived and treated within the religious community.[6]

For Kay, marriage utterly transformed how she was treated by her fellow worshippers. Now that she's married in the eyes of God and her church, she says, "We're recognized in the congregation as a family. It felt good, because it felt like now I was finally doing the right thing. I was happy because I felt, 'Now you are setting a proper example for your children.' And now we can go to meetings as a family, where before we didn't."

The social approval that religious communities give to marriage and to the married encourages people to get married in the first place and encourages them to stay married.[7]

Each case in which a social institution treats a married couple differently from singles reminds the couple that marriage matters: they are in a special relationship that's treated by society as different from any other.

Social support also means social pressure: The personal bargains individual spouses make with each other are crafted in the shadow of social expectations. When a wife urges a husband to look for a job, for example, she does not have to make an extended argument based on personal taste and preferences. Her bargaining position is immensely strengthened because she can fall back on the attitudes and expectations of the wider culture to support her position: Husbands are supposed to have jobs. Most husbands find work without ever being prodded by the wife. Increasingly, husbands are urging wives to get paying jobs, although husbands may get less leverage in this effort from social expectations, especially when children are young.

When mass unemployment strikes (as in the Great Depression, or, as some would argue, in the inner cities today), these social attitudes may inflict unjust suffering. And couples with unusual preferences—those who want the husband to stay home and take care of the kids, for example—will have to withstand a thousand little inquiries and comments from outsiders that remind them their choices are unusual.

But by and large, for most people at most times, marital roles lead men and women to act in responsible ways. The social expectations associated with marriage restrict the partners' freedom to act in ways that are contrary to the interests of the family unit.

Similarly, while husbands and wives today may negotiate actively about how many children they should have, a wife who wants a child (or who finds herself unexpectedly pregnant) is in a very different negotiating position from a girlfriend in the same state. Marriage makes a difference in what lovers expect of each other and how they behave toward each other.

Not everybody lives up to their marriage vows, of course, but the public promise of marriage as a permanent union, backed by the support of law, culture, religion, and community, makes a big difference in how men and women feel about and behave toward each other. This pervasive and implicit social recognition of the special rights and obligations of a husband to his wife and of a wife to her husband encourages the actors to play their roles fully, and in doing so, molds men and women into husbands and wives.

The Power of the Vow

The marriage contract is in one sense liberating: the security of a contract frees individuals to make long-term exchanges that leave each person better off. But any contract also necessarily constrains the parties involved: They are less "free" to break the terms of the contract. Marriage is no exception. Married people have joined their lots together. As part of this new bond, they have less freedom to act unilaterally than unmarried people—almost by definition—if they are going to live up to the promises they've exchanged.

Take sex, for example. The marriage contract specifically prohibits sex with those besides the marriage partner. By making this vow, a couple changes the nature of their sexual relationship; they are no longer free to find a new sex partner who is more attractive than the old. In exchange, each has more confidence in the fidelity of his or her partner, less anxiety about sexual performance, fewer fears of sexual abandonment, and less cause for sexual jealousy. The benefits and constraints of marriage are not so much trade-offs, as flip sides of the same coin. Marriage makes people better off in part because it constrains them from certain kinds of behavior, which, while perhaps immediately attractive (i.e., staying up all night drinking beer, or cheating on your partner) do not pay off in the long run.

Despite changing attitudes toward sex and gender roles, the substance of the marriage vow as Americans understand it has changed surprisingly little. Marriage is, above all, seen as a permanent union ("until death do us part"), which includes the promise of sexual union ("forsaking all others"), of financial union ("with all my worldly goods I do thee endow"), and of mutual support ("to love, honor, and cherish").

Each part of this public vow is part of the punch marriage packs, the secret to its power to change lives. But if one part of this package is any more important than the others, it is probably the promise of permanence.

The Promise of Permanence

Most Americans are romantics when it comes to marriage, and we are no exceptions. But to really see how marriage makes a difference, it helps to take off those rose-colored glasses for a moment and put on the grayer spectacles of an economist. For marriage is a type of partnership. And economists, it turns out, have developed the best tools for understanding how and why partnerships make partners better off. These are some of the same mechanisms that we believe underlie the impressive advantage married people demonstrate in just about every realm of life social scientists can measure, including but not limited to financial benefits.

Marriage vows include the promise to stay together, no matter what happens, until the union is broken by death. As Matt put it, "The second time, we got married with the full and complete understanding of what the institution was. . . . We were married in the sense that people and society use marriage. Not for the dishes [but] for life and forever solely with one another. That is it, we are not kids, we are not fooling around. One of us is going to die and the other one is going to be left. That is how this is going to end. No one is going away."

This long-run view is, as Matt described it, the essence of the way "people and society use marriage." Even today, with our historically high rates of divorce, most married couples define their relationship as permanent and expect it to last. More than 70 percent of adult Americans believe that "marriage is a lifelong commitment that should not be ended except under extreme circumstances." Even 81 percent of divorced and separated Americans still believe marriage should be for life.[8] And of recent marriages that are first marriages for both partners, about 60 percent will last for life.

The promise of permanence is key to marriage's transformative power. People who expect to be part of a couple for their entire lives—unless something awful happens—organize their lives differently from people who are less certain their relationship will last. The marriage contract, because it is long-term, encourages husbands and wives to make decisions jointly and to function as part of a team. Each spouse expects to be able to count on the other to be there and to fulfill his or her responsibilities. This expectation of a long-term working relationship between husband and wife leads to substantial changes in their behavior, of which the most important is, perhaps, what economists call specialization.

The Specialization Advantage

The basic purpose of any contract is to allow partners in a productive enterprise to specialize and exchange goods over time. As business people know, when the exchange between trading partners is immediate, rather than long-term, contracts aren't necessary: "I'll give you this widget now, if you'll pay me one hundred dollars now."

By contrast, contracts are made to provide the security needed to trade over time: "If I invest in expanding my widget capacity now, you'll commit to buying a set number of widgets over the next three years."

Similarly, the marriage contract gives partners the security they need to specialize and invest in each other over the long haul. Each spouse can develop some skills and neglect others, because each can count on the other to take responsibility for some of the work involved in making a home and a living.

What economists call specialization, spouses call fighting about who does what. It is sometimes a painful process in these days of shifting gender roles, but not nearly as painful over the long run, married couples tell us, as having to do everything for oneself.

Like many progressive young couples in the '80s, Matt and Dina began with the idea that, as Matt puts it, "every task should be democratically cut down the middle." What he discovered is that this is an inefficient way of divvying up the chores, because, he explains, "We both have things that we are better at. We don't split it right down the middle; you know, it is not like Thursday, you do the dishes, and I do them Friday. We fall into patterns because Dina is a classically trained girl. She knows how to cook and how to sew and how to . . . all the girl stuff—she is a total pro. So Dina tends to excel at things that are gender specific. I excel at things that tend to be gender specific: I balance the books, I keep the checkbook, I do the bills."

"He does the same amount as I do," says Dina, "I mean, we do different stuff. I do the regular scrubbing and waxing. He can't see dirt, but he does things like the shopping and the schlepping and the laundry. I don't fight with lawyers and accountants. I don't do that. He does that. That's what he does for a living. He fights with my lawyers and accountants too."

Sometimes skills and taste change over time. When she and Matt first got married, for example, Dina was the family mechanic. "[My dad] would never let me anywhere near the tools," Matt attests, "I never held a screwdriver until I moved away from home. And Dina was the first-born of parents who desperately wanted a boy and she was raised with all the attendant, you know, crawl-under-the-car-and-check-the-spark-plugs kind of stuff." As the years went by that changed. "She taught me," says Matt, "and now, as a matter of fact, I am much better than she is. I had no idea that I had aptitude for that because it was never either encouraged or explored."

Specialization increases productivity for married partners just as it does for any other economic partnership. A husband can become very good at searching for bargains or buying the highest quality products, while his wife learns to do the family finances and prepare tax forms. A wife can learn to garden and maintain the yard, while the husband becomes the expert at buying equipment and cooking gourmet meals. A wife can paint or mend, while the husband maintains the household and its machines. A husband might take the kids to the doctor, while the wife deals with the insurance company. Then husband and wife can "trade," just as countries do: one partner giving some of the goods and services he produces to his partner in exchange for goods and services that she produces.

One country might trade the steel it manufactures for the bauxite another produces; husbands and wives might trade financial management for time spent chauffeuring children. But both countries and couples are better off when they specialize and then trade goods than when they must produce everything they need all by themselves.[9]

There are a number of reasons that specialization makes partners better off. First, a partnership increases the talent pool. No one person—like no one company or no one country—can become very good at all tasks. Individuals have different tastes and skills, which point them toward different activities. Singles must accomplish all of life's tasks themselves. Even cohabiting couples, uncertain of the future, may hesitate to become dependent on each other's skill. But in a marriage, each partner can choose from among the things that have to be done, according to what he or she especially likes or does especially well. A man living alone is less likely than a married man to find that his household contains a good cook or a good financial manager.

Second, and just as important, because their partnership is permanent, married partners are able, over the course of the marriage, to specialize—getting good at some tasks because they are free to neglect others. Time and energy are limited resources. If the single man spends time polishing his cooking skills, he has less time to keep track of his money or keep his appliances functioning. Of course the same is true of women living alone, and the lack of the labor of a second adult is especially a problem for women raising children by themselves.

By specializing, husbands and wives can each master a smaller number of tasks, producing more as a team than either one could produce alone.

Specialization, Not Sex Roles

All married couples benefit from specialization, not just those who divide up life's chores along traditional gender lines. Traditionally, husbands specialized in breadwinning. Even today, men (but not women) who are high earners are more likely to marry and less likely to divorce than other men.[10]

Wives, by contrast, specialized in home and family, taking responsibility for managing the household, caring for and educating the children, doing the shopping, preparing food, and keeping order. And wives were responsible for the family's emotional life, offering support and encouragement to their husbands and a glass of milk, a cookie, and a sympathetic ear to children after school. Wives also generally managed the social life of the couple and maintained relations with the extended family, arranging holiday celebrations, recognizing birthdays and anniversaries, and organizing family visits.[11]

In America today, there is an increasing variety in the ways married couples share chores, with working wives now commonplace and househusbands not unheard of. Especially when their children are young, many couples exchange labor across traditional gender lines, but many others share both work for pay and work in the home. Seventy percent of wives now work for pay.[12] The majority of married mothers, though, either don't work or work part-time.

Some scholars have argued that strict sex roles in the family were useful because they ensured all couples would have one person who specialized in earning and one who specialized in home and family, no matter how men and women sorted themselves into individual couples.[13] But this sex-typed labor has disadvantages as well. Women were generally prepared to care for a home and family but less well prepared to support it financially, if they lost a husband to death or divorce. Even today, women living alone, and especially those raising children by themselves, are still much more likely than men in the same situation to not have enough money.[14] And men living alone are more likely than women to eat poorly, to have trouble managing their household, and to have a restricted social life.[15]

In fact in real life, both overly rigid gender roles and strict egalitarian thinking (trying to split all chores exactly fifty-fifty) can interfere with the powerful magic of specialization—the process of finding out who is good at or enjoys certain tasks.

Flexible family roles, by contrast, may increase the gains from specialization, allowing husbands and wives to take better advantage of their own individual tastes and talents. When sex roles were rigid, married couples had a harder time taking advantage of especially good fortune. Nowadays a man whose wife gets a big raise can decide to coach Little League instead of taking overtime, for example.

Marriage in Men's Lives

Even as sex differences within marriage have diminished, the role of husband still plays a unique function in the lives of men. Steven Nock argues that adolescent boys face challenges in becoming men that adolescent girls do not face in becoming women. According to Nock, "Masculinity is precarious and must be sustained in adulthood. Normative marriage does this. A man develops, sustains, and displays his masculine identity in his marriage. The adult roles that men occupy as husbands are core aspects of their masculinity."[16] The behaviors expected of married men as husbands, according to Nock, are the same behaviors expected of husbands as men. So getting married and successfully doing the things that husbands do allows men to achieve and sustain their masculinity.

When men fail to become good husbands, notes George Akerlof, they often fail to be good men. In a recent prestigious lecture, Akerlof argued that declines in marriage and parenthood for men have led to social problems such as crime and substance abuse. Akerlof argues that ". . . men settle down when they get married: if they fail to get married they fail to settle down."[17] When men delay or avoid marriage, he goes on, they continue with the often antisocial and destructive behaviors of single men. And it's the role of husband—not boyfriend or father—which seems to be key: Having children by itself does not work the same transformation in men's lives.[18]

For either men or women, when it comes to reaping the benefits of specialization, the ways in which husbands and wives divvy up life's tasks aren't the main point. Both traditional and egalitarian married couples benefit from having twice the talent pool and twice the opportunity to become household "experts" at some of the chores. Women may but don't have to become Suzy Homemaker, and men may but don't have to become Tim the Toolman to benefit from marriage. They just have to work together as a team over the long haul.

The Power of Pooling

Another secret behind the power of marriage is what economists call economies of scale and what married couples experience as the power of togetherness. The old adage "Two can live as cheaply as one" contains more than a grain of truth. Husbands and wives usually need only one set of furniture and appliances, one set of dishes, one lawn mower. They share heat and light and can watch the same TV, and in all these cases each person's use does not diminish the amount available to the other person. Similarly, by pooling their labor, married people lower not only their expenses but the amount of work that each needs to do. Cooking for two is only a bit more time-consuming than cooking for one, for example, and other chores such as paying the bills for two, may take up no more time than paying for one.

This kind of pooling means couples can have the same standard of living for much less money or effort than can an adult living alone. The two-can-live-as-cheaply-as-one argument is made official in government poverty guidelines, which are based on actual expenditures of individuals and families and suggest that two people sharing a household, meals, furniture, and a bathroom need only about 30 percent more income to avoid being poor than one person does.[19] In other words, just getting married boosts your standard of living by about a third.

True, in theory, couples don't need to make it legal to reap the economies of scale that go with living together. However, because (as we shall see) most cohabiting unions are short-lived, live-in lovers hesitate to share expenses to the degree that married people do. For when a cohabiting couple splits up, only one person will get the TV; the other will have to get either a new partner or a new TV in short order.

In theory, ordinary roommates could also benefit from economies of scale. However, money isn't everything. Few people want to share a bathroom—much less a bedroom—with someone to whom they are not particularly close. So one of the first purchases that many people make when they can afford it is a place of their own. Cohabitors and roommates can in theory enjoy most of the same economies of scale as married couples but usually for only a short period of time in practice.

"For Better or for Worse": The Marital Insurance Benefit

Married people are better off because they have someone who will take care of them when disaster strikes. A spouse acts as a sort of small insurance pool against life's uncertainties, reducing the need to protect oneself from unexpected events by oneself alone. Like the loss of a job, for example. Charnav, an Israeli immigrant, explains how she and her husband, Sam, back each other up financially: "During certain periods like when my daughter was young I stayed home with her. Both of us have gone through periods of losing our jobs, being laid off with the economic situation, and then we were just equally supportive of each other. When he had to stay home, I never resented it in any way. That's just the way it was. We share equally . . . there's no such thing as your money or my money . . . it's all ours."

But marriage also provides a kind of insurance that money can't buy. A husband may help care for his wife following her surgery; a wife may assist her husband in therapy for his bad back.[20] And if one partner becomes disabled, the other may fill in, working more to replace lost earnings, providing care for the disabled spouse, or doing the household tasks the other is no longer capable of doing: reading small print, opening jars, or getting up from a low chair. This kind of insurance explains why married couples are more likely to live independently long after disability affects one of the spouses, when a single person in the same situation would be in a nursing home or other care facility.[21]

"Cleaving unto You Alone": The Value of Primacy and Exclusivity

Marriage makes you better off, because marriage makes you very important to someone. When you are married you know that someone else not only loves you but needs you and depends upon you. This knowledge makes marriage a contract like no other.

We don't have to like the people from whom we buy a house or car, or from whom we borrow money. But most Americans marry for love. To be successful, marriage needs to meet some of the emotional needs of the partners.

Individuals may have many emotionally fulfilling relationships—with children, with parents, with their siblings, or with friends. But the emotional relationship that underlies marriage is fundamentally different from these because of the couple's exclusive sexual bond.

For example, Karen Ryback and her husband have been together eighteen years. But when asked about how to express love in marriage, she responded instantly: "I think that hot sex is number one. That your partner cares that you have a great time in bed." When asked how they celebrate their anniversary, she offered a similar story, "We try to go out and make passionate love. And generally just try to spend some romantic time together. Last year we had lobster and champagne and went skinny-dipping in a pool."

Not every marriage is as rollicking after nearly twenty years. But perhaps surprisingly the marriage bond makes a big, positive difference in the bedroom as well as in the bank account, as we will see in chapter 6. It improves one's sex life, plus one's mental and emotional health (as we shall see in chapter 5). Knowing there is someone willing to care for you, because they love and are committed to you, is in itself a great boost to one's psychological well-being.

"Love, Honor, and Cherish": The Value of Social Support

When you are married, you have another key advantage: You know that whatever problems you face, you won't have to face them alone.

Dina puts it this way: "With Matt, it's very much the way you feel with your parents, maybe even more so, that I absolutely have someone, who, no matter what, will love me and no matter what, will defend me, and who I can depend on completely."

Hundreds of studies demonstrate that those who feel they have someone they can rely on to help out in times of trouble have better mental health and greater well-being.[22] This help may take the form of practical assistance, such as someone who'll look after the kids or drive you to the hospital. But equally important is just having someone to talk to about your problems.

Just having someone to talk to about everyday hassles makes married people feel better about their lives. As we shall see in chapter 4, having a spouse improves one's immune functioning and physical health, too. Estelle, a grade-school teacher, describes the virtue of a husband this way: "I know that if I have a bad day teaching, if the principal yells at me or some first-grader throws up on another child, I can come home and Nick will patiently hear all about it. He's there. He's constant."[23]

Not every marriage partner is equally good at providing social support. But in marriages that last, partners are usually assured a certain basic level of emotional sustenance.

The Power of Trust

Every kind of partnership fosters opportunities for specialization and exchange, economies of scale, and even social support. But the marriage partnership is even more productive than most because it is fueled by a magic ingredient: trust.

Spouses expect to be able to trust each other, financially, sexually, and emotionally, not only because of their individual personal qualities but because being married means that most of their goods are jointly owned. The trust implicit in marriage reduces the need for spouses to monitor the behavior of each other closely, to catch lack of effort or stealing or dishonesty. It reduces the effort required to enforce agreements.[24]

Although not all spouses bring goodwill to the marriage, and not all spouses retain it for the entire course of wedlock, husbands and wives don't seem to need to monitor each other as much as they would, say, an employee. A husband would be less likely to watch the household expenditures of his wife, for example, than those of a housekeeper, precisely because the money being spent belongs to the wife, too.

Karen explains the role this kind of trust plays in her marriage's economic arrangements: "Something that my husband has always done, which I find very trusting—the sign of good faith in a relationship—is [to] hand me his paycheck every week. He never turns around and asks how it's spent, never. He has never said to me, 'Why did you spend that money?' I think it is a very wonderful sign of trust in our relationship, and I try to be as economical as I can."

Certainly, it would be the rare supervisor who would find total trust an effective technique for encouraging frugality in his employees. Acting as a collective, as a unit, where the good and bad times are shared by all members, married couples need to put less effort into monitoring each other's behavior and enforcing their agreements. So the marriage allows couples to be more efficient, to produce more with less.

The public vow of the marriage, enforced by love, law, and custom, is the driving power behind the bond that creates these life-enhancing changes. But the vow is not something imposed upon lovers from the outside. It is something the human heart craves.

Lloyd, a counselor for drug-addicted teenagers, asked the key questions: "Why is it that no matter where you look, men and women pair up? Why is intimacy something we want? Why even try for that one 'perfect love' when nowadays you don't have to?"[25] Lloyd answered his own queries this way: "People still reach out because something inside them yearns for human companionship. They want love, and the only way you can be sure that the person you love will be there for you is to get some kind of vow that they will. And that vow is marriage."[26]

Changing roles and expectations between men and women may require adjustments in our social understanding of marriage, but the underlying needs of men, women, and their children that point toward marriage have not changed: sexual fidelity, an economic partnership, a parenting alliance, the promise of care that transcends day-to-day emotional flux, the support of the wider community in achieving these marriage aspirations, the longing to receive and to be the source of dependable love, and the transforming power of the vow.

These things remain at the heart of what marriage means, what marriage does, what marriage is. They are, as we shall see, what give a few words mumbled before an altar or a judge the power to change lives.

But if we, as individuals, are to have the right to make this powerfully life-enhancing choice, we must first live in a society that respects, supports, enforces, and sustains the marriage vow. We must surrender the cherished myth, comforting to both the happily married and to the divorced, that our marriages are purely our own private creations, no-body's business but our own.

When what we really crave is pure freedom to shape our own rela-tionship, without any outside pressures or support at all, Americans turn to a different arrangement altogether.

3

THE COHABITATION DEAL

If you really want to understand what the marriage bargain is today, look first at what it is not: Compare the marriage bargain with the cohabitation deal. Americans sometimes talk as if marriage were a private, personal relationship. But when two people live together for their own strictly private reasons and carve out their own strictly private bargain about the relationship, without any legal or social pressures, we call that relationship cohabitation.

In America cohabitation is now more popular than ever. More men and women are moving in together, sharing an apartment and a bed, without getting married first. The latest Census Bureau figures show 4 million couples living together outside of marriage (not counting gay couples), eight times as many as in 1970. In 1970 there was one cohabiting couple for every one hundred married-couple households. Now there are eight couples living together for every one hundred married couples.[1]

Not only are more couples living together, they are doing so more openly. Thirty years ago men and women who lived together generally presented themselves as married; often the woman would use her partner's surname and the title *Mrs.* In many states their relationship became a legal, common-law marriage after a certain number of years had passed. But as the moral prohibition against premarital sex weakened and more unmarried men and women began to conduct active sex lives openly, the stigma of living together also weakened, although it has not disappeared.

In recent surveys American adults express neutrality to very mild disapproval of the idea of an unmarried couple living together.[2] Apparently, this opprobrium is too mild to act as much of a deterrent for most. About half of Americans from age thirty-five to thirty-nine have cohabited.[3]

The Cohabitation Deal

While disapproval of cohabitation is muted, what some social scientists predicted—a virtual blurring of the social boundaries between marriage and cohabitation—has not taken place. Both the general public and cohabitors themselves typically make a sharp distinction between marriage and living together. Cohabitation is not "just like marriage" but rather an emerging social lifestyle with a different set of social meanings, which generally serves different purposes. Contemporary cohabitations do not take on the protective coloration of marriage but flaunt their differences.

Of course, for some people, cohabitation is just a brief stop on the road to marriage rather than an alternative to it. Many cohabitors are engaged. And there is increasing evidence that cohabitors with definite plans to marry act and behave in ways that are similar to married couples.[4] Cohabitors without plans to marry look very different from married couples—in their health habits, in the way they spend money, in their attitudes toward divorce and marriage, leisure and money, and in their fertility patterns.[5]

Why do some people cohabit rather than marry? What is the difference between the marriage contract and the cohabitation deal? The prime difference between marriage and cohabitation in contemporary American culture has to do with time horizons and commitment. What makes marriage unique among emotional and financial relationships is the vow of permanence. With marriage, partners publicly promise each other that neither one will be alone any longer: Whatever else happens in life, someone will care about and take care of you. Even spouses who choose divorce hang on, with surprising persistence, to the ideal of marital permanence, preferring to see their own marriages as "a lie" rather than to reimagine marriage as a less-than-permanent union.[6] Eighty-one percent of divorced and separated Americans still believe marriage should be for life.[7]

Cohabitation, by contrast, is seen by partners and society as a temporary arrangement. The majority of cohabitors either break up or marry within two years.[8]

Single Parenthood with a Mate

We often think of cohabitors as young couples who aren't quite ready to marry. Over a quarter of unmarried mothers are cohabiting at the time of their children's birth, and many other cohabiting families have children from other unions.[9] Two-thirds of children entering stepfamilies do so in the setting of cohabitation rather than marriage, although many couples in these arrangements marry at some point. Half of currently married stepfamilies with children began with cohabitation.[10]

The cohabiting partner is in an awkward position in these situations; he is not the children's father or stepfather, has no legal authority over them and no legal responsibility for them. And because the future of a cohabiting relationship is uncertain, the person living with a partner's children is taking a big risk by becoming emotionally attached to those kids. Perhaps as a result of this uncertainty, children living with cohabiting couples show poorer emotional development than children from married, two-parent families do.[11]

For many cohabitors, the idea of relatively easy exit with no well-defined responsibilities constitutes cohabitation's biggest attraction. Like other Americans, these cohabitors view marriage as a bigger commitment than living together, and they do not feel ready at this time, or with this partner, to take on the larger responsibilities to another person that marriage represents. Cohabitors, in other words, have a shorter time horizon than spouses do. Even when Cohabitors have been together for long periods of time, they do not feel obligated to remain with this partner forever.

Blair, a social worker, who lives with Lauren, a speech pathologist, in a rambling suburban home with Lauren's two kids from a previous marriage, is typical of cohabitors in this regard. He explicitly contrasts the obligations of marriage with the lesser commitment he has made to Lauren. "I was dissatisfied being married 'cause I didn't like that contract. The overriding feeling of commitment was something I really didn't want." Even after years, Lauren agrees with Blair. "I still don't think of it [living together] as permanent," she says.[12]

Fear of Fidelity

This lesser commitment to one's partner extends through all aspects of life, including sexual fidelity. Cohabitors are less likely than spouses to view their sexual union as permanently exclusive. As we shall see in chapter 6, cohabitors are less faithful to their partners than are married couples, and even when sexually faithful, they are less committed to the idea of sexual fidelity. Even if they are currently monogamous, many cohabitors say they are unwilling to say their partner will be the only person they ever sleep with for the rest of their lives.

Stewart, for example, has no plans to have sex with any woman but his live-in partner: "I don't think it is a good idea if I were to get sexually involved with another woman." And yet he has told his live-in lover, "I'm not going to tell you that I'm not going to be sexually involved with anyone [else] because of our relationship. . . . I want to make that decision because of how I feel—not because of how you feel. . . ."[13]

While married couples typically define their relationship, in theory, as sexually exclusive, even if one of them cheats, cohabitors (especially those who aren't engaged) more often define their relationship, in principle, as sexually open, even if neither one has plans to have sex with anyone else.

A Bank Balance of One's Own

Cohabitors are frankly less willing to support or be financially responsible for their partners. Research into the varying reasons for divorce or breakups make this difference between married and cohabiting partners crystal clear: Whereas for married couples, income inequalities between spouses discourage divorce, for cohabitors, income inequalities between partners destabilize the relationship. Cohabitors, far more than spouses, are committed to economic independence from their partners. Such self-sufficient relationships are harder to maintain when incomes are very unequal.[14]

Because they do not see their future lives as necessarily intertwined and because they do not want to take responsibility for another person's welfare, cohabitors typically take steps to keep their time and money separate. Cohabitors, for example, are far more likely than married couples to keep separate bank accounts and split living expenses "equally" even if they have very unequal incomes.

"I don't want him to think that he is supporting me at all, and he is afraid that he will have to support somebody," explains Adrienne, who is an executive at a large corporation. "And so we always make things incredibly equal. But he makes about twice as much money as I do. . . . It's the only really tense thing between us." Stewart, who is an accountant, is very clear about his expectations: "It is hard for me to deal with community property. . . . It is hard for me to feel interdependent." He's willing to pay a bit more than Adrienne does for "common goals," such as the house they bought, but, he says flat out, "I am not going to spend money that I earned for something Adrienne wants unless I want it too.[15] I had very strong feelings about not wanting the woman I live with to be economically dependent."[16]

Married couples also monitor each other's spending, but in a way that emphasizes their joint economic future rather than each person's right to spend his or her own money. Because they see themselves as an economic unit, married couples also benefit from specialization—the partner who is better at budgeting and handling money, for example, can act for the two of them.

Lisa is a homemaker and Albert is a machinist. As Lisa puts it, "I learned how to budget the hard way. Albert never moved out of his parents' house. He owed them a lot of money for back rent, which we have mostly paid back, but we still owe them some money. I pretty much take care of this." Even though Albert earns the money, it is not his to spend as he pleases, as it probably would be if they were cohabiting. "He spends more than I think is necessary. He doesn't control it," reports Lisa frankly, "so we have to stop quite often and discuss our budget and where did all this money go to." She will ask Albert, "Why are you broke? Where did it go to?" And, Lisa explains, "If it went to good causes, I can find ten dollars more. If it didn't, tough."[17]

Even though she is not working, Lisa has no problems telling Albert how much he can spend, because the money he earns is not his but theirs. Married people almost always pool their money, sharing bank accounts and mortgages. Even when they don't, they are far more likely to accept financial responsibility for each other than are cohabitors. Spouses budget jointly, seldom tallying up who owes whom and demanding transfer payments. Married people consider their money and their property to be shared. This financial union is one of the cornerstones (along with sexual union) of what Americans mean by marriage.

In fact marriage can almost be defined as a twin union of bed and bank account. Most married couples have a single joint account, and, if they have another account, this is most often an account in the wife's name only for her housekeeping or "pin money."[18] Among Puerto Rican married couples, the husband is expected to turn over his check to the wife, who manages the money. Couples who handle their money in this way are often viewed by the community as married, even if no ceremony has been performed.[19]

The irony is that though cohabitors often try to protect themselves financially by withholding economic commitment, married couples end up far better off in financial terms, as we shall see in chapters 7 and 8. A sense of obligation to, and trust in, a life partner is a great spur to financial success. Not only do married couples have higher household incomes than cohabiting couples, but they are less likely to experience various forms of economic hardship, such as having trouble paying bills. Perhaps because (as Lisa and Albert's experience suggests) the partnership of marriage helps people to manage money wisely.[20]

Lightening the Family Burden

Cohabitation also provides a window into how the social norms surrounding marriage change people's behavior. For cohabitors are often very aware that the social expectations placed on people who live together are very different from those for married couples, a fact that sometimes pushes couples toward or sometimes vehemently away from marriage. But in any case, as Philip Blumstein and Pepper Schwartz's interviews with cohabiting couples make clear, cohabitors do recognize that even today, people still treat you differently if you are married.

For many couples living together, the social symbolism of wedding is a reminder that their relationship is "different." As one cohabitor put it, "Once in a while we go to a wedding. It's painfully obvious that we're not married."[21] A young woman, trying hard to explain why she and her live-in lover should marry, told Maggie, "It bothers me, with his parents. I want them to have to acknowledge I'm somebody. I want them to recognize my place in John's life. A wife is something a girlfriend is not." For cohabitors who aren't interested in marriage, by contrast, minimizing expectations from "in-laws" is more important than winning their recognition.

People who cohabit not only tend to value marriage less, they are more likely to value all familial relationships less.[22] Stewart, for example, doesn't want his partner's family to become his family too. "I don't want her family to think of me as family. . . . I don't want them to take me for granted. . . ." For her part, Adrienne recalls refusing to take on the "kin work" wives do: "There were a number of birthdays in his family this month. And I wouldn't send any birthday cards. . . . I wasn't going to take it upon myself because it is his family."[23]

The Benefits of Cohabitation

Cohabitation is a halfway house for people who do not want the degree of personal and social commitment that marriage represents, at least not now. As such, the cohabitation deal does offer some short-term advantages for both men and women. Men and women who live together can get some of the benefits of being married—a readily available sex partner who will share the rent and do some of the cooking—without making any long-term promises. And those who are anxious about marriage, either because they feel that they would not make a good spouse or that their partner would not make a good spouse, may decide to only live together. If your boyfriend doesn't have a steady job or has one that pays poorly, if he drinks, if money runs through his fingers, or if he has a terrible temper, you might think twice about marrying him. Living together lets you keep your money separate, avoid responsibility for your partner's debts, and leave easily if things get too bad.

Similarly, if divorce runs in your family or if you yourself have a history of failed marriages or relationships, you may seek to avoid the pain and stigma of divorce by shying away from marriage altogether.[24] So men who do not feel that they will be successful family breadwinners—or who do not want to take on this responsibility—may avoid marriage and the expectations that come with it, and choose to cohabit instead. A woman who does not want to make her career secondary to her husband's—as is often expected of a wife—might decide to live with her boyfriend rather than transform him into a husband.[25]

Less Housework

For women, *wife* and *homemaker* are synonymous, even for women holding demanding jobs. When women marry, they almost always take on—or are handed—responsibility for all the labor that it takes to maintain a home. So married women spend vast amounts of time cooking, cleaning, shopping, doing laundry, running errands, and picking up after their husbands (and children if they have them). They spend much more time at these chores than single women do and also more time than do women who are cohabiting. Just changing one's status from live-in girlfriend to wife increases a woman's time in household tasks by almost an hour a day. As we shall see in chapter 7, women—and men—do the least housework when they live at home with their parents. But when it comes to household chores, living with someone rather than marrying them gets women a little bit better—although still terrible—deal: Cohabiting women report doing about thirty-one hours of housework a week, compared to nineteen hours for cohabiting men. But married women say that they spend thirty-seven hours a week to the eighteen hours reported by married men.[26] So it makes sense that women who especially dislike traditional women's work or who are particularly determined to succeed on the job, might find cohabitation attractive. Several studies document the divergent attitudes and behavior of spouses and cohabitors. One such study, by Marin Clarkberg, Ross Stolzenberg, and Linda Waite, followed these characteristics in more than twelve thousand high-school seniors into their early thirties and found that the women (but not the men) who highly valued career success were more likely to cohabit. If a twenty-three- to thirty-one-year-old woman rated success at work as "very important" rather than "not important," the chances her first union would be a cohabitation rather than a marriage jumped from 37 percent to 57 percent.[27]

More Time for Oneself

The flip side of this reduced homemaking responsibility for women is reduced breadwinning and family responsibility for men. Men who value personal leisure highly are apt to find the cohabitation deal more attractive than the marriage bargain. Married men may do about one hour a week less in housework than cohabiting men, but they spend significantly more time in the labor market than single men, and they also experience large drops in leisure time, compared to singles.[28]

Married men not only have less leisure time, but they are more likely to spend what they do have of it with their wives, doing things "as a family."[29] When a spouse violates reasonable marital expectations of togetherness, his or her spouse will probably let it be known in no uncertain terms.

Margo's husband, George, a forklift operator, "used to go out with the guys at night," says Margo. "I didn't like that at all. It was three o'clock in the morning. I would wait up for him and give him a hard time." If he could go out at night and party, she warned, so could she: "And he decided, 'I don't want her to go out, and if I don't want her to go out, I'd better get my ass home.'"[30]

Cohabitors' free time, by contrast, is not only more plentiful, but it is more likely to be defined as their own, to do with what each individual likes. Blair describes his and his partner's cohabitation deal this way: "Lauren and I specifically said, 'Do you have other interests? Pursue them.' That means if you want to go hunting every weekend, go. If you want to get involved in other kinds of interests outside of work and home, you are free to do that."[31]

Indeed, one study that tracked the attitudes and behavior of more than twelve thousand young men and women from their senior year in high school through their early thirties found that the men (but not the women) who valued personal leisure highly were far more likely to cohabit. If a young man reported "having leisure to enjoy my own interests" as "very important" rather than "not important," the probability his first union would be a cohabitation rather than a marriage jumped from 33 percent to 53 percent.[32]

If the great theme of marriage is union, the counterriff of cohabitation is individualism. In contrast, cohabitors, by and large, cherish their individual freedom. "[C]ohabitation is attractive as an alternative to marriage not only because it is a tentative, nonlegal form of a coresidential union, but more broadly, because it accommodates a very different style of life," concluded Waite, Clarkberg, and Stolzenberg.[33]

But the price of this freedom can be high. For by consciously withholding permanent commitment, cohabitors do not reap the advantages of a deeper partnership. Because they do not feel responsible for each other's well-being, cohabitors do not seem to regulate each other's behaviors in the same way spouses do, meaning cohabitors generally do not reap the profound physical-health benefits married couples get (as we shall see in chapter 4).

Because the future of their partnership is so uncertain, cohabitors cannot risk becoming interdependent, for example, which means they forgo the benefits of specialization—of letting the more capable, interested, or experienced partner for particular tasks take care of them.

Because they aren't sure what the future holds, couples living together cannot plan for it together. Bonnie, for example, loves Rick and wants to stay with him. But she also wants to go to medical school. "There is no given that Rick will come with me," she says, "I was going through this arduous process of trying to figure where I can go and what I'm going to do." Rick encouraged her but never gave her any input on what decision would be preferable to him. "And that was upsetting me," says Bonnie. "His response is that it is real difficult for him right now to decide at this point in his life what he wants to be doing a year from now."[34]

The long-term commitment of marriage allows partners to make present sacrifices (like following your wife to med school) for future joint gain. Cohabitors, by contrast, have more individual freedom to do exactly what they like, but they have more difficulty reaping the kinds of benefits that come from jointly planning for the long haul.

Lauren has begun to think about retirement, and to think about retiring with Blair. But she still isn't sure whether or not Blair will be there, or even if she wants him to be there with her, which makes planning difficult. "I mean, something could happen. I don't know. He could meet somebody else and I could meet somebody else. He could die, I could die. I don't know. I mean, there are just a whole bunch of things like that."[35]

In addition, cohabitors, with their explicit emphasis on personal and financial independence, do not offer each other the kind of social insurance spouses do. This is both a practical and an emotional benefit of marriage: knowing that there is some other human being who will take care of you when you cannot take care of yourself. If you get sick, lose your job, or are unable to take care of yourself, your live-in partner is likely to feel much less responsible (if at all) for your welfare. As Blair put it, "The best relationships probably are made by people who don't really need them, just want them." To which his live-in lover Lauren responded bluntly, "If you ever need me, we're going to be in trouble."[36]

Cohabitation may offer short-term advantages but at a high long-term cost. Couples who live together and then get married face higher chances of divorcing than do couples who never cohabited. Cohabitors begin with less favorable attitudes toward marriage and less negative attitudes toward divorce, but the more often and the longer people live together without marrying, the more negative their attitudes toward marriage become. Cohabitation not only deprives people of the benefits of marriage now, but it makes it at least somewhat less likely they will achieve a successful marriage in the future.[37]

In matters of the heart, no less than the market, a bigger investment means better returns. The benefits that marriage (but not cohabitation) brings are not small: As the next six chapters will show, marriage for most people is the means to health, happiness, wealth, sex, and long life. In love, victory goes not to the half-hearted but to the brave: to those ordinary people who dare to take on the extraordinary commitment marriage represents.

4

IN SICKNESS AND IN HEALTH
The Medical Power of Marriage

In 1963, the Hammond report, a study meticulously following the smoking habits of nearly a half million men, released its findings. The result was a resounding warning that soon made its way onto every American cigarette pack: Smoking is hazardous to your health.

A decade later, when Professor Harold Morowitz of Yale University took a second look at the Hammond report's data, he discovered evidence that had been overlooked: Marriage also affected men's risk of premature death. Looking at age-standardized death rates, Morowitz found that divorce seemed to be about as dangerous to a man's health as picking up a pack-a-day cigarette habit.[1]

This strong relationship between marriage and health was not the quixotic finding of an eccentric researcher. A large and growing body of research conveys the same basic conclusion, which if an enterprising surgeon general ever wished to slap a warning label on, say, condom packages or divorce, the decree might read, "Not being married can be hazardous to your health."

Longer Life
How much can getting married do for you? Sometimes, it can literally save your life. Catherine Ross and her colleagues summed up the evidence to that effect in a 1990 literature review in the *Journal of Marriage and the Family:* "Compared to married people, the nonmarried . . . have higher rates of mortality than the married: about 50% higher among women and 250% higher among men."[2]

Unmarried (including divorced, widowed, and single) people are far more likely to die from all causes, including coronary heart disease, stroke, pneumonia, many kinds of cancer, cirrhosis of the liver, automobile accidents, murder, and suicide—all leading causes of death.

The risks of remaining unmarried are particularly high for causes of death "that have a large behavioral component, such as lung cancer and cirrhosis, or that kill young and middle aged adults, such as suicide and accidents." The biggest gap between married and unmarried occurs in early middle age: among adults thirty-five to forty-four years old.[3]

Being unmarried can actually be a greater risk to one's life than having heart disease or cancer. For example, having heart disease shortens the average man's life span by slightly less than six years. But being unmarried chops almost ten years off a man's life. Similarly, not being married will shorten a woman's life span by more years than would being married and having cancer or living in poverty. Statisticians Bernard Cohen and I-Sing Lee, who compiled a catalog of risks that increased chances of dying, concluded that for both men and women, ". . . being unmarried is one of the greatest risks that people voluntarily subject themselves to."[4] Physician Michael Roizen, in his book *RealAge: Are You as Young as You Can Be?*, calculates that for men, being happily married is the equivalent of being one and a half years younger than chronological age. Happily married women are, he figures, half a year younger, and divorced women two years older. But for men, being single increases their RealAge by three years.[5]

The Power to Heal

When it comes to surviving cancer, being married can knock ten years off your age, according to one study of cancer-survival rates. Researchers found that having a spouse lowered a cancer patient's risk of dying from the disease by as much as would being in an age category of people ten years younger than he or she. "A recent study of outcomes for hospitalized patients found that married surgical patients are far less likely to die in the hospital than singles."[6]

Patients who were not married also piled up bigger hospital charges and longer hospital stays. The risk of being discharged to a nursing home was 2.5 times greater for unmarried than for married patients, even after taking into account the severity of illness, age, gender, race, and diagnosis.[7]

The strong relationship between marriage and mortality has been observed across numerous societies and among various social and demographic groups. In countries as diverse as Japan and the Netherlands, the unmarried die off much faster and sooner than the married. In most developed countries, men of any given age who are single, divorced, or widowed are about twice as likely to die as married men, and unmarried women face risks one and a half times as great as married women. And despite the fashionable tendency to regard marriage as an institution of declining usefulness, the health gap between the married and the non-married in developed countries is growing rather than narrowing.[8]

Marriage not only preserves life, but it protects health. To most of us, good health is almost as important as life itself, a necessary precondition to activities and achievements that we value. And good health is also valued for its own sake: most people want to be free from pain, fatigue, and symptoms of disease, even when the illness is unlikely to be fatal.

Physicians monitor a person's health by giving him or her lab tests and physical exams. Social scientists generally ask people to rate their health, to report on their symptoms, to recall the number of days that they missed work or couldn't perform their usual activities because of illness.

Asking people to rate their own health has been shown to be a surprisingly accurate measuring tool. Research has demonstrated that your answer to the simple question, How would you rate your own health? tells us more about your future health—and even the likelihood of early death—than asking you whether you have any of a list of diseases and conditions. People seem to have a deep, perhaps intuitive understanding of the workings of their own body.[9]

Both married men and married women feel healthier than those who are divorced, separated, or widowed, according to research.[10] In their study of the health of men and women nearing retirement age, Linda Waite and Mary Elizabeth Hughes found that wives were about 30 percent more likely to rate their health excellent or very good than the same-aged single women were and almost 40 percent less likely to say their health is only fair or poor. Husbands showed similar advantages over unmarried men.[11] Married men and women are also less likely than singles to suffer from long-term chronic illnesses or disabilities.[12]

To get an idea of the size of the married advantage, consider the following thought experiment. Imagine a group of men and women, all forty-eight years old and all exactly alike in all the other important ways we can measure—race, education, household income, place of residence, presence of children or adults in the home—except for marital status. How many would make it to age sixty-five?

Using data from a large national study that began in 1968 with more than six thousand families, Lee Lillard and Linda Waite analyzed the relationship between marriage and mortality in ways that allowed us to answer that question. We followed the life changes of the men and women in this study as they got married, separated, divorced, remarried, lost their spouse, and sometimes, died. Looking at each of the periods in which these events took place, we noted other concurrent changes in people's lives that might affect health, such as moving in with others, changes in income, and additions or losses of children to and from the household, respectively. We took into account differences among people that research suggests might alter their life chances, such as age, education, and race. We noted the year in which they married for the first time or became divorced and also considered how long they had been married.

The results were startling: Even after making these extensive adjustments, both the married men and married women were much less likely to die during the study period than those who were not married.[13]

For the men in the study, avoiding wedlock was a particularly risky business. Almost nine out of ten married men alive at age forty-eight would still be alive at age sixty-five. By contrast, just six out of every ten never-married men alive at forty-eight would make it to retirement age; divorced and widowed men were almost as likely as confirmed bachelors to die before age sixty-five.

Two things are striking about this analysis: First is the amazingly large size of the survival advantage enjoyed by married men. Absent remarriage, three out of ten single, widowed or divorced middle-aged men can expect to lose their lives when they lose their wives.

Surprisingly, the risks of being without a wife affected all unmarried men equally, regardless of how they ended up alone: separated, widowed, divorced, or never married. Having been married seemed to offer no protection at all to men, once they lost that wedding band. Something about being married itself seems to help men live longer.

For women, the relationship of marriage to life span is similar, though not as strong. Nine out of ten married women alive at age forty-eight reached age sixty-five, compared to about eight out of ten never-married and divorced women.[14] Becoming a widow, however, did not seem to increase women's risk of dying early, as becoming a widower certainly did for men.

But overall, both men and women live longer if they are married than if they are not. For men, staying married boosts the chance of surviving to age sixty-five from about two out of three to almost nine out of ten; for women, wedlock ups the likelihood of surviving to old age from about 80 percent to more than 90 percent.

While marriage benefits both sexes, husbands gain larger health benefits than wives. Some have inferred from this data that marriage is either more stressful or less healthy for women. But most of the married men's health advantage appears to flow from that fact that single men behave in particularly unhealthy, risky ways that single women typically do not. Even so, married women also gain a substantially longer life, at least compared to single or divorced women. And in at least one respect, an enduring marriage provides more permanent health benefits to women than to men: Women who become widows seem to retain the health benefits of marriage, while men lose protection upon losing their spouse either to death or to divorce.

How can a "piece of paper," as the marriage license is sometimes called, actually save people's lives?

But Is It Really Marriage?

Perhaps the medicinal value of a wedding ring is a statistical illusion, a product of what social scientists call selection. Perhaps healthier people are more likely to marry than those with chronic diseases. Perhaps the reason the divorced are sicker and die younger is that marriages are more likely to crumble from the stress and strain of living with illness. Perhaps women simply dump men who continue to engage in risky "bachelor" behavior, such as drinking and driving, after they have tied the knot. Perhaps men and women who moan about minor aches and pains are simply less desirable partners, less able to attract and keep mates?

Certainly selection mechanisms such as these play some role in explaining the better health of the married.[15] But we don't think selection effects are the whole story. The evidence strongly points to a different explanation: Marriage itself gives men and women healthier and longer lives.

For one thing, researchers find that the married have lower death rates, even after taking initial health status into account. Even sick people who marry live longer than their counterparts who don't.

Surprisingly, men in poor health actually tend to marry (or remarry) sooner than healthier men do, undercutting the idea that married men are healthier only because healthy men are more likely to marry. However, men whose tastes or lifestyle or personality traits tend to keep them healthy also tend to propel them toward marriage.[16]

Moreover, prospective studies that follow the lifestyles of individuals as they move in and out of marriage show that upon marrying, people typically adopt a healthier way of living. Marriage seems to confer the strongest health advantage in avoiding those causes of death that are strongly influenced by a person's behavior (such as suicide or cirrhosis of the liver).[17]

Let's take suicide as a sad example. Married men are only half as likely as bachelors, and about one-third as likely as divorced guys, to take their own life. Widowers face about the same suicide risk as divorced men do, except for younger widowers (men under forty-five) who are up to nine times more likely than married men to commit suicide.[18]

Nor do the health benefits of marriage stem from simply living with another adult. Studies by Linda Waite and others, which take into account the presence of other people in the home, find that sharing living quarters with someone else does not confer the same protection as being married. The big health difference is between married people and the nonmarried, not between people who live alone and those who don't.[19]

Data such as these strongly suggest that something about marriage itself moves people toward a healthier way of life. What could that something be? Let's take a closer look at some of the ways that being married helps—and not being married hurts—men and women's physical health.

The Wild Lives of Single Men

Marriage confers health benefits on both men and women but not necessarily in the same ways. For men, a lot of the health advantage of marriage can be summed up in a single phrase: fewer stupid bachelor tricks.

Consider what happened when Albert met Lisa. Now happily married, the couple's first meeting couldn't have been less auspicious. "He was drunk off his behind and I'm not a drinker," says Lisa, "he kept bugging me. He wouldn't leave me alone." Once he sobered up, Albert realized he would have to try a different tack, if he wanted any chance with Lisa. "I told him I'd consider going out with him only if he didn't drink," she says now.

Marriage didn't make Albert a teetotaler, but under consistent prodding from Lisa, he has cut back considerably. "I just told him something had to be done," she says, ". . . as long as you keep it under control, fine. But the next time we have any problems, we start going to an organization for help." Albert readily credits his wife with, as he puts it, "straightening me out."[20]

A large body of research confirms the folk wisdom: Married men really do settle down, while men who aren't married voluntarily behave in ways that endanger their own life and health. Take alcohol abuse, for example. Single men drink almost twice as much as married men of the same age. In a recent national survey, one out of four single men, from ages nineteen to twenty-six, say their drinking causes them problems at work or problems with aggression. One in seven of the married men in the same age range reported these same problems with alcohol. On the flip side, only one out of six single guys drinks so little as to be a virtual abstainer, compared to one out of four married men.[21]

And alcohol abuse is not just a syndrome of the wild young never-married. Divorced and widowed men also show substantially more problems with alcohol than married men do.[22]

Nor is downing one too many the only way single men put their lives at risk. Single men are also more likely to smoke, to drink and drive, to drive too fast, to get into fights, and to take other risks that increase the chances of accidents and injuries.[23]

And of course, alcohol abuse also plays a role in magnifying many of these risky behaviors. Driving fast is always dangerous, but driving fast after five or six beers is more dangerous still. Getting into a barroom brawl always invites injury, but when one or both parties is inebriated, the likelihood that words will escalate into blows or worse, gunshots, increases. Excessive drinking can precipitate fights, arguments, and accidents.[24]

By contrast, when men marry, they dramatically alter this kind of behavior. This change is not just a statistical artifact of selection—sober-minded men marrying and staying married more often. Instead, the evidence suggests that men actually mend their ways as they first approach and then actually get married.

Single men who are heading toward marriage, for example, reduce their drinking up to a year before the ceremony. Although they start with the same heavy-drinking patterns as their friends who stay single, by the time they make it to the altar, young men drink much less than they did a year earlier. Meanwhile, their bachelor friends continue to down many more drinks and to experience more symptoms of alcohol problems.

As young men begin to think of themselves as husbands rather than bachelors, their values and their behavior apparently change: Light drinkers, moderate drinkers, and heavy drinkers all imbibe less after they marry.[25]

Jerald Bachman and his colleagues trace patterns of smoking, drinking, and drug use in young adulthood, using a large national study of high school seniors that follows them into their thirties. This data set allows us to directly compare cigarette consumption, marijuana and cocaine use, and drinking during the senior year of high school with these activities later.[26]

As young adults move away from the parental nest, they typically indulge in a wide variety of previously discouraged behaviors: They start smoking, or they smoke more often; they drink more overall and get smashed more often. Use of cocaine increases dramatically. Only marijuana use tends to fall soon after the end of high school.

But marriage actually changes these self-destructive patterns. In the year before marriage, both young men and women smoked less, drank less, snorted less cocaine. Even marijuana use, which tends to drop off after high school, drops two to three times more rapidly among those who marry than among their single counterparts. Meanwhile, their classmates who do not marry increase their use of cocaine and experience more bouts of heavy drinking instead.

Similarly, other studies show that when men lose their wives, either to death or divorce, they once again resume their bachelor habits: they smoke or drink more than they did when they were married.[27]

The sharp drop in risky behavior upon marriage helps explain why, in the analysis Waite made with Lillard, men's risks of dying early drops immediately and substantially upon getting married.[28] The day a man says, "I do" (or indeed merely sets a wedding date), he holds the Grim Reaper at bay.[29]

The Virtues of Nagging

Men also benefit from what social scientists call social support and husbands call nagging. Wives monitor both their own and their spouse's health habits. Wives not only discourage drinking, smoking, and speeding, but they cook low-fat or low-cholesterol meals, add more fruits and vegetables to the family diet, and encourage regular sleeping habits. For example, not only did Lisa get Albert to cut back on his drinking, but she also curbed his tendency to stay up watching TV, eventually falling asleep on the couch. "I didn't get married to go to bed alone," she says.[30]

Wives schedule checkups and monitor their husband's compliance with the doctor's orders. They negotiate with medical bureaucracies such as hospitals, doctor's offices, pharmacies, and insurance companies on behalf of the family, making appointments and finding and contacting specialists.[31] Lisa, for example, has already begun collecting information on alcohol-treatment programs in her area to be ready just in case Albert's drinking ever slips out of control in the future.

Sociologist Debra Umberson found that married men were much more likely than single men to report that someone monitors their health. That person was almost always the wife (although sometimes it was the mother). Married women, by contrast, reported no more health monitoring than did single women. Eight out of ten married men said their wives reminded them to do something to protect their health, compared to just six out of ten married women who said their husbands did the same for them.

A spouse's nagging can have a powerful impact on one's health for both men and women. Umberson looked at the behavior of people who said their spouses sometimes told them to do something to protect their health. Three years later, the nagged husbands and wives had reduced their cigarette smoking, and the nagged wives had increased their average hours of sleep and their physical activity.[32]

Another health benefit men get from being married stems from the emotional support they receive, which can have profound effects on physical well-being. The emotional support of a spouse seems to help people recover better when illness strikes or to manage a chronic disease (such as diabetes) better over the long term.[33] There is even intriguing evidence that social support of the kind marriage provides can actually boost the immune system, making the married less likely to catch even the common cold.[34]

According to one study, which monitored the mental and physical health of a group of people over fifty for a period of fifteen months, the severely depressed were four times more likely to die during the study period than others, even after controlling for a prior history of hypertension, heart attack, stroke, cancer, or physical disability. And married people (as we shall see in chapter 5) were less likely to be depressed than the unmarried. "By protecting and improving psychological well-being," suggested Catherine Ross and her colleagues, "social support also improves physical health and survival."[35] While both men and women benefitted from marriage in this way, men were more likely to depend exclusively on their spouses for emotional intimacy.[36]

Not all marriages are equal, of course. The quality of the relationship between the spouses makes a difference: As a marriage improves over time, so does the reported health of the husband and wife.[37]

The power of a good marriage is visible even on the biological level. Professor Janice Kiecolt-Glaser and her colleagues have studied both newly married couples and those married a long time to assess the impact of marital quality on the functioning of the immune system.

Kiecolt-Glaser and her colleagues also studied short-term changes in products of the immune and endocrine systems during marital conflict between newlyweds and between those who have long been married. They found that even in a laboratory setting among couples with very high levels of marital happiness, endocrine levels changed substantially during conflicts for women but not for men. But both men and women who displayed more negative behavior during conflict had immune systems that functioned relatively poorly.[38]

People who showed negative behaviors during problem-solving also experienced larger and more sustained increases in blood pressure than others. Men and women who used positive or supportive problem-solving behaviors showed no immunological or blood-pressure changes.[39]

Here is at least one important mechanism through which poor marital quality appears to cause poor health later: Conflict in marriages leads to poor immune function, which leads to more illness. Conversely, marriages of high quality—which most are—foster high levels of immune function and thereby better health. As Professor Kiecolt-Glaser suggested to us, in marriages of average or better quality, coming home to one's spouse at the end of the day—to a safe haven—dampens down maladaptive stress, improving physical well-being.

Kiecolt-Glaser and her colleagues find that people in marriages of poorer quality had lower immune functioning than people in better marriages had. They also found that women whose marriages had ended within the last year had poorer immune function than did a matched sample of married women. Perhaps most interesting, Kiecolt-Glaser and her colleagues expected that they would find no differences between married people and people who had been divorced for some time. But they did. They found higher levels of depression among divorced people, as others have found, and as we will see in the next chapter. They also found significantly lower levels of immune function for the divorced on three of their measures, suggesting that something about being married improves immune function or that something about being divorced depressed it, even years after the divorce occurred.[40]

Someone to Talk To

As we will see in the next chapter, married men and women show better emotional health, on average, than unmarried men and women. Getting married improves mental health for both men and women across many dimensions of well-being. Scholars have long thought that just having someone to talk to accounted for much of the powerful marriage boost for emotional health. But recent research shows clearly that talking about deeply held emotions or distressful or traumatic events in itself improves physical health.

Psychologist James Pennebaker has tested this idea by having people write or talk about their deepest emotions or thoughts. The subjects get no feedback on their efforts but show significant improvements in both mental and physical health. He finds that even among relatively healthy people, writing or talking about emotional topics improves immune-system functioning. Talking or writing about personal topics also lowers heart rate, electrodermal activity, and muscular activity—indicators of the body's "fight or flight" response. Pennebaker was especially interested in explaining the benefits of psychotherapy for individuals. But marriage remains more common than psychoanalysis; especially over the long haul, many more people talk to their spouses than to a therapist about their worries and disappointments. So perhaps some of the health benefits of marriage come from having a spouse with whom to talk over one's troubles.[41]

Likewise, sexual intimacy provides people with an arena of self-disclosure; during sex, people reveal both their physical, and, often, their psychological selves at their most naked and unprotected. Marital therapist David Schnarch feels that monogamous couples in long-term, committed relationships construct what he calls the sexual crucible. This sealed pressure cooker formed by a monogamous sexual bond gives couples a mechanism for forging individual growth and change.[42] More on that in chapter 6, but it seems clear that the self-disclosure forged in the marriage bed and over the kitchen table can actually help couples ward off physical illness.

What Money Can Buy Women

For women, the pathways through which marriage protects health are not exactly the same as for men. Like married men, married women live longer, healthier lives than their nonmarried counterparts, but the benefits of marriage for women are not quite as pronounced. The basic conclusion of most research on the subject is that, as Debra Umberson put it, "The effects of marital status on health behaviors are similar for men and for women. The baseline levels of health-compromising behavior are higher for men than for women, however."[43] The benefits of settling down are less for women because single women already lead relatively settled lives, compared to single men.

However, just as for men, marriage does encourage women to lower their already low levels of risky behavior. For example, although they begin with far lower levels of substance abuse than men, women also reduce their drinking, smoking, and drug use upon marriage.[44] And a recent survey showed that divorced and widowed women were much more likely than married women to engage in a variety of risky behaviors: They sometimes get careless and have accidents around the house, driving, or on the job; they sometimes take risks that endanger others; or they have serious arguments or fights at home or away. Both previously married women and men show elevated levels of risk-taking, compared to the married.[45]

Married women not only engage in less risky behavior themselves, but they are less likely than are single women to spend a large amount of time around men who do these things. For example, although single women themselves may be unlikely to drink and drive, they probably more often find themselves in cars driven by intoxicated men than do married women, who go home—or stay home—with their husbands. Single women are also far more likely to meet violence at the hands of men than are their married counterparts, both on the streets and in the home (more about that in chapter 11).

But unlike men, women do not seem to experience sudden large drops in their mortality risk upon marriage. Instead, Lillard and Waite found that for women, the health protection marriage provides grows with each passing year. The longer women stay married the greater the protection from early death they receive. (For men, too, the age-adjusted risk of dying continues to drop for each year the marriage endures, but the decrease connected with the duration of marriage is not as pronounced for men as it is for women.)[46]

So while married women engage in fewer risky behaviors than single women do, most of the health benefits of marriage for women seem to come from a different source: more money. Lillard and Waite found that after controlling for other factors, the economic advantages of marriage seem to play a crucial role in boosting married women's health. Married women have far higher household incomes than single, divorced, or widowed women. (Married men are also better off economically, on average, than singles, but as we shall see in chapters 8 and 10, the financial advantages of marriage are greater for women than for men.)[47]

Higher income gives women access to better housing and safer neighborhoods and the security and social prestige that comes with, for example, owning one's own home.[48] Marriage also gives women access to private health insurance, an increasingly precious commodity in the contemporary United States. A recent study by Beth Hahn showed that just over half of divorced, widowed, and never-married women had private health insurance, compared to 83 percent of married women. Women with private health insurance rate their health significantly higher than do women who go without it. Health insurance both improves health directly, by giving women access to health-care services, and indirectly, by giving people a sense of security about their health care.[49]

So while women don't need the same push away from unhealthy habits that marriage gives men, marriage does give women a type of health advantage men don't need as much—more money. And for both sexes, more money is consistently associated with better health.[50]

The advantages of marriage continue into old age. A recent study of elderly Medicare recipients found that marriage reduced men's chances of dying during the study period very substantially. This finding is not a surprise; we have seen this pattern in many studies. The findings for older women, however, are quite striking. Even at quite old ages, married women were much less likely than unmarried women to become disabled. Having a husband around protects elderly women from many of the worst trials of old age, including the loss of independence and physical functioning. Perhaps as a result, elderly married women—like their male counterparts—are much less likely than unmarried elders are to enter a nursing home.[51]

The Picture of Health

By now, a strong picture of all the varied ways marriage protects health emerges: Consider the lives of David and Mark, two men of the same age. Knowing nothing else besides the two men's marital status, we can make strong predictions about how they live: Mark, the bachelor, is far more likely to, among other things, smoke, drink regularly, drink excessive amounts of alcohol and show other symptoms of problem drinking, and also use illegal drugs such as marijuana and cocaine. Bachelor Mark is more accident-prone than husband David, perhaps because he is more likely to drive too fast, ignore traffic regulations, become sleep-deprived, and get behind the wheel while drunk.

Being married, David probably spends less time hanging out in bars or at parties where, under the influence of too much alcohol, people have disagreements that sometimes flare up into brawls or homicides. Married men don't need to spend evenings in singles bars to find a sex partner or just someone to talk to. Married men spend less time with hard-drinking bachelors and more time with their wives, who discourage drinking and drug use, often deliberately.

If David does drink, it's more likely to be at home; if he drinks too much outside of home, his wife is likely to be willing and able to be the designated driver for the evening. Or, knowing he is responsible for driving someone he loves home, David may drink less, or drive more carefully than the fancy-free bachelor Mark.

There are other differences between David and Mark that might affect their health as well: David's wife, Karen, may nag him to quit smoking or get enough sleep. She may actively seek to cut the fat in his diet or introduce more fresh fruits and vegetables into it. Certainly, if he drives too fast, she's likely tell him to slow down. If he has heart palpitations, she's probably the one who will schedule a doctor's appointment or insist on a trip to the emergency room.

When David or Karen falls ill, the loving support from the other spouse will help him or her recover more quickly. Both David and Karen benefit from the higher incomes and bigger bank accounts that accompany marriage, but Karen benefits even more. Especially if she has children, she is unlikely to be able or willing to earn the kind of money David will bring to the family. Being married, she will live in a better house in a safer neighborhood and enjoy better access to medical care than her single peers (especially single mothers). And being married she is also far less likely to suffer injuries or death from violence committed either by strangers or by intimates.

Why Do Men Get More Health Benefits from Marriage?

Marriage improves women's health, but it improves men's health more. That's primarily because, as we saw earlier, single men often lead unhealthy and risk-filled lives, but single women rarely do. However, women also seem to make more specific contributions to the health of their mate. They seem to do a better job than do men of managing the nontechnical aspects of health, negotiating the health-care-delivery system, dealing with doctors and pharmacists, and following medical regimens. Single women do this for themselves, and married women do it for their families, but men without mates miss out.[52] Wives often monitor their husband's health, as we pointed out earlier, but husbands tend not to provide the same service to their wives, who get this support more often from friends or female relatives.[53] Single men also tend to be more isolated than single women, who tend to have stronger social supports through kin and friends.[54] So the social support of marriage, while good for both sexes' health, is more indispensable for men.

The Medical Consequences of Meaninglessness

But along with all these factors there is one more advantage the married enjoy. Marriage—and the parenthood that often accompanies it—also seem to provide individuals with a sense of meaning in their lives. In good marriages, husbands and wives know their partners' well-being depends on them. A wife feels licensed to nag in a way that a girlfriend does not, precisely because both the wife and her husband know their lives are intertwined; a husband may respond better to his wife's urging to take care of himself because he knows that she and their children depend upon him. In marriage there is no such thing as a victimless crime.

Even without the prodding of a spouse, married people seem to monitor their own health more closely. A spouse's illness, injury, or death could devastate the family, and that knowledge makes married men and women more cautious and careful.

It is precisely this sense of responsibility for another that distinguishes marriages from alternatives such as cohabitation. If marriage were just a piece of paper, then cohabiting couples who share a home and bed should behave just like married couples. Instead, research confirms that in this country, living together is very different from being married. This is partly because the people who choose to be legally married are different to begin with than those who opt to avoid the entanglements and obligations of marriage. But research also shows that cohabitation itself is a different institution than marriage, with different expectations and effects on the individual.[55] For both of these reasons, cohabitation does not confer the same kind of health benefits to either men or women as does marriage.

People who choose cohabitation do so largely because one or both partners wish to escape (at least for the time being) the heavier commitment marriage represents. Because they do not feel certain their future lives will be spent with their current partners and because they do not feel as responsible for their partners' well-being, lovers who live together do not exhibit the same healthy behaviors as husbands and wives.

For example, Monitoring the Future, a survey that follows the attitudes and behavior of high-school seniors through the next decades of their lives, found that young men and young women who cohabit in adulthood are different from their peers who don't, even while still in high school.[56] As high-school seniors, cohabitors drank more and also used more marijuana and cocaine than those who made the choice either to marry or to live singly.

But unlike getting married, merely moving in together did not seem to motivate young men and women to reduce unhealthy behavior. During their twenties, young men and women who live together showed very high and increasing rates of health-destroying and dangerous behaviors. Those who married, by contrast, started out with moderate levels of smoking, drinking, and drug use during high school but improved on all fronts, often dramatically. Only on heavy alcohol use does cohabitation seem to provide some protection, but far less than marriage does.

The evidence from four decades of research is surprisingly clear: a good marriage is both men's and women's best bet for living a long and healthy life. Especially, as we shall see, if they wish to live both long and happily ever after.

5

HAPPILY EVER AFTER?

Marriage, Happiness, and Mental Health

In most cultures, marriage marks the end of carefree adolescence and the beginning of serious adult responsibility. Marriage is both the end point of romantic longing but perhaps also, we fear, the end of romantic love.

Most of us carry within us, unresolved, both images of marriage: a source of happiness, satisfaction, and gratification and a source of restriction, frustration, and curtailment.

Thus, in his study of successful men, Robert Weiss reports, "When men who have been married fifteen or twenty years are asked how marriage changed their lives, their first thought is apt to be lost freedom."

"If I weren't married I'd probably have one hell of a time" is Mr. Brewer's first, immediate response. "I'd probably spend my summers in Newport and my winters on the Caribbean." In the next breath, Mr. Brewer offers a different vision of life without the burdens of marriage: "Much as I wouldn't want to admit it, I'd probably be lonesome with life. Because I know quite a few guys that got divorced and what it really comes down to, a lot of them go home at night to a cold home."[1]

Now that women have the same sexual license as men do and more economic opportunity, they, too, voice a similar ambivalence about the relationship between marriage and happiness. Today's young women live with both the fairy tale and its negation, the old yearning for a happily-ever-after and the modern disillusioned "knowledge" that pinning one's hopes for happiness on a husband is a recipe for disaster. Women, experts warn, may be "casualties of a marital subculture that crushes their emerging identities."[2]

These two competing visions of marriage—the wedding as a doorway to happiness and the wedding as an obstacle to individual growth—subsist side by side in contemporary American culture. Each has resonance; each perhaps reflects some hard-won bits of personal truth.

Is there any objective way to sort out the probabilities of these competing points of view? Is marriage generally good for one's mental and emotional health, or is living with one person for the rest of your life enough to drive a sane person bonkers? When people consider getting or staying married, the question often at the forefront of their minds is, Will getting married (or getting a divorce) make me happy?

A Measure of Happiness?

For a social scientist, the first step to answering such a question is defining the terms. For one thing, the line between physical and mental health is nowhere near as sharp and bright as people commonly assume. Emotional distress (as we saw in chapter 4) often leads to physical illness, while chronic physical illness frequently results in mental distress, including depression. Moreover, mental disorders such as anxiety or depression often manifest themselves in a series of physical symptoms, such as sleeplessness, fatigue, sweaty palms, racing heartbeats, or a loss of appetite. Separating the mind from the body is not so easy.

And mental health and happiness, though intimately related, are not exactly the same thing either. Researchers have developed various measures to help capture subjective well-being. Psychological well-being consists of feeling hopeful, happy, and good about oneself. Those in good emotional health feel energetic, eager to get going, and connected to others.

Psychological distress, by contrast, comes in a variety of forms, including depression, or feelings of sadness, loneliness, and hopelessness. Psychological distress may also appear as anxiety, tenseness, or restlessness. Anxiety can also produce other physical symptoms such as acid stomach, sweaty palms, shortness of breath, and hard, rapid beating of the heart in the absence of exercise.[3]

Like physical health, emotional well-being is both a good in itself and a means to other goods, the necessary precondition to functioning effectively in our various roles and fulfilling our diverse ambitions.

How does marriage influence our odds of achieving a sense of emotional well-being or avoiding psychological distress? Does marriage more often make us happy or frustrate our desire for emotional growth? Overall, perhaps surprisingly, the evidence gathered by social science points more in the direction of an older, rosier view than the bleaker modern suspicion. Marriage appears to be an important pathway toward better emotional and mental health.

Escaping the Abyss

When it comes to avoiding misery, a wedding band helps. Married men and women report less depression, less anxiety, and lower levels of other types of psychological distress than do those who are single, divorced, or widowed.[4]

As one researcher summarized the international data on marriage and mental health, "Numerous studies have shown that the previously married tend to be considerably less happy and more distressed than the married."[5]

One study of the more than eighty thousand suicides in the United States between 1979 and 1981 found that overall, both widowed and divorced persons were about three times as likely to commit suicide as the married were.[6] Although more men than women kill themselves, marriage protects wives as well as husbands. Divorced women are the most likely to commit suicide, following by widowed, never-married, and married (in that order).[7]

When it comes to happiness, the married have a similarly powerful advantage. One survey of fourteen thousand adults over a ten-year period, for example, found that marital status was one of the most important predictors of happiness.[8] According to the latest data, 40 percent of the married said they are very happy with their life in general, compared to just under a quarter of those who were single or who were cohabiting. The separated (15 percent very happy) and the divorced (18 percent very happy) were the least happy groups. The widowed were, perhaps surprisingly, just about as likely to say they are very happy as singles or as cohabitors—22 percent.[9]

On the other end of the scale, married people were also about half as likely as singles or cohabitors to say they are unhappy with their lives.

The divorced were two and a half times more likely, and the widowed were almost three times more likely than spouses to confess they are "not too happy." The most miserable were the separated, who at 27 percent were almost four times more likely than the married to say they are "not too happy with life."[10]

Does Marriage Make You Happy or Do Happy People Get Married?

Why are married people so much healthier mentally and happier emotionally than those who are not married? One possibility is that happy, healthy people find it easier to get (and keep) mates. Divorced and widowed people may be unhappier, because the gay divorcées and merry widows disproportionately remarry. The happiness boost from marriage may be more apparent than real, a function of the selection of individuals into and out of the married state.

In recent years social scientists have extensively investigated this theory, tracking people into and out of the married state to see if marriage really is a cause of mental health and happiness. This powerful new body of research clearly comes down against the cynics: The selection of happy and healthy people into marriage cannot explain the big advantage in mental and emotional health husbands and wives enjoy.

Certainly happily married people do not doubt that the love of their spouses helps them weather the storms and shocks of life. "Before my father died, we went on a vacation together where we talked and talked. We told each other how much we loved each other. . . . Matt was there with me and for me, always, to get through these terrible things, as I was with him when his parents died," said Sara, a slim woman in her early fifties.[11] "[S]he shares and defends my interests," her husband, Matt, an environmental policy analyst, chimes in. "She understands what I do. None of what I do now would have happened without her active support. She encourages me all the time."[12]

Economists write a great deal about the economic specialization that takes place in marriage; spouses just as often spontaneously offer stories of emotional specialization, a balancing act that leaves both partners better off. "I've learned I need balance, to be cautious. Otherwise I'll get into a lot of trouble," notes Helen, the livelier and less emotionally inhibited member of her marriage. "And [Keith] provides that. [He] is not a risk taker. I add spice to his life. I want quick solutions and I tend to jump ahead. He's slower to act and react."[13]

Tina acknowledges the role her tumultuous marriage played even in providing the support she needed to resolve her childhood traumas: "As crazy as he [her husband] was—and he was crazy—I never had to wonder if I was alone," she said. "Sometimes I felt alone, but I knew I wasn't alone. Because I wasn't alone, I could feel how lonely I used to be. I felt safe and protected and loved. And by my midthirties I could finally begin to face that I had been unsafe, unprotected, and unloved throughout my whole childhood. . . ."[14]

When Nicholas, a very successful executive, went to the hospital with an anxiety attack, he credits his wife with knowing just what he needed to help him recover: "During that entire frightening time, she was wonderful. She was calm, sympathetic, reassuring, but never intrusive and certainly never hysterical. Whatever she suffered—and I'm sure she did, we both did—she protected me. She gave me the support and the space that I needed."[15]

Spouses can help in these times of crisis in a way that a friend or lover cannot precisely because of what marriage means: someone who will be there for you, in sickness or in health. Living with someone "until death do us part" provides a particular kind of intimacy—a spouse comforts partly because he or she has the knowledge that comes from long, emotional acquaintance but also because only a spouse can offer the peculiar reassurance that whatever life tosses at you, as Tina put it, at least you won't face it alone.

The most convincing evidence that marriage causes better emotional health comes from studies that follow people's life changes over a number of years, as some marry and stay married, some marry and divorce, and some remain divorced or never marry.

Nadine Marks and James Lambert did precisely this kind of work, looking at changes in the psychological health of men and women from the late 1980s to the mid-1990s. They took into account the psychological health of each individual in the year the monitoring began and watched what happened to him or her over the next five years. They measured psychological well-being in amazing detail, along eleven separate dimensions, including many measures that psychologists have used for years, such as depression, happiness with life in general, and self-esteem, as well as other, newer measures: personal mastery (which reflects the feeling that one has control over his or her life and can reach the goals set for oneself); hostility (feeling angry, irritable, or likely to argue); autonomy (being independent of influence by others); positive relations with others (having close personal relations, being a giving person); having a purpose in life (which reflects one's aims in life); self-acceptance (liking oneself); environmental mastery (being able to meet the demands of everyday life); and personal growth, which reflects one's learning, changing, and growing.[16]

When people married, their mental health improved—consistently and substantially. Meanwhile, over the same period, when people separated and divorced, they suffered substantial deterioration in mental and emotional well-being, including increases in depression and declines in reported happiness, compared to the married—even after Marks and Lambert took into account their subjects' mental health at the start of the study. Those who dissolved a marriage also reported less personal mastery, less positive relations with others, less purpose in life, and less self-acceptance than their married peers did.

Divorce, Marks and Lambert found, was especially damaging to women's mental health; divorcing women reported more of an increase in depression, more hostility, more of a decline in self-esteem, less personal growth, and less self-acceptance and environmental mastery than divorcing men.[17]

Because they had measures of people's mental health both before and after marriage, Marks and Lambert were able to rule out selection as the explanation for the mental-health advantage of married people. Instead, they found the act of getting married actually makes people happier and healthier; conversely, getting a divorce reverses these gains—even when we take into account prior measures of mental and emotional health.

In a similarly powerful study aptly titled "Becoming Married and Mental Health," researchers Allan Horwitz, Helen Raskin White, and

Sandra Howell-White examined changes in psychological well-being among young adults over a seven-year period. They paid particular attention to those men and women who got married during the study period. The researchers measured the emotional health of each person at the beginning of the study, using that data as their starting point, and looked for changes when certain events occurred, especially marriage. They compared the mental health of those who got married with that of people who stayed single over the entire study. They used two measures of mental health: depression and problems with alcohol.

Once again, marriage made a big difference: Young adults who got married experience sharper drops in levels of both depression and problem drinking than did young adults who stay single. Interestingly, although more of the men than the women were problem drinkers, getting married led to bigger declines in problem drinking for women.[18] By the same token, more of the women were depressed than the men, but getting married reduced depression for the men but not for the women.[19] Horwitz and his colleagues concluded that "adequate statements about the relative advantages of marriage for men and women cannot be based on single mental health outcomes." They also concluded that marriage advantages both men and women, but does it through different mechanisms.[20]

Selection played a surprisingly small role in who marries, at least with regard to depression and alcohol abuse. Horwitz, White, and Howell-White found that alcohol use has no impact on entry into marriage; problem drinkers were just as likely as abstainers to find someone to marry. The same was true of depression, at least for the men; relatively high levels of depression do not preclude marriage or even reduce a person's chances of marrying. More of the depressed women did face increased chances of remaining single. But the strong positive impact of getting married remained even when the researchers took into account initial levels of depression and alcohol abuse for the individuals. Their conclusion? "Selection effects do not account for the lower rates of depression among people who become married, compared to those who remain single."[21]

The Lonely Heart?

Researchers who first noticed this correlation between mental health and marital status speculated that simply living with other persons—which almost all married persons do—was the source of the emotional-health advantages of the married. Living alone, they theorized, causes distress, and those single men and women who live with others probably are as psychologically healthy as the married.

But social scientists who have tested the idea found, to their surprise, that living arrangements cannot explain the emotional advantages of marriage. Walter R. Gove and Michael Hughes compared mental-health measurements of married adults and unmarried adults who lived alone with those of people who lived with someone else. Even single adults who lived with others were more depressed than the married.[22]

The latest studies confirm these findings. In their joint research, Linda Waite and Mary Elizabeth Hughes examined two different measures of emotional health among adults in their fifties and early sixties. They found that all the single adults, whether living alone, with children, or with others, described their emotional health more negatively than did the married people. Just 17 percent of older wives characterized their emotional health as either fair or poor, compared to 28 percent of the older single women. Similarly, just 14 percent of the husbands versus 27 percent of the single men described their emotional health as fair or poor. At the other end of the happiness spectrum, 50 percent of the wives versus only 38 percent of the unmarried women described their emotional health as either very good or excellent. Meanwhile, 53 percent of the husbands but only 42 percent of the older unmarried guys rated their emotional health so high.

The husbands and wives also reported substantially fewer symptoms of depression than the single adults did, who were more depressed, on average, than the married even when they were living with their children or other people.[23]

To married couples, these results must not have been so surprising. For marriage changes not just people's outward physical arrangement but their inner relation to one another. The tendency among social scientists has been to conceptualize marriage as an external, structural category and to look beneath the piece of paper for the "real" reasons married people appear happier and healthier. But in American society, marriage is not just a label, it remains a transformative act—marriage not only names a relationship but it creates a relationship between two people, one that is acknowledged, not just by the couple itself, but by the couples' kin, friends, religious community, and larger society.

Almost by definition, married people share their lives with each other to a much greater extent than single adults do. Roommates, parents, adult children, friends, even live-in lovers, all have separate lives from those of the people they live with and expect more independence and autonomy from each other than spouses do.

The Limits of Cohabitation

Indeed, researchers have found that a desire to retain one's autonomy—to keep a life apart—is one of the prime factors that drives individuals toward cohabitation over marriage. Cohabitors, for example, are far more likely to spend leisure time apart from their lovers than spouses are. Cohabitors also place a higher value than do the married on having time for one's own individual leisure activities.[24]

In the short term, cohabitors may gain some (though not nearly all) of the emotional benefits of marriage. But over the long haul, it appears cohabitors may be no better off than singles. Another large study, this time of more than 100,000 Norwegians, found that for both the men and women, "the married have the highest level of subjective well-being, followed by the widowed."

Even the divorced or separated people who cohabited did not seem to be much better off than those who lived alone, with one important exception: Those who moved in with a new partner within one year after divorce or separation reported very high rates of happiness, higher even than those of the married.

This phenomenon may reflect, as the study suggests, a buffering effect that protects an ex-spouse during the strains of divorce. But it may also reflect the likelihood that those who move in with a partner immediately following a divorce began the relationship before the end of the marriage. The glow of happiness these couples report may reflect the underlying social reality: It is far more pleasant to be the one who dumps one's spouse for a new love than to be traded in for a different model. But this newfound happiness of live-in lovers appears to be short-lived (at least among those who do not quickly remarry). "[A]mong those who have remained divorced for three years or more the level of well-being is much lower and very similar for the single and cohabiting," the study concludes.[25]

Cohabitation provides some—but not all—of the same emotional benefits of marriage, yet only for a short time and at a high price. Breaking up with a live-in lover carries many of the same emotional costs as divorce but happens far more frequently. People who are cohabiting are less happy generally than the married and are less satisfied with their sex lives. In America, long-term cohabiting relationships are far rarer than successful marriages.[26]

Of course, marriage can be a source of stress as well as comfort. The strong emotional benefits of marriage come only from relationships that spouses rate as "very happy."[27] Those who describe their marriages as "pretty happy" are somewhat better off than singles, but not as well off as those in "very happy" relationships.[28]

Not surprisingly, the men and women in the relatively small number of "not too happy" marriages show more psychological distress than do singles. Horwitz and his colleagues find that the quality of the marriage is the most consistent determinant of both depression and problem drinking; both husbands and wives who say they have a good relationship with their spouses also report lower levels of depression and fewer problems with alcohol.[29] People who say their relationships are unhappy, that they would like to change many aspects of their relationship and that they often consider leaving their spouses or partners have higher distress levels than people without partners at all.[30]

Fortunately for the mental health of the country, most married people describe their marriages as "very happy." Among the nearly twenty thousand married men and women questioned over the last several decades as part of the General Social Survey, 66 percent of the husbands and 62 percent of the wives give their marriage the highest possible happiness rating. Almost no one—2 percent of the married men and 4 percent of the married women—described their marriage as "not too happy."[31] So the emotional damage from an unhappy marriage is quite a rare occurrence, and the vast majority of married men and women get emotional benefits—usually very large ones—from being married.

Nor do unhappy marriages necessarily stay that way: 86 percent of those who rated their marriage as unhappy in the late eighties and who were still married five years later said their marriages had become happier.[32]

The Marital Transformation

New marriage partners together create a shared sense of social reality and meaning—their own little separate world, populated by only the two of them. This shared sense of meaning can be an important foundation for emotional health.[33]

Ordinary, good-enough marriages provide the partners with a sense that what they do matters, that someone cares for, esteems, needs, loves, and values them as a person. No matter what else happens in life, this knowledge makes problems easier to bear.

Over a century ago, sociologist Émile Durkheim found that people who were integrated into society were much less likely to commit suicide than people who were more socially marginal. Life is uncertain and often hard, he argued, but being part of a larger group one loves gives people the strength and will to cling to life in the face of difficulties.[34]

Marriage and family provide the sense of belonging that Durkheim had in mind, the sense of loving and being loved, of being absolutely essential to the life and happiness of others. Believing that one has a purpose in life and a reason for continued existence, that life is worth the effort because one's activities and challenges are worthy comes from having other people depending on you, counting on you, caring about you. Married people have a starring role in the lives of their spouses; their shared universe would cease to exist if something happened to one of them. When the shared universe includes children, the sense of being essential, of having a purpose and a full life expands as well. Marriage improves emotional well-being in part by giving people a sense that their life has meaning and purpose.[35]

The enhanced sense of meaning and purpose that marriage provides protects each spouse's psychological health. Russell Burton examined reports of psychological distress for a national sample of adults. As other sociologists have, Burton found that multiple social roles seem to protect people's mental health. Men who were employed, married, and parents, for example, were less distressed than other men.[36] Men who were employed and married or married and a parent but not employed also felt that their lives had more meaning and purpose than other men did. Burton found a similar picture for women: Employed single women, employed wives, employed single mothers, married mothers, and employed married mothers were less distressed than women who were single, childless, and not employed. But while having more than one social role can boost one's health, marriage appears to be the key role. Married women—regardless of whether they worked or had children—reported greater purpose and meaning in life, and neither work nor children, in the absence of marriage, increased women's feelings of purpose and meaning. The sense of meaning and purpose marriage creates, concluded Burton, seems to be in itself responsible for the better psychological health of husbands and wives.[37]

Oddly, contemporary experts have often failed to notice the immense transformative power of the marriage act. Perhaps because, in the age of divorce, sensible people naturally place a great deal of emphasis on finding the right partner, experts tend to talk as if a marriage license were only a "piece of paper," as if the relationship were everything and the marriage ceremony merely a public certification of a preexisting condition.

The ideas that happiness is a purely individual rather than an interpersonal achievement, that marriage is simply a sum of the characteristics of the individuals that enter into it, that getting married cannot change an individual's outlook, behavior, or internal feelings is surprisingly influential in contemporary America. Noting that married people say they are lonely less often than do singles, a recent college textbook on marriage and family concludes, "It would be ludicrous to suggest that young adults who experience loneliness and stress should marry to alleviate their problems. Obviously, the same personal characteristics that resulted in their distressful state in singleness would also be reflected in marriage."[38]

As Professor Norval Glenn stated in a critique of textbooks, "[M]ost social scientists who have studied the data believe that marriage itself accounts for a great deal of the difference in average well-being between married and unmarried persons. Indeed, loneliness is probably the negative feeling most likely to be alleviated simply by being married."[39]

The latest research shows the skeptics are wrong: In real life, the public legal commitment represented by that "piece of paper" makes a big difference. The married really are emotionally healthier than their single counterparts because they've chosen to live in this particular type of committed relationship. The commitment married people make to each other is reinforced and supported not only by their own private efforts and emotions, but by the wider community—by the expectations and support of friends, families, bosses, and colleagues who share basic notions about how married people behave.

The emotional support and monitoring of a spouse encourages healthy behavior that in turn affects emotional as well as physical well-being: regular sleep, a healthy diet, moderate drinking. But the key seems to be the marriage bond itself: Having a partner who is committed for better or for worse, in sickness and in health, makes people happier and healthier. The knowledge that someone cares for you and that you have someone who depends on you helps give life meaning and provides a buffer against the inevitable troubles of life.

In contemporary folklore, marriage may represent the end of the period of happy, carefree youth. But science tends to confirm Grandma's wisdom: On the whole, man was not meant to live alone, and neither was woman. Marriage makes people happier.

6

WITH MY BODY
I THEE WORSHIP

The Sexual Advantages of Marriage

What does marriage do to your sex life? For men, the supposedly boring qualities of married sex have long been satirized in popular culture—taken for granted and transformed into the butt of jokes. "What's the best food to curb your sexual appetite?" the old joke asks. "Wedding cake" is the sobering answer.

Over the last generation, a new element to the old "ball-and-chain" story has been added: Women, too, we are now increasingly likely to believe, must choose between marriage and sexual fulfillment.

"What is it about marriage," Dalma Heyn writes in her latest book *Marriage Shock*, "that so often puts desire at risk? . . . [A] favorite question on book jackets and magazine covers is 'Is there sex after marriage?' and inside the books and the magazines is advice on how to bring the spark back into your marital bed, counsel that often sounds labored, as if this will require work, like jump starting a dying battery."[1]

"There is sex after divorce, and for almost all of these women it is better and more frequent than it had been before . . . ," claims journalist Ashton Applewhite in her 1997 book *Cutting Loose: Why Women Who Leave Their Marriages Do So Well*. "Marriage results in familiarity, and familiarity does have a way of dampening ardor—after all, nobody needs premarital aids."[2]

So these days, for both men and women, marriage is often portrayed as a sort of large wet blanket thrown on one's sex life. Is it true? Do we have to choose between emotional bonds and sexual pleasure? Does marriage sentence us to a life of sexual self-denial or does monogamy make sex better?

The Shocking Truth about Marital Sex

Thanks to two new large sex surveys, we now know far more about the sex lives of Americans today than we used to and are far better equipped scientifically to answer questions such as those above. One investigation, conducted by Edward Laumann and his University of Chicago colleagues and popularly known as "The National Sex Survey," was based on interviews with a nationally representative sample of nearly 3,500 American adults in 1992. Researchers asked adults not only about their sexual behavior but about their fantasies, ideals, preferences, and satisfaction.[3] A second major study, conducted by psychologists Scott Stanley and Howard Markman, interviewed about a thousand American adults, asking them about sex, satisfaction with their relationship, conflict, and violence.[4]

What these prominent researchers found may shock you: Married people have both more and better sex than singles do. They not only have sex more often, but they enjoy it more, both physically and emotionally, than do their unmarried counterparts. Only cohabitors have more sex than married couples, but they don't necessarily enjoy it as much. Marriage, it turns out, is not only good for you, it is good for your libido too.[5]

Getting Any?

According to the National Sex Survey, 43 percent of the married men reported that they had sex at least twice a week. Only 26 percent of the single men (not cohabiting) said that they had sex this often, and the divorced men were no more active than the never-married guys. The picture is much the same for women: Wives had more active sex lives than all types of single women except cohabitors; 39 percent of married women had sex two or three times a week or more, compared to 20 percent of single women.

Married people were also far more likely to avoid the specter of absolute celibacy than were singles. Staying single dramatically increases the chance that you won't have any sex at all. Single men were about twenty times more likely to be celibate than married men; at the time of the survey, one out of four or five unmarried men hadn't had sex in the past year, compared to about one in a hundred married men. Single women were even more likely than men to lead sexless lives: Thirty percent of all never-married women and 34 percent of all previously married women had had no sex at all in the last year, compared to 3 percent of married women.[6]

Why is the conventional wisdom so wrong? Is there something about marriage itself that improves one's sex life, and if so, what?

Wives Are Easy

One simple reason that married people have more sex is logistics: They have easy access to a sex partner. For the single person, finding someone to have sex with or even finding the time to have sex with them is almost always a far more complicated and arduous endeavor than for the married.

Imagine the experiences of twin brothers James and John. Both are healthy, handsome thirty-year-old professional men. James is married and John is still a bachelor. Legend has it that John the bachelor should have a much more scintillating sex life. We know from research the cold hard fact is that James most likely gets far more sex than John.

After all, the first prerequisite for a satisfying sex life is that you have to find someone willing to have sex with you. In these days when "nice girls do," that's a lot easier for bachelor John than it used to be. Still, as for other singles, if John wants to have sex, he has to invest considerable time, money, and effort into finding a partner. On Friday night, after a hard week's work, he can't just roll over and make nice to the woman in bed with him. He has to shower, dress, drive to a bar or a party, and chat with a lot of women, most of whom aren't ever going to sleep with him.

Even if John enjoys the process, all this effort takes time (and money) that must somehow be squeezed from his regular routine. The girl at the bar won't regard his day at the office as time spent partly on her behalf. He must invest, at the very minimum, hours in courting her, if he hopes to persuade her to have sex with him. In this sense, each act of sex for singles is costly, compared to that of married people.

Even after he's located and secured a regular partner, John must invest more time in getting sex than the married must. At the very minimum, he has to get in the car, drive to his girlfriend's home, and make an appropriate amount of small talk before jumping in the sack. Afterward, he must get out of bed, dress, drive home, and undress before finally going to sleep in his own bed.

The same basic sexual truth holds for women. Locating someone who is both attractive and interested takes a great deal of effort—including many hours invested in "blind alleys"; people don't always pan out, as any dating woman can attest.

For James, by contrast, figuring out who to have sex with is easy. (As one married man of our acquaintance explained to us, "If you're a married man and want to have sex, at least you know where you have to go to get it.") James doesn't have to sift through lots of potential partners, strike up a conversation, get to know the person, establish a relationship, and negotiate the sexual partnership. These things have already been done. And of course his sexual partner is right there, conveniently in bed next to him every night.

Familiarity does not seem to dampen ardor as much as facilitate it. One reason married people have more sex is that any single act of sex costs them less in time, money, and psychic energy. They have already made the huge investment in establishing and maintaining a sexual relationship and can lie back and enjoy the dividends. For the married, sex is more likely to happen because it is so easy to arrange and so compatible with the rest of their day-to-day life.

Easy access to a sex partner is one benefit of marriage that is also enjoyed by cohabiting couples. For them, too, dinner and small talk with their lovers is not a special date—time out that must be somehow subtracted from regular life—but part of their daily routine. Consequently, live-in lovers also have a lot of sex, at least as much, on average, as married couples have.

In fact, cohabiting relationships seem to be built around sex to an even greater extent than marriage. Cohabiting men have the most active sex lives—55 percent have sex two or three times a week or more. Sixty percent of never-married cohabiting women and 51 percent of previously married cohabiting women have sex two or three times a week or more. According to the National Sex Survey, cohabiting men and women made love on average between seven and seven and a half times a month, or engaged in about one sex act more a month than did married people.[7]

In the National Sex Survey, the slight advantage in sexual quantity holds even after we take into account the length of the relationship (men and women report the most sex in the early years of a marriage or co-habitation, and most couples who live together either marry or break up within a few years). But Stanley and Markman's survey found no difference in sexual activity between cohabiting people and married people, once they took the length of the relationship into account. And while celibacy is extremely rare among the married, it is virtually unheard of among cohabitors. None of the cohabiting men and women in the National Sex Survey were celibate in the last year.

Sex appears to be the key part of the cohabiting deal. While sex is a very important part of marriage, it is not (as it is for cohabitors) the defining characteristic of the relationship. Celibate spouses are considered an aberration, in other words, while sexless cohabitors are just roommates.

The Joy of Married Sex

Quantity isn't everything of course. The National Sex Survey also asked men and women to describe the way that sex with their primary partner made them feel, both physically and emotionally.[8] Stanley and Markman asked people how strongly they agreed or disagreed with the statement "We have a satisfying sensual or sexual relationship."

Both surveys showed that husbands and wives were more satisfied with sex than the sexually active singles; 42 percent of married women interviewed in the National Sex Survey said they found sex extremely emotionally and physically satisfying, compared to just 31 percent of single women who had a sex partner. Whatever its advantages, divorce does not seem to improve one's sex life: Only 27 percent of those previously married women with sexual partners were extremely emotionally satisfied and only 36 percent were extremely physically satisfied with sex with their primary partners.

When one combines sex and satisfaction, the sexual advantage of marriage becomes even more pronounced: Married women are almost twice as likely as divorced and never-married women to have a sex life that (a) exists and (b) is extremely emotionally satisfying. About four out of ten wives have a sexual partner who leaves them extremely emotionally satisfied, compared to only about one out of four never-married women, and one out of five previously married women.

What about cohabitors? While cohabiting couples have at least as much sex as the married, they don't seem to enjoy it quite as much. For men, having a wife beats shacking up by a wide margin: 48 percent of husbands say sex with their partner is extremely satisfying emotionally, compared to just 37 percent of cohabiting men. Fifty percent of married men find sex physically satisfying, compared to 39 percent of cohabiting men. Married women are only a bit more likely than cohabiting women to say they find sex extremely satisfying emotionally (42 percent of wives versus 39 percent of cohabiting women). Perhaps the cohabiting women are more similar to wives than cohabiting men are to husbands, because cohabiting women are more likely than cohabiting men to believe the relationship will end in marriage. But after controlling for age and other differences, married men and married women are both significantly more satisfied with sex than cohabiting or single men and women.[9]

So convenience is not the only plus that marriage adds to one's sex life. Something other than ease of access explains the sexual advantages of marriage. What else makes marriage a recipe for a rich, satisfying sex life?

The Sexual Power of Commitment

The answer, both theory and evidence suggest, is that the secret ingredient that marriage adds is commitment. For women, the idea that committed sex is better sex is almost a truism. This conventional wisdom that emotional content of the relationship matters more to women than men in terms of sexual satisfaction has recently been buttressed by the theories of evolutionary biology: Women, not men, get pregnant. Therefore women have a stronger incentive than men to make sure their sexual partners care for them and are likely to care for their children.

Because of the subsistence conditions under which our ancestors lived, the children of women who did not take care to secure the commitment of their sexual partners were far less likely to survive than children of more discriminating and sexually exclusive females.[10]

The new data available in the National Sex Survey allowed us to test the conventional wisdom directly for both sexes. Does an emotional commitment increase sexual satisfaction, and if so, how? Does it have the same benefits for men as for women? Are men and women equally likely to be unfaithful, and are both sexes equally attracted to casual sex?

Kara Joyner and Linda Waite looked closely at the National Sex Survey for new answers to these questions. Several queries measured the relationship between sex and commitment. For example, respondents were asked to what degree they agreed with the statement "I would not have sex with someone unless I was in love with them." They were also asked to explain why they had sex with their partners the last time that they had done so. Those who answered that they had sex "to express love or affection" seemed to the researchers to be demonstrating emotional commitment to their sexual partners.

People were also asked how strongly they agreed or disagreed with the statement "I try to make sure that my partner has an orgasm when we have sex," a rather direct measure (at the very least) of a commitment to one's partner's sexual satisfaction.

Both husbands and wives were more likely to see love and sex as intrinsically connected than either cohabiting or single men and women were. Twenty-six percent of married men felt strongly that they wouldn't have sex unless they were in love with the person, compared to just 15 percent of cohabiting men and 9 percent of single men. Married men were less likely than cohabiting or single men to say (in theory) that they find sex with a stranger very appealing—27 percent of married men versus 41 percent of cohabiting and 40 percent of single men. Nonetheless more than 90 percent of the men in all these types of relationships said they had sex last time to express love for their partners, and about the same percentage—nearly 40 percent—strongly agreed that they try to make sure their wife or girlfriend has an orgasm.[11]

As predicted, women were more likely than men to make commitment a sexual bottom line. Single women, for example, were almost four times as likely as single men to make love a condition for having sex. But married women were the most adamant about connecting sex and love. Forty-six percent of married women felt strongly that they would never have sex with someone unless they were in love with that person, compared to 30 percent of cohabiting women and 33 percent of single women in ongoing sexual relationships.

But very high proportions of all sexually active women had sex last time to express love (96 percent married, 94 percent cohabiting, 97 percent single). Women were less likely than men to strongly agree that they always try to make sure their partner had an orgasm (36 percent married, 30 percent cohabiting, and 33 percent single). And only a small minority of women said they find sex with a stranger appealing (9 percent married, 11 percent cohabiting, and 9 percent single).

Stanley and Markman asked their respondents directly about their commitment to their relationship.[12] They asked whether or not people agreed with each of four statements: "My relationship with my partner is more important to me than almost anything else in my life"; "I may not want to be with my partner a few years from now"; "I like to think of my partner and me more in terms of 'us' and 'we' than 'me' and 'him/her'"; "I want this relationship to stay strong no matter what rough times we may encounter." They found that cohabiting people with no plans to marry were significantly less committed to their partners than husbands and wives were to each other. Men who were cohabiting scored lower on commitment than anyone else in the survey.

These measures of emotional commitment, along with data on actual instances of infidelity, allowed us to assess not only how much sex Americans have with their partners but how that sex makes them feel: Do they feel extremely satisfied or somewhat less fulfilled? What we found surprised us. Both the conventional wisdom and evolutionary biology predict that for women but not for men, emotional commitment plays a very strong role in sexual satisfaction. But the data clearly show that commitment increases sexual pleasure for both sexes.

Both men and women who said they had sex last time to express love, who said they wouldn't have sex unless they were in love, and those who said that they tried to make sure their partners had an orgasm all reported they had more satisfying sex with that person. The emotional content of the relationship was just as important to men as to women.

Of course commitments vary. The commitment bachelor John has to his regular girlfriend is likely to be quite different from the commitment husband James has made to his wife. And Stanley and Markman showed that men living with women they are not engaged to have very low levels of commitment to their partners and the relationships.

Which kind of commitment is most likely to boost one's sex life? Does it have to be "until death do us part" or is an affirmative answer to the question posed in the old Carole King song "Will You Love Me Tomorrow?" sufficient? And is the relationship between the strength of the commitment and sexual satisfaction the same for men and women?

The National Sex Survey did not ask married or cohabiting couples about how long they believed the relationship would last. However, it did ask single men and women who said they had a regular sex partner how much longer they expected the relationship to last. Answers could range from a few more days to a lifetime.

Joyner and Waite looked at these answers to determine whether or not men and women who expected to be together a long time were more sexually satisfied with each other than those who had a more short-term outlook. For men as well as for women, commitment and sexual satisfaction were strongly related, but in different ways.

Men who said they expected their current relationship to last at least several years were more likely to find sex extremely satisfying emotionally than less committed men. Only 5 percent of dating men who said they didn't expect their relationship to last very long said they were extremely emotionally satisfied with sex, compared to 13 percent who expected a long relationship (and 37 percent of cohabiting and 48 percent of married men). Men also found committed sex more physically pleasurable by about the same margins, giving the lie to the popular notion that men find sex more fun with a new woman.

For women, time horizons were somewhat different: The kind of love that adds zest to sex is one they viewed as endless. Unlike men, women did not seem to distinguish between very short and somewhat longer relationships when it came to sexual satisfaction. Women who expected their current relationship to last several years were no more satisfied with sex than those who expected the relationship to end soon.

What did make a difference for the women was an expectation of permanence: Women who believed they'd would spend their whole lives with their current boyfriends were much more emotionally satisfied with their sexual relationship than were other single women.

Only 7 percent of dating women who saw their sex partners as relatively short-term propositions said they were extremely satisfied physically with sex with them, compared to 11 percent of dating women who expected a long relationship (and 39 percent of cohabiting and 41 percent of married women). Very few women in sexual relationships who were not married to or living with their lovers said that sex with their partners left them extremely satisfied emotionally, no matter whether they expected their relationships to be long or short.

The general rule seems to be that nothing less than the prospect of a lifetime commitment boosts a woman's sex life, while men see a bigger difference between quickies and longer-term sexual relationships, short of marriage.

How committed to their partners are the unmarried? Once again, the sexual stereotypes have a basis in fact: women are far more likely than men to see their current partnership as "lifelong"—headed presumably for marriage. For men, the time horizons divide neatly into thirds: Out of three single men in ongoing sexual relationships, one expects it to last only a few more days; one expects it to last several years; and one expects it to last a lifetime. Among single women in sexual partnerships, one in four expects it to last a few more days; three in ten expect it to last several years; and just under half expect it to last a lifetime.[13]

In one way, however, men and women are alike: a permanent commitment to one's sexual partner makes a big difference to both sexes' sexual satisfaction. Married men are far more likely than either single or cohabiting men to be extremely emotionally satisfied. But single men who say they have made a lifetime commitment to their partner and consider her committed as well are also more sexually satisfied emotionally than less-committed single men. Twenty-four percent of single men in sexual partnerships they see as short-term said that sex left them either somewhat or not at all satisfied, compared to 15 percent of men with long-term girlfriends.

What does this information add to our understanding of the sexual power of marriage? Some argue that the causality goes entirely in the other direction: People with great sex lives tend to be—or become—very committed. Science may not be able to provide a definitive answer to this question, but we don't think that's the whole story. There are strong reasons for believing that the lifelong, permanent commitment embodied in marriage itself tends to make sex better.

Consider the difference between the sexual incentives for spouses and those for dating partners. We've already pointed out how marriage gives much greater access to a sexual partner. But let's take a look at other differences marriage makes as well.

Practice Makes Perfect

By marrying Lucy, James has emotionally closed off the option of finding a "better" sex partner. He believes that Lucy will be the only woman he will make love to in his life. Thus, he has a strong incentive to figure out how to please her, believing at the most basic level that how often he ever has sex again depends on whether and how often she is willing. Lucy has similar sexual incentives: If she wants great sex, she has to figure out how to please her husband and teach him to please her.

Paradoxically, by closing off their other options, James and Lucy increase the energy and attention that each devotes to the needs of their one partner, increasing the likelihood that satisfying sex will result. In sex (as in cooking), marriage likely increases what Laumann and his colleagues call partner-specific skills.

In real life, married men and women easily recall the way that over time, sex in marriage continues to improve. "I think for sex you need time, time to get in sync, time to know your partner, time to get to know what the other person likes or doesn't like," muses Beth McNeil, a hospice nurse who has been married for more than a decade to Kit Morgan. She consciously invested in building a good sex life: "I would physically show him what I wanted. I would participate more. I think this was something he wasn't used to. And it gave him permission to accept that I was giving to him, and not to have that performance anxiety. I was used to good sex. I didn't want to settle for anything less."[14]

Here is one important way a permanent commitment improves both men and women's sex lives: The long time horizons of marriage gives your partner both the time and the motivation to learn how to please you. The husband who satisfies his wife can expect the same attention to his sexual needs and vice versa. And keeping an eye on the long-term can help put the occasional sexual disappointment in perspective as well.

Jean has been married for thirty years to her businessman husband, Keith, who calls her "marvelous" and "a little warmhearted pussycat." They both agree that over the years sex has gotten better: "It's a learning relationship that gets better as we learn more," says Keith. Jean recalls that with time, they've become both more understanding of sexual limitation, and more grateful for sexual pleasure. "You figure, he's either had a busy day or there's a multitude of reasons. . . . Oh, darn. Oh, well. And I learned you should count to ten and be grateful for what you got and not fuss over one time. You get a longer-range view."[15]

The Power of Love

Emotional commitment improves one's sex life in other ways as well. For example, sex with someone you love literally doubles your sexual pleasure: You get satisfaction not only from your own sexual response but from your partner's as well. Emotional commitment to a partner makes satisfying him or her important in and of itself. Demanding a loving relationship before having sex, using sex to express love, and striving to meet the sexual needs of one's partner all increase satisfaction with sex. Love and a concern for one's partner shifts the focus away from the self in a sexual relationship and toward the other person. This selfless approach to sex, paradoxically, is far more likely to bring sexual satisfaction to both men and women.

"I think the sexual bond is essential [to marriage]," reflects Matt who has been married for sixteen years to a woman he's "never not felt in love with."[16] "[I]t is a clear indication of how close and open we are with each other. I'm talking about the times when we are really making love. It's a voyage. It's what we love and what we look for during intimacy. It doesn't happen all the time, and we don't expect it to happen all the time. But sometimes when I've made love to Sara, I disappear. It's really incredible."[17]

For both men and women, the most important component of commitment by far was saying that you had sex last time to express love. Those who used sex to express love were at least twice as likely to be extremely satisfied with both the emotional and physical dimensions of sex with their spouse or partner than those who had sex for other reasons. Forty-five percent of men who said that they had sex to express love were extremely physically satisfied with sex, compared to 18 percent of men who did not give this reason for having sex. The figures for women for physical satisfaction were 41 percent of those who gave this reason versus 12 percent of those who didn't.

When it comes to emotional satisfaction, the "love gap" is even larger: 41 percent of men who said they had sex to express love were extremely satisfied emotionally versus 7 percent of those who did not give this reason. Thirty-eight percent of women who gave this reason were extremely satisfied emotionally, compared to 13 percent who did not give this reason.

People want powerful sexual feelings to have a meaning. And the meaning that is most satisfying appears to be: "I love you. Our lives are as joined as our bodies." Or in the words of the old Anglican marriage service: "With my body, I thee worship."

Sexual Exclusivity

A second aspect of marriage that may improve sex with one's partner is the commitment to sexual exclusivity it normally entails. Infidelity—breaking the promise of sexual exclusivity—constitutes such a profound threat to the marital union that a spouse seeking divorce may start an affair to deal a death blow to the marriage.[18]

Kit is one of many husbands who can testify to the sexual power that faith in one's partner's fidelity gives. "I felt reborn sexually with Beth," Kit says, speaking of his wife of more than ten years, "it was like night and day, compared with my other experiences. I like women a lot, and when I was in my twenties I had a lot of sexual encounters. I also lived with one woman for two years before Beth and I got together." Like many cohabitors who are not engaged, his former live-in lover didn't want a sexually exclusive relationship. "I just couldn't handle that," recalls Kit, "I suffered with premature ejaculation. I was really feeling badly about myself as a man." By contrast, sex with his wife makes Kit feel good. "With Beth I feel mature and comfortable. And it continues to be absolutely satisfying."[19] One reason men find marriage more sexually satisfying than we predicted is that it reduces the threat of outside competition, and hence, the performance anxiety associated with sex.

Our ideas about the relationship between sex and marriage have changed a great deal over recent years, especially when it comes to premarital sex. But when it comes to ideals of marital fidelity, little has changed. Almost all people who are married or even living with someone say they expect the relationship to be sexually exclusive. In the National Sex Survey, 94.6 percent of cohabitors and 98.7 percent of married people expected their partner to be sexually faithful to them.[20]

But married people are far more likely to be true to their vows. In the National Sex Survey, men were twice as likely as women to report infidelity in the past year. Still just 4 percent of married men compared to 16 percent of cohabiting men said they had been unfaithful over the past year. Thirty-seven percent of the single men in ongoing sexual partnerships had other sex partners at the same time they had girlfriends. Only one married woman in a hundred said she had an affair in the past year, compared to 8 percent of cohabiting women and 17 percent of single women in ongoing sexual relationships.[21]

Just 2 percent of married and cohabiting women said their husbands or boyfriends had had other sexual relationships, suggesting that most men—especially cohabiting men and boyfriends—who were unfaithful managed to keep that fact a secret.[22]

Women had fewer affairs and less often kept them secret: 5 percent of women reported having sex with someone else and 3 percent of men said their wives or girlfriends had other sexual relationships. So only a minority of unfaithful women succeed in keeping their partners in the dark about their affairs.

Many scholars argue that satisfaction with a sexual relationship is increased when the partners do not have sex with others in large part because other alliances create problems in the primary relationship. It stands to reason that husbands or wives who are paying less attention to their partners because their attention is focused elsewhere will be less satisfied with sex at home.

Some of the problems caused by having more than one sex partner are logistical: Resources such as time, money, and emotional energy are limited; those who spread these resources across several partners give less to each one.

Other roadblocks infidelity places in the way of sexual satisfaction are emotional. Those who have extramarital sex almost always do so without the knowledge and consent of their partners, bringing the problems of dishonesty, secrecy, and guilt to their marriages. Sexual jealousy, competitiveness, feelings of betrayal[23] may reduce a wife's satisfaction and her inclination to satisfy her husband . . . and she may impose new costs (such as having to respond to his wife's unhappiness) on a husband.

If, as we have seen, people are most satisfied when using sex to express love, it makes sense that those who dilute (or "adulterate") this meaning of the sexual act are less satisfied sexually than those who remain faithful.

In their book, *American Couples*, Philip Blumstein and Pepper Schwartz interviewed both married and cohabiting couples. One theme that came up again and again in their portrait of cohabitors was ambivalence toward the idea of exclusivity, particularly on the part of men. Biff has been happily living with Abbey for three years. But he's still not sure how he'll behave sexually, when she leaves on an extended business trip. "We talked about her going away for ten weeks. . . . I said, 'I really don't know whether I want to say to you I won't mess around with someone else while you're gone. I don't think I should, but who knows what I'll do?'" In the end, he guesses, "We'll probably be faithful while she's gone."

Rick has been living with Bonnie for two years. "I'm totally monogamous," he says. "In the abstract, we say that monogamy is not something we're really suited to. We should be able to have relationships with other people that might enrich yourself and our relationship together." Bonnie, who had "started to think it [her and Rick's bond] was a long-term monogamous relationship," had an affair when Rick told her to stop thinking of the relationship in those terms. "It was then I realized I needed to do something so that I would not be quite so dependent on him," Bonnie says.[24]

People who are living with someone are keeping their options open, particularly if they are not engaged. The National Sex Survey found that cohabiting men were about four times as likely as husbands to report infidelity in the past year. Women were more faithful in general, but still cohabiting women were eight times more likely than wives to cheat on their partners.

Renata Forste and Koray Tanfer found strikingly similar figures in the National Survey of Women. Married women in their survey were least likely to have had a secondary sex partner—4 percent, compared to 20 percent of cohabiting women and 18 percent of dating women. And this phenomenon did not appear to be merely an artifact of selection: Women's behavior changed dramatically when they married, with a huge decline in the chances of their having a secondary sex partner. Forste and Tanfer concluded that marriage itself increases sexual exclusivity.[25] By contrast, when people marry, they tell the world—and their husbands or wives—that they are in this for keeps, forsaking all others.

One of the most intriguing results from the National Sex Survey is the evidence that it is our beliefs about infidelity, rather than our behavior, which may have the strongest relationship with sexual satisfaction in marriage. Two questions in the survey dealt directly with ideas about sexual exclusivity and casual sex. People were asked, "What is your opinion about a married person having sexual relations with someone other than the marriage partner—is it always wrong, almost always wrong, sometimes wrong, or not wrong at all?" Men and women who said that extramarital sex is always wrong believed strongly in sexual exclusivity within marriage.

The survey also asked Americans to rate the appeal of "having sex with someone you don't personally know" from "very appealing" to "not at all appealing." Analyzing the data with Kara Joyner, Linda Waite found that large majorities of both men and women condemned extramarital sex. Eighty-one percent of women and 73 percent of men said extramarital sex is "always wrong." Men are far more likely than women, however, to find the idea of casual, impersonal sex tempting: One-third of men said they find the idea of sex with a stranger appealing, compared to less than one woman in ten. And women were twice as likely as men to find the prospect of anonymous sex "not at all appealing" (44 percent of men, compared to 82 percent of women).

Married men and women were just a bit more committed to the ideal

of monogamy than either cohabiting or dating men and women; 75 percent of married men, compared to 64 percent of cohabiting men
thought that extramarital affairs are "always wrong." Eighty-four percent
of married women, compared to 77 percent of cohabiting women held
this view.[26]

These beliefs about sexual faithfulness inside marriage and about the
appeal of casual sex turn out to have a strong relationship with sexual satisfaction both inside and outside of marriage. Men who are very attracted
to casual sex, for example, are less often very satisfied with sex with their
wife or girlfriend. Perhaps they hunger for casual sex because they are
dissatisfied at home, or perhaps these are men for whom committed sex
carries less-powerful emotional meanings. The very few women who say
they find the idea of sex with a stranger appealing are no more or less
sexually satisfied with their partners than other women, perhaps because
these are women who find sex generally appealing.

The Erotic Meaning of Marriage

For women, beliefs about sexual fidelity are key. Women who say that
extramarital sex is "always wrong" are more likely to be highly satisfied
with sex with their husbands or boyfriends than women who are more
tolerant of extramarital liaisons. This phenomenon suggests that the marriage commitment has more than an instrumental relationship with sexual satisfaction. Married people enjoy sex more not only because their
sex partners are more available, less distracted, more eager, and more able
to please, but also because marriage adds meaning to the sexual act. Pope
John Paul II may have been onto a wider sociological truth when he advised Catholic spouses, in essence, you can have sex whenever you want,
but you have to mean what your bodies are saying.

At least, if you want a satisfying sex life.

Sex is an integral part of the marriage commitment; it is such a basic
part of our conception of marriage that we are shocked and distressed to
discover sexually inactive married couples, unless extreme age or ill
health accounts for the hole in the center of the marriage. A sexless marriage is apt to be viewed as a "lie" or a "pretense" or at best a divorce
waiting to happen.

Marriage thus legitimates the sexual relationship between a man and a woman, giving the blessing of church, state, and family to the sexual union. For the religious, sex becomes a sign and a symbol of the union between a man and a woman. The *ketubah,* the Jewish marriage contract, gives a wife explicit, legally enforceable access to her husband's sexual services; his failure to provide these give her grounds for divorce. Similarly, in Catholic canon law, the sexual act actually creates the couple's final union; sexual impotence or a failure to consummate the marriage sexually is grounds for an annulment—an indication that the marriage did not actually take place.

Even Saint Paul, considered by some to have a dour view of sex, explicitly advised Christian married couples that they should not abstain from sex for long periods, emphasizing the reciprocal physical union marriage represents: "A wife does not have authority over her own body, but rather her husband, and similarly a husband does not have authority over his own body, but rather his wife. Do not deprive each other, except perhaps by mutual consent for a time, to be free for prayer, but then return to one another, so that Satan may not tempt you through your lack of self-control [1 Corinthians 7:5]."

One intriguing bit of evidence that marriage changes the meaning of the sexual act in ways that boost sexual satisfaction comes from a poll of 1,100 randomly selected adults that was conducted by the Voter/Consumer Research Firm for the Family Research Council. In this survey, not only were married people more sexually satisfied than singles, but married people who attend church weekly and married people who strongly believe out-of-wedlock sex is wrong were much more likely to be sexually satisfied than married people with less-traditional views. Seventy-two percent of married traditionalists were "very satisfied" with their sex lives, compared to 59 percent of married people who were less traditional. Spouses with three or more children, as well as one-earner married couples, also appeared more likely to report high sexual satisfaction. But after researchers controlled for age, gender, and other demographic factors, the factor most strongly related to sexual satisfaction among married couples was not age or gender or work status but traditional attitudes toward sexual morality. Homemakers were not more sexually satisfied than working wives; but wives (and husbands) who see sex as a sacred union, exclusive to marriage, a sign and symbol of their conjugal commitment, got something out of the sex act that less–sexually traditional people didn't. What we think sex means can have a profound effect on how much satisfaction we get from it.[27] Every time a married couple makes love, they may be reminding each other of the marital promises: to love, honor, cherish, and care for each other—and their children—until death do they part.

Married Sex Is Better Sex

The latest research suggests that there are strong reasons for believing marriage improves sex in a variety of ways. Marriage provides:

- Proximity—sex is easier for married people, because it is more comfortably fitted into their everyday lives.
- A long-term contract—married people have more incentive to invest time and energy in pleasing their partners, have more time in which to learn how to please them, and are more confident that the gifts they give to their partners will be reciprocated.
- Exclusivity—without other sexual outlets, married people put more effort into working out a mutually agreeable sex life than the less committed do.
- Emotional bonding—in marriage, sex becomes a symbol of the union of the partners, of their commitment to care for each other both in bed but out of it. By giving sex this added meaning, marriage increases the satisfaction men and women draw from sexual activity—both their own and their partner's.

Married sex really is better sex. Over the long run, there is no better strategy for achieving great sex than binding oneself to an equally committed mate. For both men and women, marriage as a social institution facilitates the development and maintenance of an emotionally committed, long-term, exclusive union, which typically brings spectacular sexual rewards.

7

THE WAGES OF WEDLOCK

In 1745 Benjamin Franklin gave this classic rejoinder to a bachelor friend who claimed he was too poor to marry: "A single Man has not nearly the Value he would have in that State of Union. He is an incomplete Animal. He resembles the odd Half of a Pair of Scissors. If you get a prudent healthy Wife, your Industry in your Profession, with her good Economy, will be a Fortune sufficient."

Two hundred and fifty years later, the debate over the relationship between marriage and income still rages. Married couples are far more affluent, on average, than singles. Married men in particular make significantly more money than do bachelors. But are higher earnings a cause or a consequence of marriage for men? And how does marriage affect women's earnings?

Consider the experience of Cathy and Doug, an attractive college-educated Oregon couple in their early thirties. When Cathy married in 1989 at age twenty-five (about the median age for women to marry), she was employed full-time as a sales rep in a large corporation. Doug, at twenty-seven, was a regional account manager for a software company.

The impact that impending marriage had on Cathy's career was more dramatic for her than most wives immediately face. "I was offered a promotion to sales manager that would require a move to San Jose," she recalls, "they told me I'd have to change cities every few years. Doug told me to take it—he didn't want to feel guilty the rest of his life. But I knew I wanted to spend the rest of my life with Doug."

She turned down the promotion and quit the company in order to move to the city where Doug lived. She soon found another position as a sales rep, but at a lower salary.

On the day they married, Cathy made about $25,000 a year and Doug, $34,000. Marriage made them both instantly better off financially. Together they made almost double what each enjoyed previously, but now they only had to pay for one apartment, one utility bill, and they could split the labor needed to care for house and home.

But with the birth of their first child, Doug and Cathy's employment histories began to diverge drastically. Cathy quit her job, a decision made easier by the fact that she was not satisfied with her current position. Staying home with a baby created a natural break in which she could regroup and plan for a new career.

Doug was not particularly satisfied with his job either. "He worked constantly," Cathy remembers, "I never saw him, and when he was in town he was a total bear." But because both he and his wife saw him as the primary breadwinner, taking time off for retooling was not an option for Doug.

Eight years into married life, Doug, like the typical husband, has experienced dramatic wage growth; he now earns $65,000 a year. Cathy, by contrast, returned to work two years ago, employed part-time in her dream job in the investment business. She now makes a base salary of $24,000 annually, about the same as when she married.

Both husband and wife are, in their different ways, success stories: Doug has gained income and experience enough to begin the process of launching his own company. Cathy meanwhile has a permanent part-time position in the field she desires. Though her overall earnings remained stable, her pay per hour has more than doubled. Plus, she is able to continue in what is, for her, the cherished role of primary caretaker of her children.

In many ways Cathy and Doug's experience is typical. Overall, both men and women who marry enjoy higher average household incomes than do singles. The 1997 Statistical Abstract of the United States gives the median income of all married-couple families in the United States as $47,129, compared to $26,023 for single men and $15,892 for single women.[1]

However, when it comes to personal earnings, marriage affects men and women quite differently. Married men make more money than single men do. But some argue that the higher salaries of husbands are merely a statistical illusion: Perhaps husbands make more because successful men are more likely to win and keep a wife than the financially less well-endowed. Are the higher wages husbands get a consequence of marriage or merely a prerequisite for getting (and keeping) a wife?

Meanwhile, the affluence enjoyed by wives has also become a source of suspicion and a subject of debate. Wives are financially better off than single women, despite wives' lower personal earnings, because they share their husbands' earnings. But what if the marriage doesn't last? When divorce occurs, some women (particularly long-married mothers) find themselves substantially worse off than their single peers who worked continuously.

Given the high rates of divorce, does marriage really make women such as Cathy, who cut back their workforce participation, financially better off? Or is the support of a husband less an asset than a temptation and a snare, a trap that will leave women such as Cathy dangerously dependent, perhaps even just a divorce away from welfare?

When it comes to making money, sex makes a difference. So let's look at how tying the knot influences the salaries of men and women separately.

Success and the Married Man

For men, the data leave little room for doubt: Marriage itself makes men more successful. In fact, when it comes to earnings, for men, getting and keeping a wife may be as important as getting an education.

Doug's experience is typical of husbands, according to a wide body of research by labor economists. The wage premium married men receive is one of the most well-documented phenomena in social science. Husbands earn at least 10 percent more than single men do and perhaps as high as 40 percent more. The longer men stay married, the fatter their paychecks get, relative to single men's earning power.

One recent study of young men, for example, found that husbands in their twenties and early thirties earned $11.33 an hour, while single men earned $10.38, and divorced or separated men earned $9.61.[2] For older men, the wage gap between husbands and bachelors is even larger. A study of men from age fifty-five to sixty-four found that married men earned 20 to 32 percent more than their nonmarried counterparts.[3]

Nor is men's marriage premium a strictly American phenomenon. Economist Robert Schoeni compared men's earnings in fourteen developed countries. In virtually every country studied, married men earn much more than unmarried men. In the United States, Schoeni found married men earned 30 percent more than never-married men.

To put the size of men's marriage premium in perspective, a man who completes one year of college earns 7 percent more than a male with just a high-school diploma. If Schoeni's data is correct, a married high-school graduate in the United States earns as much, on average, as a never-married college graduate.[4] In the United States, according to some estimates, getting a wife increases a man's salary by about as much as a college education.

If discrimination by employers could explain away husbands' higher earnings, we'd expect to see a one-time jump in earnings, as men switch from the disfavored category (bachelors) into the favored category (husbands). If selection of higher-earning men into marriage were the only cause for husbands' increased wages, we'd expect little or no change in men's earning trajectories over the course of marriage. Instead, married men's wages actually rise faster while they are married than do earnings of comparable single men. Even when researchers take into account characteristics such as a man's occupation, industry, the hours and weeks that he works, and his tenure on the current job, married men's wages rise faster than those of comparable unmarried men.[5]

Just as with men's health habits, men's earnings begin to improve in the year before they marry, as grooms-to-be shrug off bachelor habits and begin to assume the outlook and priorities of married men. Conversely, when a marriage breaks down, the husband's wage premium erodes.[6] The same man who begins to earn more when he moves toward marriage earns less as he moves away from it. This pattern strongly suggests that something about the working partnership with a wife (rather than selection or discrimination) is responsible for a husband's higher earning capacity.[7]

Economists who've attempted to control for selection, conclude that men really do make more money because they are married. According to Sanders Korenman and David Neumark, less than half the earnings advantage of married men can be attributed to the fact that men who make more money are more likely to marry.[8] The majority of husbands' higher earnings comes from the increase in men's productivity that marriage itself causes.

One economist estimated that younger husbands earn about 5 percent more than the same men would have earned if they had not married.[9] And the longer men are married, the bigger the wage premium they receive. Married men experience faster wage growth than do single men, indicating that being married (rather than getting married) actually helps men earn more.[10]

One study that followed the earnings of Swedish workers over a number of years found that married men earned substantially more than unmarried men—even after taking into account their work hours and working conditions, their education and work experience, and whether or not they had supervisory responsibility. Over a four-year period, married men experienced a much greater growth in earnings than unmarried men did. In fact, marriage had a bigger impact on the trajectory of earnings of men than it had on the initial difference between the salaries of husbands and bachelors.[11] For the male worker, a wife is a secret weapon, giving him, over time, a powerful competitive advantage over his unmarried coworkers.

Married men's earnings advantage is largest where their marriages are most secure—further evidence that something about being married leads to higher earnings. Jeffrey Gray looked at men's marriage premiums in different states, comparing the premiums of states that have no-fault divorce provisions in their laws with those of states that don't have these provisions. As some states shifted from fault-based to no-fault laws, men's marriage premiums declined. Gray argues that where marriage can be ended at will by either spouse, wives are less willing to invest in their husband's earning power and, as a result, married men are less advantaged.[12]

The Secret to Success

What is it about marriage that makes men more financially successful? One possibility is that married men put a higher premium on money than single men do. Because they must provide for a family, husbands may more often seek out less interesting or riskier work that pays better.

The type of work husbands choose is part of the explanation, but it is not the whole story. One study looked at how much of the gap between husbands and bachelors can be explained by the kinds of jobs they take. After controlling for family responsibilities, researchers found that married men still earned 17 percent more than did single men with similar responsibilities. Even after controlling for a man's household responsibilities (the number of children under the age of eighteen living at home or the number of hours that the man said he spent on housework, for example) and for the characteristics of the jobs (level of risk, training required, amount of control granted the worker, and mental and physical demands of the job), the researchers determined that the marriage premium for men dropped only somewhat: Married men still earned a hefty 11 percent more than did similar single men holding down comparable jobs.[13]

The Power of Specialization

Married men earn more because, within marriage, they specialize in making money. Even when wives work full-time at demanding careers, they typically do the vast majority of housework, child care, and family work, arranging holidays and family events, keeping in touch with family and friends.[14] As a result, almost all husbands specialize to some extent in earning money—they do more of the earning and less of everything else than do wives. So married men have more time to devote to work because of their wife's time and effort getting dinner, doing the laundry, and driving the car pool to soccer. Economic theory argues that this is one reason that husbands make more money: They specialize, with the support of their wives, in earnings.[15] Economist Shoshana Grossbard-Shechtman refers to the time wives spend in activities that directly benefit their husband as spousal labor. She argues that both men and women are better off when her efforts increase his earnings and he shares them with her.[16]

Does this mean that married men make more money because they do less housework? The answer, surprisingly, seems to be no. While time spent on housework does affect the earnings of wives, some evidence suggests that husbands who spend more hours on household tasks do not earn less money as a result. One study of factory workers paid by the piece for making men's suits, for example, found that married men's earnings did not vary depending on the number of hours of housework they did. Instead, the more children a husband had to support, the more productive a worker he was. Another study compared the hourly wages for workers in all types of jobs, collected in a large national survey. It, too, found that for men, hours spent doing housework had no effect on their wages.[17]

However, men typically spend less time on housework than do women, and differences between the men who do the least household chores and those who do the most are modest. This gender gap in house-keeping predates marriage; even single men living alone—or with their parents—do substantially less housework than women do in the same sit-uation.[18] So, it seems that most men don't do very much housework, per-haps little enough that even among men who do more housework than most, it rarely interferes with their jobs. Or perhaps men are, in general, more willing and able to put their work first and their housework second to avoid conflict.

Smart Husband Tricks

Married men make better workers than single guys do, because they lead more settled lives. They have lower rates of absenteeism from work and are less likely to quit or be fired than are single men. When we can mea-sure productivity directly, married men produce more on average than single men at the same job. One study of naval-reserve recruiters found that married men succeeded in getting 9 percent more recruits, on aver-age, than did single men. Two researchers used personnel records from a single firm to compare the work output of married and single men. They found that married white male managers and professionals were more likely to be promoted, entirely because married men received higher performance ratings from their supervisors.[19]

Cohabitation produces some, but not all, of the benefits of marriage for men. According to economist Kermit Daniel, cohabiting men receive just half the earnings premium of marriage. And while most cohabitations are relatively short-lived, the returns to marriage increase with each passing year. And the earnings advantages of marriage for men are even greater in the later years of marriage than in the first few. The close working relationship between a man and woman in marriage seems key to increasing men's earnings.

Two Heads Are Better Than One

Simple as it sounds, married men make more than their single counterparts because they have wives. Benjamin Franklin was right: Men do better when they are joined in marriage to a woman whose "job" is to take care of them in certain key ways.

One indirect measure of how wives help to raise their husband's earning power comes from research that documents the effects a wife's education has on her husband's moneymaking abilities.

We may not have any direct way to determine how good a particular woman is at providing support for her husband's career. But the amount of education the wife has is a very rough indicator of the knowledge and skill she brings to assisting her husband's work. One study found that, after researchers controlled for the husband's own education, married men whose wives were high-school dropouts earned 11.8 percent less than comparable single men. By contrast, men whose wives had a high-school diploma earned 4.3 percent more than comparable single men, and men whose wives had some college earned 7.1 percent more, while men married to college graduates earned 11.5 percent more than comparable single men. Wives' education remained a powerful predictor of husbands' earnings, regardless of whether or not they had children and regardless of whether or not they themselves are employed.[20] The wives' help seemed to matter more for husbands who were relatively well educated and when the husbands' jobs reward performance. The evidence, as economist Shoshana Grossbard-Shechtman argues, suggests that a wife and husband collaborate to improve his job skills and work performance.[21]

Some of the pathways by which wives contribute to husbands' health and wealth may be connected: Married men are less likely to show up for work hung over or exhausted, because (as we saw in chapter 4) wives monitor their husbands' health and health-related behavior. Perhaps as another of Franklin's old adages succinctly suggests, early to bed, early to rise, really does make a man healthy and wealthy, if not wise.

Clearly wives make some fairly direct contributions to their husbands' careers, in ways that highly educated wives do better than those with less schooling. Wives, for example, may gather or analyze information that helps their husbands at work. They may help them make better work and career decisions, offer input on how to manage professional relationships, or they may provide skilled support services regularly or on crucial occasions.

Asked about whether she made any direct contributions to her husband's career, Cathy can recall at least one example vividly. "I found him his current job," she says instantly. "He told me the criteria he had, including very little travel, not much of a commute, and a small company where he could have an impact. . . . I started looking."[22]

Cathy used her own skills and initiative she developed as a sales rep to locate the kind of company her husband, Doug, was looking for: She went from door to door in the community in which they both wanted to live until she found a likely prospect, a small software company.

"I remember walking in and asking for the sales manager, gathering information about the company, and finding out to whom he could send his resume." When the company placed an ad looking for a software sales rep, Doug applied and got the job.

Through some combination of more information, more managerial skills, better connections, more understanding or ability, educated wives such as Cathy help their husbands succeed at work.

The Wages of Wedlock for Women

For women, the relationship between marriage and money is a bit more complex. Like men, women get an earnings boost from marriage. White childless wives, for example, get a wage premium of more than 4 percent, and black wives without children earn 10 percent more than comparable single women. The partnership of marriage appears to help both men and women on the job.[23]

Women do assume different risks than do men in marriage, risks magnified by the inadequacy of most divorce settlements and the failure of the law to enforce the marriage contract. In choosing to marry, women share the advantages of husbands' higher earnings. Married women are far more affluent than single women. But during marriage, women may specialize in ways that leave them worse off if the marriage ends, especially given the inadequate legal protections available under no-fault divorce. As long as the marriage lasts, both Cathy and Doug will enjoy the financial benefits of marriage. But if the marriage fails, Cathy's decision to cut back on her workforce commitments will leave her much more financially vulnerable than her husband will be.

Still, even in the event of divorce, a woman such as Cathy will likely remain better off as an ex-wife than if she had chosen instead to become an unwed mother. For one thing, if she becomes a single mother through divorce, her children, supported through infancy on her husband's earnings, will be older, and her child-care costs proportionately much less. And the child support she receives as an ex-wife, however inadequate, will be much higher than the average unwed mom receives, at least in part because a husband's income is typically far higher than that of an unwed father, and because the dad who was married to his child's mother is more likely to pay for child care than an unmarried father is.[24]

But even when marriages survive and wives work full-time, marriage is often portrayed as a handicap to women's careers. Marriage, critics charge, expands men's opportunities but limits or squelches women's opportunities. Are they right?

The Problem of Housework

Marriage does increase the burden of home management on women but not by as large an amount as most people assume. The increase isn't as large partly because single women do a lot of housework, far more than bachelors—even if the women live alone or with their parents.

Single women living independently spend about twenty-five hours a week on housework, while wives spend a hefty thirty-seven hours a week on tasks such as preparing meals, doing dishes, cleaning, laundry, shopping, chauffeuring, maintaining the car, paying bills, and outdoor maintenance. But much of this rise in household duties comes not from marriage but from children. When the impact of marriage is separated from the effects of motherhood, marriage alone increases the time women spend on housework only about six and a half more hours a week, compared to single women living on their own.[25]

This small increase in housework attributed to marriage appears to have no impact, one way or the other, on women's earnings. Marriage by itself neither increases nor decreases women's personal earnings, according to most evidence. Many working women report getting substantial help in their careers from their husbands, which helps offset the extra burdens at home.[26]

The Motherhood Penalty

What puts a woman's career and earnings at risk is not tying the knot but cutting the umbilical cord: Married women without children earn as much or more than comparable single women. Mothers, married or single, do not work as much or earn as much as childless women.[27]

Unlike men, women show no clear pattern of gaining earning power as they move toward marriage and losing earning capacity as they move toward divorce. Divorced women, in some studies, actually earned more than either married or single women.[28] But regardless of marital status, research shows that children have a large negative impact on women's wages.[29] Even when mothers work continuously, the demands of child-rearing detract from their earning capacity. Comparing women with similar work histories, Jane Waldfogel found that one child still reduced a woman's earnings by almost 4 percent and two children or more reduced hourly earnings by almost 12 percent. Women do not pay a marriage penalty, but they do pay a substantial motherhood penalty, whether or not they marry.

In most married couples with children who are minors, the husband is employed full-time.[30] In about half of these families, the wife also works for pay. In the other half, she takes care of the home and family full-time.

Married women have the option of reducing their work commitment and relying on their husband's income, and married women who have a baby often do work less or leave their jobs altogether. But even when they work full-time, married mothers earn less than working wives without children or working single mothers who cannot rely on a second income.

White married women pay a wage penalty ranging from 3 percent for one child to 16 percent for three kids, compared to single women without children, according to Kermit Daniel. For black wives, kids reduce but do not eliminate the wage premium they get from marriage.

Part of the reason married moms earn less may be that they more often work part-time, and part-time work pays less per hour than the same work done full-time. For white (although not black) married moms, taking into account the amount of hours worked eliminates the effect of children on earnings. White married moms earn less because they choose to work less.

The High Cost of Housework

There is some evidence that the "second shift" affects married women's job performance. In one factory that makes men's suits, where workers are paid by the piece, the more hours a married woman spent in housework, the fewer suits she finished and the less she earned per hour. (Men's productivity in this factory was unaffected by their hours of housework.)[31] Other researchers have found that the wages of both men and women fall as they spend more hours in household chores.[32]

When married women cut back on work to care for children, the family may benefit, but the women themselves are taking a risk—gambling that their marriage will last. Women enjoy a large share of men's earnings only when they are married. After divorce or widowhood, women's financial well-being declines dramatically, as does their children's.[33] Recent changes in divorce law seem to have exacerbated this situation, even while increases in women's education and work experience have moderated it.[34] Faced with high rates of divorce and laws that fail to protect wives and children when marriage dissolves, women will be more reluctant to invest in their husbands' careers and more eager to invest in their own.[35]

Still it is not marriage, per se, but having a child that puts a woman's financial future at risk. A woman who marries and remains childless will enjoy all the emotional, sexual, and physical advantages of marriage and will be financially better off, to boot, enjoying both her own and her husband's earnings.

If she marries and has children, she will probably work less and earn less than she would if she had remained single. If the marriage lasts, she will be far more affluent, on average, than her single sisters. If the marriage fails, she assumes considerably more financial risk than her husband, but she and her children will almost certainly be better off financially than if she had had children out of wedlock.

The risks of divorce have changed married women's behavior considerably. They invest less in their husbands' careers and more in their own. They invest less in children generally, by having fewer of them (although the resources parents devote to each child have risen).[36] Even in enduring marriages, the lack of protection our current divorce law affords mothers has profound effects on family life.

Women who don't want children will risk nothing, career-wise, by getting married, and they gain a share of their husbands' incomes. For the overwhelming majority of women who want children, marriage today provides imperfect protection in exchange for family labor, but certainly a wedding ring still offers mothers a better financial deal than women are likely to receive without it. Inequities caused by divorce (or housework) may be a serious reason for social concern and reform, but they are not good reasons for women to avoid marriage.

Both men and women, it is fair to say, are financially better off because they marry. Men earn more and women have access to more of men's earnings. Though both men and women sometimes kvetch about the financial burden marriage imposes, the research suggests the truth is as Ben Franklin suspected: If more money is your aim, getting married makes it far more likely that you will attain that part of the American dream.

8

FOR RICHER OR FOR POORER

The Wealth and Poverty of Spouses

Tiffany and Lisa are both young mothers, but their lives could not be more different: At sixteen, Tiffany Clay lives with her toddler in a rat-infested apartment with a bullet hole in the front door. She lives on welfare mostly, sharing the apartment with her mother, her eighteen-year-old sister, and her sister's two small kids. A few weeks ago, a man was shot down in his bedroom in the apartment next door. Tiffany, only a sophomore in high school, has no firm plans for the future.[1]

Lisa, an attractive woman in her early twenties, has one toddler and is expecting her second child. Like Tiffany, Lisa has no job. But unlike Tiffany, Lisa lives in a nice two-bedroom home that she co-owns. Money is tight; she clothes her baby boy in garage-sale finds and hand-me-downs. Still, in dramatic contrast to Tiffany's economic situation, Lisa's balance sheet is actually improving even during these difficult years when she is caring for a small child. Not only is Lisa accruing equity with each mortgage payment she makes, she's even managed over the last three years to pay off some back debts.[2]

Why is one young mother building modest wealth while the other languishes in poverty? Obviously, there are many profound differences between Lisa and Tiffany that affect their respective bank ledgers: age, education, ethnicity, family background, work experience, neighborhood characteristics, not to mention choice in men. But surely one important difference influencing Lisa's and Tiffany's financial portfolios is that Lisa is married and Tiffany is not.

Some people argue that marital status is a reflection rather than a cause of wealth and poverty. "Certainly, marriage has clear economic benefits for people with access to steady jobs and stable homes. . . . But marriage has fewer benefits and some surprising costs to people living in poverty," argue Stephanie Coontz and Donna Franklin. "The economic stability of married couples may be the precondition rather than the consequence of marriage."[3]

Perhaps unwed mothers such as Tiffany are so often poor because poorly educated women with few career choices more often choose to have children in this way. Perhaps. Many things besides marital status affect wealth and poverty, of course. (Tiffany's household income could hardly be boosted by marrying a man in jail, for example.) Still, most would suspect that Lisa's relative comfort has something to do with the fact that she is married, and few doubt that Tiffany would have been better off financially if she had avoided unwed motherhood.

What can research tell us about whether, how, and how much marriage affects money? In the larger scheme of things, just how important is marriage to the business of building wealth and the even more urgent task of staying out of poverty? Let's look first at the wealth side of the equation, where the relationship between marriage and money is less well known than that between nonmarriage and poverty but is no less profound.

The Wealth of Spouses

How much wealthier are the married? Consider first the wealth accumulated in families such as Lisa's and Tiffany's, those raising children. Sociologist Lingxin Hao studied how family structure affects net worth, which she argues may be a better measure of financial well-being than income. Family households are mostly young households, saddled with the costs of child-rearing, so the amount of wealth accumulated is not high, on average, for any marital status. In Hao's study, married families had accumulated the most money, with a median net worth of almost $26,000. Remarried families were almost as well off ($22,500) as were single-dad families ($22,930). At the bottom of the heap were both single mothers and (perhaps surprisingly) cohabiting couples who, in marked contrast to married couples, had a median wealth of just $1,000. Single moms typically had *no* assets at all.[4]

But this portrait of wealth as a particular snapshot in time underestimates the true advantages of marriage. For the wealth of spouses grows with each passing year. Economists Joseph Lupton and James P. Smith looked at the net worth of couples in their fifties and early sixties—the peak years for wealth acquisition, after a lifetime of working, but before retirement makes demands on savings. They use a measure of wealth that is quite broad: real assets, financial assets, value of the home—minus debts.

The median married couples (including remarried couples) had a net worth of just over $132,000, or about $65,000 apiece. Each spouse's net worth was almost twice as much as that of the typical divorced person ($33,670). Never-married individuals were only slightly better off, with a median wealth of about $35,000. Widows and widowers fell in between, with a median net worth of just over $47,000. The most disadvantaged were the currently separated with assets of only $7,600.[5]

Next Lupton and Smith measured the wealth of these older Americans, using an even more comprehensive measure. In the United States today a very substantial amount of people's wealth comes from their entitlement to future income from pension plans and Social Security. Despite the fact that Social Security has provisions that are designed to redistribute wealth (low-wage workers get better "returns" than high-wage workers), when these forms of wealth are added in, the financial advantage of the married remains dramatic.

On the verge of retirement, the typical married couple had accumulated about $410,000 (or $205,000 each), compared to about $167,000 for the never-married, just under $154,000 for the divorced, about $151,000 for the widowed, and just under $96,000 for the separated.[6] As Lupton and Smith conclude, "Married couples apparently save significantly more than other households, an effect that is not solely related to their higher incomes nor the simple aggregation of two individuals' wealth. If marriage is related to household savings, the sharp decline in the fraction of American households who are married may be part of the reason for the secular fall in U.S. private savings rates."[7]

The Savings Advantage

Some of the advantage married people have is undoubtedly due to selection—to the fact that educated people and people with higher wages are more likely to get and stay married. But being married in itself seems to encourage the creation and retention of wealth. Smith, for example, investigated people's savings behavior over a five-year period. Couples who stayed married throughout the period saw their assets increase by slightly more than 7 percent a year. By contrast, the assets of individuals who remained divorced over the five years grew at just half that rate. Those who divorced over the five year period actually lost assets, as did the widows.

The marital advantage remained even after taking into account characteristics such as education and health that affect savings. (Since, as we saw in chapter 4, marriage actually causes better health, this study may actually underestimate the effects of marriage on the accumulation of wealth.) The high earnings of married people can account for less than a third of the disparity in wealth.

Looking again at the wealth of Americans in their fifties and early sixties, Smith found that the longer married people stayed married, the greater their wealth accumulations. Conversely, the longer divorced individuals stayed unmarried, the fewer their assets. Spouses who had been married less than five years, for example, had a median net worth of $96,000. Couples who had been married fifteen to nineteen years had a net worth of $125,000, while couples married thirty-five years or more had assets totaling almost $158,000. People who had been divorced less than two years, by contrast, had a median net worth of $41,900; those who had been divorced from fifteen to nineteen years were worth just half as much ($21,400). And those who had remained single for twenty years or more were worth just $7,200.[8]

The story for families with children is similar: The longer marriage lasts the greater the family wealth children enjoy. The number of divorces and remarriages significantly reduces family wealth because divorce is costly and divides assets. Strikingly, for cohabitors (unlike spouses), the length of the relationship has no effect on wealth accumulation.[9] Something about being married causes people to save and acquire more. What might these things be?

A Virtuous Wife (or Husband) Is Beyond Rubies

Albert, who is Lisa's husband, has no doubt: In his case, the thing about being married that helps him to save is his wife. Albert, a machinist who sometimes works two jobs, credits homemaker Lisa for their financial stability. "In this society, you can't get by without money. Lisa takes care of it for us. She's kind of the penny-pincher and I spend it more at whim. Without her, we wouldn't have savings 'cause I can't save. So she's in charge."[10]

Married people, who can take advantage of specialization as Albert and Lisa do, are, as we saw in chapter 2, more productive together than either would be as a single individual. The power of specialization applies not only to goods that are produced and traded in the marketplace (i.e., earnings) but goods that are produced and consumed within the household. Both kinds of production can increase a couple's net worth—the first by directly boosting earnings, the second by cutting expenditures. For example, a parent may cook gourmet meals rather than paying for meals out, or help children with reading difficulties rather than hire an outside tutor.

"She's a great budgeter—one of the great shoppers," said Leonard about his wife, Holly. "I think she belongs to a club that tells you how to get a lot of free things from coupons and she makes a lot of the things we use. She made this suit. Yes, she did . . . she keeps a garden. . . . She's responsible for our having a fine life. I give her money and she makes it go farther than I could ever make it go. She makes a lot more money for us at home than she could [at work]."[11]

Even when both partners work, they can specialize and exchange in ways that leave the family financially better off. Irwin's furniture business, for example, benefits from his wife's expertise as a bookkeeper. "She comes into the office once a month and reconciles the books, tells me what money I have to spend, what to put away for taxes, the whole schmere. I never have to think about it. Anytime I've had to get somebody else to do it, it's never been done as well."[12]

Married people also benefit from economies of scale—two can live as cheaply as one (or at least as one and a half). Married people can share a couch, a bed, a TV, and a microwave, for example. So married people spend less for the same lifestyle than the same individuals would if they lived separately.

Better Than a Piece of the Rock

Husbands and wives offer each other companionship, sex, partnership, but they also offer each other a type of insurance that is better than any policy either of them could buy to protect themselves against life's unexpected events. None of us know how long we will stay healthy or whether or not we will become disabled. We don't know how long we will live or the shape we will be in when we die. This uncertainty makes it hard to know how much to spend now and how much to save against these unforeseen events.

Married couples agree explicitly as part of their marriage vow to support each other "in sickness and in health." In the case of their death, spouses almost always leave their worldly goods—and their Social Security and pension benefits—to their wives or husbands. This promise and their shared fortunes act as a kind of insurance policy; the promise to share until death and bequeath future support acts as an annuity. Of course, people can simply buy annuities—policies that allow people to pay a sum of money now in exchange for a specified stream of payments as long as the person is alive. In practice, though, insurance companies have to charge more to cover the costs of running the business. They also have to charge more because the people who are most likely to buy annuities are precisely those who need them most—those who expect to live an especially long time. So purchased annuities are much more expensive than the same level of insurance that comes with marriage.

Economists Laurence Kotlikoff and Avia Spivak calculated how much spouses gain from pooling their risks in marriage. Just getting married creates an annuity value that is equal to increasing one's wealth by 12 to 14 percent at age thirty and by 30 percent at age seventy-five, compared to staying single. We don't count these windfalls in wealth from marriage in any official statistics, so the astoundingly greater wealth of the married that we noted earlier is really even bigger than it looks.[13] Marriage is, to put it crudely, a valuable commodity in and of itself.

Early to Bed, Early to Rise

Of course, higher earnings and lower costs need not lead to greater wealth. Married people could in theory spend their extra money by, say, taking more expensive vacations (or having more children). But instead, it appears that even at similar income levels, married people save more.

The married lifestyle institutionalizes obligations to children on the parts of both parents (and both sets of grandparents). The social norms associated with marriage encourage people to do things that build wealth: buy a house, save for children's college, acquire a car, and a set of furniture suitable for entertaining.[14]

Married people behave more responsibly about money because they have more responsibilities: both someone to be responsible for and someone to be responsible to. When a single person is struck by the impulse to splurge rather than save, it is nobody's business but his or her own. But when a married person such as Albert thinks about splurging, he or she also has to think about how to explain it to a spouse.

Cohabiting couples often acknowledge, in a backhanded sort of way, this power of marriage over the purse. Both men and women who cohabit often say they relish the freedom it gives them to spend their money any way they see fit. Jane is a pediatrician living with Morton, a lawyer. "Morton was not particularly thrilled when I took the bonus and traded in the Volvo for the Alfa. Well, too bad. I let him alone and I expect him to let me alone." Morton agrees, somewhat wistfully. "I would not always make the same decisions she does. I would save and invest more. But it's her money and I don't dare interfere."[15]

Trading in the Volvo for the Alfa may be fun, but in the long run, it's hard on the bank account. This lack of responsibility for, and accountability to, one's partner may explain why cohabitors seem to reap few if any of the economic gains of marriage. In theory, cohabitors should benefit from economies of scale and opportunities to specialize too.

In theory, for example, Nola and John (who live together) only need one set of silverware. But even after six years together, says Nola,

"He has a drawer for his silverware and I have a drawer for mine. Most of my income I just spend on me and most of his income he just spends on him. I don't have any say over him and he doesn't have any say over me."[16]

In practice, cohabitors' lesser commitment to each other and greater emphasis on personal autonomy prevent the development of the kind of interdependence that produces long-term economic gains. Consequently, while for married people (especially those in a first marriage), the longer the marriage lasts, the greater the family wealth, the duration of cohabitation has no effect on wealth. Merely living together, even for long periods, does not create wealth in the same way that marriage does.[17]

The institution of marriage, and not just the quality of relationship, affects people's economic behavior in profoundly productive ways. Blumstein and Schwartz, for example, found that husbands and wives who do not believe marriage is forever are far less willing to pool their money than other husbands and wives. "Only couples who are committed to the institution of marriage, not simply to each other, feel safe enough to be able to trust their resources to one another."[18]

Marriage is more than a private relationship between two people. The institution of marriage, created and sustained by the norms of the wider society, boosts spouses' confidence that the partnership can be trusted. This confidence allows spouses to order their lives differently than singles or cohabitors do. By pooling money, labor, and time, married people create far more opportunities for building wealth.

The Value of In-laws

Marriage, by transforming a biological stranger into kin, also strengthens the commitment of other relatives to the new family unit. One reason married families have greater wealth than single-parent families do is that spouses get far more financial help from their extended families. About a quarter of families with children received financial transfers in the past five years, with the overwhelming bulk of such personal wealth transfers coming from kin. About 29 percent of married couples received such financial help compared to 28 percent of stepfamilies, 24 percent of cohabiting couples, 19 percent of formerly married moms, and 14 percent of never-married moms.

Even more important, married couples receive help from both sides of the family. Single parents do receive significant family support, but only from their own relatives. Single parents uniformly lose financial support from the relatives of the absent parent. Almost 17 percent of married couples report that they received help from the father's kin (18 percent also received help from the mother's kin). By contrast just 2 percent of divorced moms and no unwed mothers got financial support from relatives of their child's father.[19] Similarly, cohabiting families were only about half as likely as married families to receive help from the father's kin. Marriage not only changes the way spouses behave, it changes the way that spouses' relatives behave as well.

And the returns to marriage seem to be increasing, not decreasing, despite the greater acceptance of alternative family forms. Using a measure of family income adjusted for size and composition of household, economist Lynn Karoly found that married families (along with older adults and the educated) have been the big winners in the economic changes that have taken place since the early seventies. Between 1973 and 1993, for example, female-headed families' income was virtually unchanged, while the income of single-father families dropped 18 percent. Meanwhile, married families' adjusted income increased more than 11 percent.[20]

The Costs of Divorce

When a marriage ends, the same processes that worked to build family wealth now work in reverse to drain the savings account. Two households need more money than one to have the same standard of living—about one-third more income just to break even in terms of lifestyle.

So even if the income is divided fairly between the former spouses, the standard of living of the family drops by about 25 percent. No amount of child support can change the basic math: It costs more to live separately than together, and the money must come from somewhere.

Typically it comes out of the bank accounts of women and children. Annemette Sørensen estimates that the proportion of U.S. families in poverty would almost double if all families had to support two households with the same income. Although overall poverty rates are lower in two European countries she studied (Germany and Sweden), the impact of divorce on poverty is very similar in each nation.[21]

Men who are not married make less money than do husbands, and men who are not married also share less of their income with children and mothers than do married men.[22] Meanwhile, former wives who specialized in child care and homemaking now find themselves disadvantaged in the labor market.

Even wives who are not homemakers can specialize in ways that put them at a disadvantage when a marriage ends. When Paulette was married, she recalls, "We both agreed that he was the brilliant one." So she worked to put him through the Stanford graduate school. "Sure enough, in his last year—not his first year, mind you—he had this affair with someone he was in class with. He was honest about it, I'll say that for him, but he also didn't return the tuition money. . . . He got to get ahead in his career and mine was not even started . . ." says Paulette.[23] Especially when children enter the equation, even former wives who worked find that as single moms, they face new constraints on their hours and travel, because with the marriage's end, they now must shoulder both new breadwinning and new homemaking responsibilities.

Child-support orders tend to be too small to distribute the costs of divorce evenly between mothers and fathers, and many women do not receive even the modest support ordered. About 60 percent of single mothers have a court-ordered child support award, and of these the average award due was only $2,500 a year.[24] Once again, marriage—even a failed marriage—appears to influence the likelihood of receiving support from the father's side. Only 8 percent of never-married mothers receive child support, compared to 43 percent of ever-married mothers.[25]

The net result of these factors is that mothers and children experience large drops in their income after a divorce. Richard Peterson, for example, looking at a sample of divorces in Los Angeles County in the late seventies, found that wives' standards of living dropped 27 percent, while men's standards of living increased by about 10 percent.[26]

Sometimes the drops are even more dramatic. The average mother and child whose family was not poor prior to the divorce suffers a 50 percent drop in income when the parents separated.[27] The average white married mother who experiences a divorce in her child's teen years, for example, sees her family income plunge from $62,000 (in 1992 dollars) to less than $37,000 a few years after divorce. Meanwhile, her stably married counterpart's family income continues to rise over the same period, from $61,500 to almost $67,000.[28]

The effects of divorce on net worth are long-lasting and cumulative. One sociologist compared the assets of people in their fifties who had originally married in their twenties. Getting and staying married was by far the best strategy for accumulating assets. Having been divorced, by contrast, reduced wealth quite substantially, and early divorces had a bigger impact than late-life divorces. Each year spent unmarried decreased total wealth by 3.5 percent. Those who divorced young and did not remarry were particularly disadvantaged as they approached retirement.[29]

When Death Parts Us

Divorce is not the only way marriages end. And financially, the death of husbands can also be a disaster for wives. Women are far more likely to be widowed than men, because husbands tend to be older than wives and because women live longer than men. Most men spend their final hours as husbands; most wives spend their last years as widows.

While widows are far better off than divorced women in terms of assets, the end of marriage still poses substantial financial penalties on women. Even with Social Security, specifically designed to protect widows' financial security, the death of a husband is hardly less devastating than divorce (though far less likely to plunge children into economic distress).

In one national survey, 26 percent of recent widows fell into poverty, whereas only 14 percent were poor prior to their husbands' death.[30] Cathleen D. Zick and Ken R. Smith estimate that 17 percent of women who were not poor prior to their husbands' death became poor because of it.[31] In fact women see their standards of living fall by an average of about one-third when their husbands die, about the same decline in economic well-being that accompanies divorce. Men, by contrast are actually less likely to experience a decline in their financial well-being following the death of their wives than prior to it.[32]

For whatever reason, husbands tend to severely underinsure themselves through the purchase of life insurance against their possible death, failing to protect their wives from economic decline.[33] And Social Security fails to compensate adequately.[34]

The Poverty of Singles

Marriage is not just an emotional but an economic relationship as well. Married couples not only have far more wealth, but they are far less likely to slip into poverty than are single people (especially single mothers). In 1996, for example, 11.5 percent of children younger than six who lived in a married-couple family were poor, compared to almost 59 percent of young children living with a single mother.[35] Not only are children raised outside of intact marriages more likely to experience poverty, but their poverty tends to be deeper and last longer than for impoverished children with married parents.

The amount of extra income that would be needed to pull a poor family over the poverty threshold, for example, is about $1,500 per person for poor married families, but more than $2,000 per capita for single-mother families because poor single-mother families are poorer than poor married-couple families.[36]

Christopher Jencks, looking at causes of rising homelessness, found that for women (but not for men) declines in marriage were key. Low earnings do not themselves put women at risk for poverty. But extremely low incomes among unmarried women is another story. According to Jencks, it was not declines in marriage alone but "the fact that unskilled women not only married less but continued to have children that pushed more of them into the streets."[37]

Sara McLanahan and Gary Sandefur, looking at family income when a child is sixteen (usually the peak of parents' earning powers), found that black teens in single-parent families were more than twice as likely to live in poverty as black children in intact families and white teens were about three times as likely to be poor if they lived with a single mother.

Likewise, 87 percent of two-parent families in McLanahan and

Sandefur's data set owned a home, compared to only 50 percent of single-mother families. Two percent of married families with a sixteen-year-old lived without a car, compared to 30 percent of single mothers of a teen.[38]

One important reason that single mothers and their children are more often poor is that they are younger and less educated than married mothers. But even after researchers take education into account, marital status of the family head has a powerful effect on the likelihood a teen will experience poverty. Forty percent of single mothers (with a sixteen-year-old child) who have no high-school diploma are poor, compared to just 12 percent of married-couple families in which the parents have this much education; more than 14 percent of single mothers with a high-school diploma are poor (during their child's adolescence) compared to just 3 percent of married couples who are high-school graduates.[39]

Economic distress is both a cause and a consequence of marital failure. The government's own official poverty threshold testifies to the protection provided by marriage. The federal poverty guidelines, based on actual expenditures of individuals and families, suggest that a married couple sharing a household needs only about 30 percent more income to avoid being poor than a single person does: the poverty threshold for a single person is $7,299 versus $9,395 for two married people (or any two-person family).[40]

And not only does the end of marriage put women at risk, but getting married is an important route out of poverty for single moms. When Kathleen Mullen Harris followed the progress of a group of black teenage mothers first interviewed in Baltimore in the late seventies, she found that 21 percent of teen moms who left welfare did so through marriage or cohabitation (three-fifths through marriage, two-fifths through moving in with a boyfriend). Despite the fragility of teen marriage, teen moms who were married at their first child's birth had a much better chance of leaving welfare later than those who were unmarried when their first child was born.[41]

In their famous study of poverty, Mary Jo Bane and David Ellwood similarly found that "marriage is an important road out of poverty for [female-headed families], though not as important as work." About a third of single mothers escaped poverty by working, while just over a quarter of single mothers moved out of poverty through marriage.[42]

Marriage plays a powerful role in both the attainment of wealth and the plunge into poverty. When people marry, they are immediately better off, because they now have a claim on not only their own, but their spouses' future income. Over time, the advantages of marriage increase, as couples benefit from higher earnings created by specialization, a lifestyle that encourages savings, the help of a partner in restraining impulse spending, and the reduced costs sharing a life permits.

When it comes to building wealth or avoiding poverty, a stable marriage may be your most important asset.

9

BEING FRUITFUL

Why Married Parents Are Better

It's been twenty-five years since her parents' divorce, but for Karen, it remains the great tragedy of her life. Karen, now twenty-eight, remembers, "I would go days at a time without speaking one word." Another child of divorce, who participated in the same study as Karen did, echoed her sentiments: "I was always angry. My mother wasn't around. I had no one."[1]

Karen is just one of many white middle-class suburban kids whose development was followed by clinical psychologist Judith Wallerstein and for whom the trauma of their parents' divorces lingered for years.

Anecdote and proof are two different things, of course, but a large body of research confirms the general findings of researchers such as Wallerstein. Whether or not parents get and stay married can have long-term consequences for their children, and even their children's children. On average, children of married parents are physically and mentally healthier, better educated, and later in life, enjoy more career success than children in other family settings. Children with married parents are also more likely to escape some of the more common disasters of late-twentieth-century childhood and adolescence.

Divorce is not exactly a random event, striking some families like a bolt of lightning and leaving others miraculously untouched. Many divorces follow years of conflict between spouses, which also takes a toll especially on children. Perhaps single parents have personality characteristics that make them both poor spouses and also less-effective parents. Alcoholics, for example, or people with emotional illnesses would have trouble functioning in either role. Maybe divorce doesn't create problems for kids; maybe difficult children drive their parents to divorce.

Do we have any evidence that the divorce itself causes problems for children? The answer is simple: Yes, a great deal. In a snapshot, the risks of divorce and unwed childbearing for children look like this: Children raised in single-parent households are, on average, more likely to be poor, to have health problems and psychological disorders, to commit crimes and exhibit other conduct disorders, have somewhat poorer relationships with both family and peers, and as adults eventually get fewer years of education and enjoy less stable marriages and lower occupational statuses than children whose parents got and stayed married.[2] This "marriage gap" in children's well-being remains true even after researchers control for important family characteristics, including parents' race, income, and socioeconomic status.

As researchers, who were at first skeptical of the idea that divorce can cause long-term harm, began checking out alternate explanations for the negative impact on children of nonintact families, the power of marriage itself to protect kids has become clearer. One study by Andrew Cherlin, Lindsay Chase-Lansdale, and Christine McRae explicitly took into account predivorce characteristics of the child and family, such as the child's emotional problems and the family's economic situation. The researchers found that "part of the negative effect of parental divorce on adults is a result of factors that were present before the parents' marriage dissolved. The results also suggest, however, a negative effect of divorce and its aftermath on adult mental health. Moreover, a parental divorce during childhood or adolescence continues to have a negative effect when a person is in his or her twenties and early thirties."[3]

Similarly, Sara McLanahan and Gary Sandefur used various sophisticated statistical techniques to isolate the effect of family disruption from the characteristics of couples prior to divorce. This analysis suggested that "coming from a disrupted family reduces child well-being by a considerable amount, even after adjusting for unobserved differences [between single-parent families and families in which parents stay married]."[4]

Of course, the idea that losing a parent might hurt kids is not some arcane, difficult-to-understand notion—it is the idea that underlies the virtually universal impulse in human society to push the principle of "legitimacy," the idea that children "ought" in some sense to be born inside marriage.

Why does it matter to kids whether or not their parents are married? What are the pathways by which the marriage of parents shapes the future of their children? A short answer is this: Marriage shapes children's lives first and foremost by directing the time, energy, and resources of two adults toward them.

Marriage Means More Money

The first obvious advantage of an intact family is a better standard of living. Divorce costs children many of the advantages that money can buy. On average, divorce causes a child's standard of living to drop by about one-third. For middle-class children, the losses may be even larger. "The average decline in income of a mother and child who are living in a nonpoor family prior to separation is 50 percent," report McLanahan and Sandefur.[5]

Having one parent generally means having less money, because fathers who don't live with their kids share relatively little of their income with them.[6] In fact, children in single-parent families are often doubly disadvantaged; they have access to the earnings of only one adult, and that adult is usually a woman.

But even kids raised by single fathers have a lower standard of living than children raised by both their parents. In 1994, according to the Census Bureau, 31 percent of single fathers were in the bottom fifth of the income distribution, compared to 49 percent of single mothers and just 12 percent of married-couple families.[7] Children in single-parent families lose the built-in economic advantages of the married partnership: economies of scale (that reduce expenses) and specialization (that boosts productivity both inside and outside the home). Men who aren't married make less money than husbands (as we saw in chapter 7). And when divorced men remarry, they acquire new obligations to share the wealth with a person who may not be thrilled about sharing family income with someone else's kids.

When marriage fails (or fails to form), poverty rushes in. Sociologists Sara McLanahan and Gary Sandefur estimate that almost half of black children living with one parent are poor, compared to less than one-fifth in two-parent families. For whites, the marriage gap is just as large, although poverty rates for whites are much lower than for blacks.[8]

Living in poverty is in itself difficult for children, increasing stress, poor health, weak social support, and maternal depression.[9] Poverty also has important indirect effects that create psychological distress for children. Poor parents, for example, find it harder to maintain a warm, consistent parenting style; they give their kids less positive emotional responses and are more likely to resort to harsh discipline.

Less money is part of the reason children of divorce do less well than children in intact marriages, but it is not the whole story. McLanahan and Sandefur's research indicated that about half the worst outcomes for children in single-parent families were due to lower incomes. The other half was due to children's access, or lack thereof, to the time, attention, and social resources of two parents. Money is not all that parents have to offer their kids, after all. Sociologist Susan Mayer discovered in her national study that absent extreme deprivation, what parents do with the money they have, rather than the amount they earn, makes the most difference for children. She stated, "The activities, possessions, and housing environments that are important to children's outcomes are only modestly related to parents' income. Whether children have these amenities depends on parents' tastes and values."[10]

Time Enough for Love

Two parents are better than one in part for the simple reason that they have between them twice as many adult hours to give to their kids. But two married parents can also give their children the benefits of specialization. They can divide work for pay and work in the home between them, while single parents must do it all themselves. Two-job couples can divide child care between them by working different shifts or coordinating their hours to arrange more parental time with their kids.[11] Having Mom and Dad in the same home means more parental supervision, more help with homework, another shoulder to cry on after a hard day.[12] Two parents make it twice as likely that a child will find a good math tutor in his home, as well as someone who can help out with the art projects, than a child with only one parent to turn to. In one national study,

81 percent of children in two-parent families said that they get homework help from their fathers, compared to just 56 percent in single-parent families and 68 percent in stepfamilies.[13]

Less access to Dad is compounded by the other usual consequences of divorce: less time with Mom, who is suddenly pressured to do all the jobs in running a home and earning a living that she used to share with Dad. So children in single-parent families also get less time with their *mothers* than do children in two-parent families. One 1997 study of children's time use found that children in one-parent families got about nine hours less from their mother and about thirteen hours less from either parent per week than did children in two-parent families, even after researchers controlled for socioeconomic characteristics.

The consequences of less time with parents can be profound: fewer hours spent supervising homework may explain why children in single-parent families perform less well in school and are more likely to get into trouble, on average, than are children with married parents.

Stronger Family Bonds

Less time and money also translate into weaker emotional bonds between parents and children. The most obvious casualty of divorce is the relationship with fathers. Except where fathers have custody, time and attention from Dad dwindles. With the passing of years, often the divorce itself results in the child's total loss of relationship with his or her father.[14]

But you may be surprised to learn that the single-parent family takes a toll on the mother-child bond as well. Adult children whose parents divorced, for example, are about 40 percent less likely than children whose parents remained married to say they see either their mother or father at least several times a week. When asked to rate their relationship with their parents, adult children raised by married parents describe their current relationship with both their mothers and fathers more positively than do children raised in unwed or divorced families.[15]

How does divorce weaken family bonds? A combination of less time and more stressful family relationships translates into less frequent contact and weaker emotional ties, on average, between single parents and their adult children.

Moreover, the departure of a parent from the family home presents children with a model of family bonds as optional relationships. A divorce, after all, is a public declaration that two people who used to be each other's "next of kin" are now no longer related at all. Children in single-parent households learn that family members come and go and that family relationships don't necessarily last. These lessons linger long into adulthood.

Less Social Capital

Children in single-parent families typically have less contact with other adults in the community as well, less of what sociologist James Coleman calls social capital. Social capital consists of the bonds between parents and their children's friends' parents, their children's teachers, coaches, religious leaders, as well as other adults. These ties with other adults help parents to supervise and guide their children's lives.[16]

Where fathers play only a marginal role (as is typical with unwed or long-divorced families), children grow up with only half the kin network and half the adult friendships that can provide support, guidance, and access to technical expertise, school recommendations, and job referrals.

The social capital created by married families benefits not only the children of that marriage, but other kids in the neighborhood too. The risk that a teen will engage in juvenile crime, for example, is heavily influenced not just by whether or not his own parent is married, but whether or not he lives in a neighborhood where single-parent families are common.

Sociologist Robert Sampson suggests that two-parent families are more effective in controlling the minor delinquent acts—"hanging out," truancy and vandalism—that set the stage for more serious crime. In communities composed primarily of single parents, people are less involved in community politics, in recreational and service organizations such as the YMCA, or even educational organizations such as the library, which teach teens important skills, link them to other adults and wider social institutions, and help parents teach values and beliefs that encourage responsible behavior.[17]

Similarly, a loss of social capital—of the wider network of relationships with adults and the community—is one of the most wrenching parts of divorce for many kids. Because two households cannot live as cheaply as one, divorce usually requires custodial mothers to move—either to sell the house or move to a smaller apartment, often in a cheaper neighborhood, in a different school system.[18] And because divorce generally lowers children's standard of living, their new house, new neighborhood, and new school are probably not as nice as their old ones.

That makes for big differences: The more threatening the neighborhood, the more the teens who live there display symptoms of depression, anxiety, oppositional defiant disorder, and conduct disorder.[19]

More Sickness and Less Health

Divorce itself appears to be literally making some children sick. Using the National Health Interview Survey to track the health of children prior to and following their parents' separation, one researcher found divorce made it 50 percent more likely a child would have health problems.[20]

For children, just as for adults, married homes are healthier homes. Children living in female-headed homes are more likely to be hospitalized, to have chronic health conditions such as asthma, heart ailments, or convulsions than are children in two-parent homes. Fifty-eight percent of white married parents rate their children's health as "excellent," compared to just 46 percent of white single mothers. Black children receive a similar, though not quite as large, health boost from marriage: 38 percent of black married mothers say their child's health is "excellent," compared to less than 31 percent of black single mothers. The health advantage of married homes for children remains sizable, even after taking into account the lower average education and income of female-headed families.[21]

For babies, marriage can make the difference between life and death. White babies born to unmarried moms are 70 percent more likely to die in the first year of life, while black infants born out of wedlock are 40 percent more likely to die before their first birthday. Even for college-educated white mothers (the demographic group whose babies have the lowest infant-mortality rate), being unmarried increases the risks a baby will die by 50 percent.[22] The greater danger babies of unmarried mothers face can be found in other countries too. A study of Sudden Infant Death Syndrome (SIDS) fatalities in Denmark, Norway, and Sweden found that all babies put to sleep on their stomachs faced higher risks of SIDS but that this risk varied greatly depending on whether or not the mother was married. If a married mother put her baby to sleep on its stomach, her baby was almost thirteen times more likely to die of SIDS. But a baby's risk of sudden death was fifty-six times greater for stomach-sleeping babies of unmarried mothers than for back-sleeping babies of married mothers. It is not clear how a mother's marriage helps an infant avoid SIDS, but the impact is huge.[23]

How does having married parents protect kids' health? Probably in some of the same ways that married adults are healthier. Married parents have more money and are also more likely to have private health insurance, advantages their children share. Married women drink less than single women and are also less likely to use illegal drugs, which may have direct effects on infant mortality.[24]

Another reason children in married families are healthier is that they are more closely supervised, which means reduced risk of accidents. A New Zealand study, for example, found that white children in single-parent families were more likely to be killed or hospitalized as a result of pedestrian injury than children in two-parent families. (Extended kin networks seemed to protect children of Pacific Island origin in single-parent families).[25] The lack of emotional support from a partner may also make it harder for a single mother to manage a child's health problems effectively.[26]

Whatever the reasons, parents' decision to divorce creates health risks for their kids that persist long into adulthood. Parents' divorce knocked four years off the life expectancy of their adult children, according to one study that followed the life course of a group of highly advantaged kids— white, middle class, with an IQ of at least 135—through their seventies. Forty-year-olds from divorced homes were three times as likely to die from all causes as forty-year-olds whose parents stayed married.[27]

In another Swedish study adults who had been raised in single-parent families were one-third more likely to die over the sixteen-year study period than were adults from intact families. Even after researchers took economic hardship into account, adults from "broken families" were 70 percent more likely to have circulatory problems, 56 percent more likely to show signs of mental illness, 27 percent more likely to report chronic aches and pains, and 26 percent more likely to rate their overall health as poor.[28]

Better Mental and Emotional Health

Most children find their parents' divorce to be at least temporarily traumatic. In the immediate aftermath, they frequently show signs of anxiety, depression, and disruptive behavior.[29] The vast majority recover, but some do not. Analyzing one study of seventeen thousand children born in a single week in 1958 whose mental-health characteristics were tracked until they were twenty-three years old Lindsay Chase-Lansdale, Andrew Cherlin, and Kathleen Kiernan looked at rates of psychological symptoms, including headaches, violent rages, worrying, sleep troubles, and other indicators of emotional distress. They found that 11 percent of young adults from divorced families had seven or more symptoms, indicating a high likelihood of mental illness, compared to 8 percent of those from intact two-parent families.[30]

Remarriage does not improve the psychological well-being of children, on average. And children in cohabiting couples also show poorer emotional health than children from married, two-parent families—closely resembling children in remarried and single-parent families.[31]

As adults, children whose parents divorced show slightly higher levels of behavioral and psychological problems on average than do those whose parents remained married, according to Paul R. Amato and Alan Booth.[32] But these averages disguise the quite different effects of two distinct types of divorce. When divorce occurs after a sustained period of high conflict between parents, children's psychological health may actually improve as a result. But when, as in the majority of cases today, divorce occurs in families with lesser levels of conflict, the divorce is especially traumatic to the child (more on that in chapter 10).[33]

Less Education

Over time, less money, less time, less social capital, and more stress in single-parent families translate into less education for children of divorce. Children of married parents get more schooling than children in single-parent families, even after researchers control for family characteristics such as income and education.

The education gap begins early and persists into adulthood. One quarter of children in mother-only and remarried families repeat a grade in school, compared to 14 percent of those in married families. Twenty-three percent of kids in mother-only families and 18 percent of children in stepfamilies have been suspended or expelled, compared to less than 10 percent in mother-father families. Fifty-two percent of children in mother-only and 48 percent in remarried families are in the bottom half of their class, compared to 38 percent of children whose parents are still married.[34]

Living in a single-parent family approximately doubles the risk that a child will become a high-school dropout: 29 percent of children in one-parent homes dropped out of high school, compared to 13 percent in two-parent families, according to McLanahan and Sandefur's research. This gap is not due to differences among families in income, education, family size, or the part of the country they live in—all of which McLanahan and Sandefur took into account.

Children whose parents stay married are also more likely to get a college education. Sixty percent of children in intact families enroll in college, compared to 50 percent of children in one-parent or stepparent families. Children with two married parents are about one-third more likely to earn a college degree than children from one-parent or stepparent homes.[35]

How does divorce disrupt college plans? Consider the experience of Frank, a college senior expecting to graduate with honors from an elite private university in the Midwest. He came to see Linda about the senior thesis he had to write. He was having trouble finding time to spend on his paper because he was working four jobs. "Why are you working so much?" Linda asked. Frank's parents had recently divorced. His parents had encouraged him to attend the expensive private college over an excellent state institution, promising to pay. Now his mother, a high-school teacher, wasn't able to pay for college tuition. His father had stopped supporting him at all. With neither parent paying any of his college expenses, Frank had to take out loans and work several jobs to stay in school. Frank was able to finish his degree (albeit with a heavy load of debt). But many from divorced families aren't able to overcome these obstacles.

Married parents have more time to help with homework, and they move less frequently, which translates into fewer disruptive changes of schools for children.[36] Married parents have more money, which means better schools in safer neighborhoods and higher aspirations for college.

More Crime and Delinquency

Both divorced and unwed parenting dramatically increase the risk that a child will get into trouble with the law. Even after researchers control for factors such as neighborhood characteristics, race, mother's education, and cognitive ability, boys raised in single-parent homes are twice as likely (and boys raised in stepfamilies three times as likely) to have committed a crime that leads to incarceration by the time they reach their early thirties.[37]

Teens in both one-parent and remarried homes display more deviant behavior (and commit more delinquent acts) than teens whose parents stayed married.[38] Twice as many young teens in single-mother families and stepfamilies reported having tried marijuana, for example. (Young teens living with single fathers were almost three times as likely to try marijuana.) When it comes to cigarettes and booze, young teens in stepfamilies were even more likely to indulge than teens in single-parent homes, while young teens in married homes are the least likely to experiment with tobacco or alcohol.[39]

Why do married parents do a better job of keeping their kids out of trouble? Certainly better schools and neighborhoods help. But the main pathway may be straight through the heart. In the late eighties, two criminologists, Ross Matsueda and Karen Heimer, assessed the impact of family structure on adolescents' own reports of delinquent acts over the past year. Teens in one-parent families, they found, were less attached to their parents and more attached to peers than teens with two parents. Consequently, the opinions of single parents simply have less influence on the way their child defines the world on such important issues as whether or not it is important to follow the rules, keep out of trouble, and work hard.

Teens from single-parent families are more apt to develop beliefs such as "Most things that people call 'delinquency' don't really hurt anyone" or "It is all right to get around the law if you can get away with it." Combined with lower levels of parental supervision, these attitudes set the stage for delinquent behavior.

Black children are particularly put at risk of delinquency by the lack of two parents, perhaps because they are more likely to live in neighborhoods with a high proportion of single-parent families. Not only do they have attitudes and beliefs conducive to delinquency, but so do more of their peers, magnifying the effects of single parenthood. But all children are more likely to get into trouble at school and on the streets, if they are raised without both parents in the home.

More Child Abuse

Living without both parents not only increases the risk that a child will commit a crime, but it increases the likelihood he or she will be the victim of a crime as well, especially the devastating crime of being abused in your own home. Children in single-parent families are also more likely to become a victim of domestic violence. Stepfathers and mothers' boyfriends are disproportionately likely to sexually and otherwise abuse children. Indeed, a large body of research confirmed that as Martin Daly and Margo Wilson put it, "[S]tepchildren constituted an enormously higher proportion of child abuse victims in the United States than their numbers in the population-at-large would warrant."

One recent study of women seeking refuge at a battered women's shelter in Canada found that women who had children from a previous union were twice as likely as women who had only their present partner's children to report their abusive partner assaulted the children as well. "Living with a stepparent has turned out to be the most powerful predictor of severe child abuse yet," concluded Wilson and Daly.[40]

The Married Advantage

For children, the advantages of having married parents last long into adulthood. Less education means that as adults, children raised outside of intact marriages have on average, lower incomes, less prestigious jobs, and greater unemployment rates than their more fortunate peers.

Adults raised by one parent work in occupations of lower status, are more likely to experience economic hardship as adults, and more likely to report they ran out of money for basic necessities over the past years.[41]

McLanahan and Sandefur found that even after taking parental socio-economic status into account, children whose parents divorced or never married were about one and a half times more likely to be "idle"—out of school and out of work—in their early twenties than children whose parents stayed married. Differences in academic ability as measured by tests accounted for only about a fifth of the higher rates of idleness among young adults raised in single-parent families.[42]

Unto the Fourth Generation?

When two parents' marriage fails (or fails to form), the effects can extend far into the future. For children raised outside of intact marriages are disadvantaged not only in terms of education, career, and financial success, but as adults, they face greater challenges in building a satisfying family life as well. Children whose parents divorce or never marry begin sex earlier, get pregnant out of wedlock more often, and more frequently become a teen parent (both married and unmarried). They are less likely to be happily married and more likely to divorce than children whose parents got and stayed married.[43]

Divorce in one generation leads to a big increase in illegitimacy in the next. Young women whose parents divorced, for example, were more than three times as likely to have an out-of-wedlock child as were women whose parents stayed married. (Seventeen percent of young women whose parents divorced had an out-of-wedlock child, compared to just 5 percent of women whose parents stay married.) Parental divorce also almost tripled the chances that young women left home early because of friction and doubled the chances that they cohabited before marriage.[44]

Men whose parents divorced were also disproportionately likely to leave home early, to cohabit, and to have out-of-wedlock children. A parental divorce tripled the likelihood that a boy would leave home early because of family conflict, more than doubled the likelihood of cohabitation before marriage, and nearly doubled the chance that he would be a father before marriage.[45]

One reason children in single-parent families are at greater risk for out-of-wedlock births is that they start having sex at much earlier ages. Only 11 percent of teens from age twelve to fourteen who are living with both of their parents have ever had sex, compared to 21 percent of those living with a mother and stepfather, 23 percent of those living with a single mother, 27 percent of those living with a single father, and 28 percent living with a father and stepmother, according to one study.[46]

Daughters of single mothers often observe their mother dating, or more. When a mother has a boyfriend sleep over, it may be more difficult for her to enforce prohibitions against teen sex. The daughters of mothers who divorce and remarry develop a more liberal view of sex outside of marriage than do daughters of married mothers whose sex lives are apparently more discreet, or, at any rate, are much less likely to be visibly nonmarital. Even worse, the men whom a single mother brings home may, as we have seen, pose a threat to teenage girls, or these men may introduce their single friends and acquaintances in the home, putting the girls at risk for premature sexual activity.[47]

The divorce itself, in other words, may have not just long-term consequences but intergenerational ones as well. When parents are unable or unwilling to build a good-enough marriage, the consequences may be felt not only by their children, but by their children's children who will be far more likely, as a result, to experience and pass on the deprivations of poverty, the trauma of fatherlessness, and the health risks and economic handicaps of living outside of marriage.

The Divorce Itself

Influenced by the mounting weight of evidence, most first-rate family scholars now believe that family structure matters, but the idea that children are better off when they are raised by their two, married parents is not an uncontested one. Academics have engaged in an active debate over how, if at all, the legal status of parents—a mere piece of paper—can have such broad, profound, and long-lasting effect on the health and happiness of their kids.

Those who doubt that marriage itself has a strong impact on children generally make one of two arguments: First, some argue that when it comes to children, it is money, not matrimony that actually matters. Poverty, not the absence of two parents, explains the difficulties children outside of marriage experience.[48]

Others say the damage apparently caused by divorce is actually a result of family conflict. Family structure (i.e., an intact marriage), they say, is not in itself important for predicting children's well-being; what matters is rather the underlying family processes, the emotional environment in which kids are raised.

As Arlene Skolnick, a major advocate of this point of view, put in her recent family-studies textbook, "The majority of well-designed studies . . . find that family structure—the number of parents in the home or the fact of divorce—is not in itself the critical factor in children's well-being. In both intact and other families, what children need most is a warm, concerned relationship with at least one parent."[49]

Both these arguments, we believe, represent a classic case of the false dichotomy. No reputable family scholar (not to mention any normal human being) doubts that either poverty or intense infighting between parents creates serious problems for children. But since divorce in itself makes kids poorer, reduces the likelihood that a child will have a good relationship with both mother and father, and can sometimes even increase conflict between parents, these arguments strike us as very poor evidence for the idea that marriage itself does not matter.

Certainly, it makes no sense to try to distinguish the effects of the divorce itself from the effects of less income, if one of the most consistent consequences of divorce for children (in every country we know of) is a lower standard of living. Nor can we conclude that it is not marriage that matters but rather warm parental bonds, if it is marriage that creates the conditions under which warm, affectionate, consistent parenting is most likely to take place.

One recent study of two thousand married families by Paul Amato and Alan Booth sought to distinguish the long-term effects of marital conflict and divorce on children's well-being. In many outcomes, both divorce and poor marital quality seemed to have independently harmful effects. If married parents didn't get along, their children reported less affection from both parents (relationships with fathers suffered the most). But even after Amato and Booth controlled for predivorce marital quality, divorce itself further weakened relations between parents and children. "[R]elations with parents appear to suffer, on average, more when parents divorce than when unhappily married parents stay together," reported the researchers.[50]

For children's ultimate socioeconomic attainment, the quality of parents' marriage appears to matter far less than its durability—it is divorce that influences how much education children get, what kind of careers they pursue, and how much money they will make as adults. When it comes to educating and launching children into the world of work, the structural supports marriage provides are more important than the emotional ones.

Of course this does not mean that all children of divorce are doomed to lead substandard lives. A majority will surmount the various tensions and disadvantages imposed by growing up outside of an intact marriage and go on to graduate, work, marry and become healthy, happy, productive citizens. The absence of a stable marriage is a risk factor in a child's life, not a prophecy of certain doom.

The same of course could be said about many other risks Americans are concerned about. Many, perhaps even a majority, of cigarette smokers lead long and healthy lives. Nonetheless, both families and societies are urgently interested in cutting rates of smoking, particularly among teenagers. As Sara McLanahan and Gary Sandefur point out, parents routinely try to head off much smaller risks to their children's well-being than those posed by divorce: "[W]hile the chance that a middle-class child will drop out of high school or become a teen mother is very low, it is higher than the likelihood that he or she will be severely injured or killed in a car accident. Yet parents take the latter very seriously."[51]

When parents divorce, they do put their children at risk of

long-lasting damage. On average, children lucky enough to have married parents lead emotionally and physically healthier, wealthier, longer, better educated, and more financially successful lives as a result.

Of course, no one doubts that there are cases when divorce or separation really is the best answer for everyone. There are circumstances in which children are better off when parents part. The question for struggling spouses is, When?

10

WHEN SHOULD PARENTS PART?

Suppose for the moment that your only concern as a parent is what's best for your kids. Your marriage is ho-hum, struggling even. Or maybe it's not you but your son or daughter, friend or neighbor who is feeling trapped and thinking about divorce. In any case, you want to know: When is a divorce really better for everyone concerned?

In America today, both inside and outside the academy, there are two schools of thought. For people such as Brian and Elisa, divorce is the enemy. They are an engaged couple madly in love, and as one reporter described it, "Brian and Elisa have to pause, untwine hands and count on their fingers to add up the ruined marriages of their baby-boomer parents: nine."

On the eve of becoming one of the first wave of young couples in Louisiana to opt for covenant marriage, with its modest restrictions on divorce, Brian and Elisa can recount a parade of stepparents—"the one who drank, the one who hit, the one who made everyone laugh, the one who left without a word."

The one strong impression left on this young couple by the ever-changing cast of family characters: "Divorce is like a bad word to us," says Brian. Brian's quadruply divorced mother, Sandy, left her first husband after five years and three babies because he was too critical, demeaning, and, says Sandy, "emotionally uninvolved." In her own mind, a divorce was bad, but the worst thing was a bad marriage, like the kind her parents had. "For many years my mother stayed with my father for the sake of the children. And I left the boys' father for the same reason. I felt that together, we could do them a lot of harm."

That was 1976. So at twenty-five she found herself with a high-school diploma, three small boys, and a minimum-wage job. The fears that she couldn't support her sons drove her into, as she says now, "relationships and marriages that were not good choices." Husbands Number Two and Number Three had drug and alcohol problems. Husband Number Four brought three teenage stepchildren (plus her own three kids) into a small three-bedroom house. She got pregnant again. The marriage lasted eighteen months.

In 1998 she watched her son consciously strive for commitment and fidelity, being friends for a year before dating, and postponing sex until marriage. "I think we have a generation of kids trying to change things now, wanting to get back to the basics. We lost that commitment and got into this mind-set of everything being too easy—get in, get out. Myself included," Sandy observes. "The baby boomers have kind of messed this marriage thing up."[1]

The debate taking place in the hearts and minds of Sandy and her family is echoed in homes and hearts across the country. When it comes to the idea of getting married, most Americans remain notably enthusiastic. Ninety-two percent of Americans tell pollsters that having a successful marriage is very important to them. Just 8 percent consider marriage an outdated institution.[2]

For most people, the really pressing question they are likely to wrestle with at some point in their lives is not, "Should I get married?" but "Should I stay married, maybe even for the sake of the kids?"

This heartfelt debate is central to the future of marriage as a permanent commitment. And it is a debate that is taking place, not only among people but within people. On the one hand, Americans hate divorce and long for enduring marriage, for dependable love for themselves and their children. On the other hand, we are very much afraid of being trapped in a loveless relationship. Almost three-quarters of adults agree that "marriage is a lifelong commitment that should not be ended except under extreme circumstances."[3] Seventy percent in a 1993 poll viewed parents' getting divorced as "a big problem." Yet at the same time, when asked whether they believed that a couple with young children "should not get divorced even if they are unhappy," 61 percent of Americans said that was a view they "no longer believe in."[4]

So many of us see a 50 percent divorce rate as a necessary antidote to something even worse: the bad marriage. Maybe in today's world, we reason hopefully, the good marriages, the kind that promote health, wealth, and happiness continue to thrive, while our divorce culture encourages the bad marriages to dwindle away.

Maybe what really counts, as some social scientists have argued, is not marital status per se but emotional closeness. Maybe as two scholars suggested in an influential review of the literature, "The conflict associated with divorce, rather than the breakup of the family, is primarily responsible for many of the problems seen in children whose parents divorce."[5] Maybe, as three researchers noted, "[C]onflict may be more influential than divorce per se in a child's adjustment."[6] Maybe some assume that "divorce is bad for children," but as University of Pennsylvania professor Demie Kurz, put it, "Other highly reputable data, however, show that children in a strife-torn marriage can face hardships, and that it is very difficult to demonstrate that divorce makes children worse off than children in such marriages."[7] Maybe we need to ask, as sociologist Constance Ahrons has, "If these unhappy families stayed together, would that be better for the kids?"[8]

Maybe, as one popular magazine interpreted this sort of expert's thinking, "It takes a lot more character to end a wrong marriage than to stay in it. It's not easy, but for the children's sake and yours, it is right. . . . [I]f you don't show your children the kind of relationship you want them to have, you're training them to repeat the same scenes in their own marriage."[9]

Maybe, as one middle-class unwed mother put it, "Single parenthood is not a bad second to a superb marriage, and a poor marriage is a poor third."[10] Maybe, as one divorced Albuquerque mother put it, "Staying is counterproductive."[11]

Maybe. Or maybe not.

For the Sake of the Children?

While staying together for the sake of the children was once the norm, today's Americans are more likely to tell an unhappy couple that they should divorce—sometimes, as Brian's mom put it, even for the sake of the children.

Two psychologists from the University of California at Berkeley stated in a 1997 letter to the *New York Times* that "children are at risk when their parents fight a lot—and it is this conflict, not divorce, that is so harmful to children."[12]

Under the influence of such ideas, ordinary parents say things such as this mother said: "What pushed me over the edge [to divorce] was that I was training my children to think this is what a relationship is about—total emptiness."[13] Is she right? Are children usually better off when unhappy parents divorce? Our conclusion, after we looked at the best scientific research on the topic, is that in the majority of divorces, the answer is no.

How can this be, when every family expert agrees that intense marital conflict is very damaging for children? Well, for one thing, there's a big difference between fighting a lot and being unhappy with your marriage. Research suggests that marital dissatisfaction is probably not in and of itself psychologically damaging for children: what counts is whether, how often, and how intensely parents fight in front of their children both before and after divorce.

As two influential researchers sum up the evidence, "encapsulated conflict," or conflict of which children were not aware, was not associated with behavior problems. Similarly child problems were found to be more highly associated with unhappy marriages that were quarrelsome, tense, and hostile than to unhappy marriages characterized by apathy and indifference."[14]

Adults may prefer to be joyously in love, but children don't much care whether parents zoom to heights of romantic ecstasy or not. Your children don't care whether your marriage feels dead or alive, empty or full. As long as Mom and Dad don't fight too much, they thrive under the love, attention, and resources two married parents provide.

Moreover, while divorce ends marital conflict, it doesn't necessarily stop (and may even increase) what really bothers kids: parental conflict. Divorced parents can (and often do) keep fighting. When this happens, children can be especially devastated. Researchers at the University of Georgia conducted a study of fifty-six young teens, dividing them into four groups, based on their parents' marital status and quality: high-conflict intact marriages, low-conflict intact marriages, low-conflict divorces, and high-conflict divorces. Teachers rated adolescents from high-conflict divorced families as functioning significantly more poorly than the remaining groups, which was reflected in their grades as well. For example, children from high-conflict intact families, where parents had thoughts of divorce, had an average GPA of 3.6, while teens from divorced high-conflict families had an average GPA of just 2.4.[15]

When it comes to helping kids succeed in school, the structural benefits of marriage—more money, better schools and neighborhoods, and more time for supervision—seem to matter more than whether or not parents have a close and warm marital relationship.

Similarly, the structure that marriage provides appears to help parents maintain the kind of consistent, moderate discipline to which children respond, even when the marriage is less than ideal. One study investigated the relationship of marital status and marital quality to children's compliance, interviewing 117 mothers who were attending a parenting clinic to deal with their young children's conduct disorders. As expected, maritally troubled moms had a harder time getting their children to behave than more happily married mothers. But even after researchers controlled for income, single mothers reported more discipline problems than unhappily married mothers and perceived themselves as more stressed than either group of married mothers.

And while maritally distressed mothers may have been distracted by ongoing troubles in their marriage, single moms reported "ongoing chronic conflict with ex-spouses or repeated conflict and separations from boyfriends."[16]

Divorce, while it may relieve some sources of emotional distress, often creates brand-new ones. And single mothers must deal with these new emotional stresses while at the same time coping with the structural strains of taking on the disciplining, nurturing, and caretaking of children, and the breadwinning for them, all by themselves.

A recent Dutch study, for example, directly investigated the question of whether or not children in single-parent families are worse off than children in conflicted intact families. They found, to their surprise, that while children in troubled marriages did do less well than children from happier intact families, children in single-parent families were even worse off. When it comes to relational problems and employment difficulties, the researchers observed, "Youngsters from single-parent families are the worst off, despite the fact that the divorce may have taken place ten years ago, and even controlling for income."[17]

The divorce optimists who see keeping an unhappy marriage together for the sake of the kids as pointless, often point to a study conducted by Andrew Cherlin and his colleagues on how parental divorce affects children's mental health.[18] While mental health was the only outcome they studied, Cherlin and his colleagues did find that most of the apparent effects of divorce on children were actually due to family and child characteristics prior to divorce.

But in reexamination of the issue in two more recent studies, Cherlin and his colleagues have concluded that the divorce itself does have additional long-term negative effects on children's psychological well-being. Even after controlling for predisruption differences, for example, they found that twenty-three-year-olds who experienced a parental divorce before age sixteen had poorer mental health, on average, than children from intact families.[19] Similarly, when Cherlin and fellow researchers followed the effects of divorce on a large sample of British kids until the study participants reached age thirty-three, they found that the mental health of adults from intact and divorced families continued to diverge years after the divorce.

"Part of the negative effect of parental divorce on adults is a result of factors that were present before the parents' marriages dissolved," the researchers summed up. "The results also suggest, however, a negative effect of divorce and its aftermath of adults' mental health. Moreover, a parental divorce during childhood or adolescence continues to have a negative effect when a person is in his or her twenties and early thirties."[20]

The most ambitious attempt to distinguish between the effects of divorce and the effects of marital quality on children appears in a study by Paul Amato and Alan Booth in which they tracked the characteristics of more than two thousand married people over a fifteen-year period.

On most measures they found that both a poor marriage and a divorce depress children's well-being. For example, even after controlling for predivorce conflict, Amato and Booth determined that over the long haul, parental divorce led to more problematic relationships between parents and child, increased the likelihood that adult children would divorce themselves, and lowered children's future education and career success. In other words, reported Amato and Booth," [L]ow parental marital quality lowers offspring well-being and parental divorce lowers it even further."[21]

Even after the researchers controlled for income, education, race, sex, and other factors, they found that a parental divorce lowered the number of years of education that a child finished by about half a year. They pointed out that half a year of schooling, more or less, may not sound like much, but since each year of education raises annual income by $4,000, when you multiply the loss in yearly income by the number of years that people typically work over their lifetime, the loss in lifetime earnings is very large.[22] And of course controlling for income may underestimate the true impact of divorce, since in the real world, lower income is one of the most predictable consequences of the breakup of a marriage.

Moreover, suggested Amato and Booth, the average effects of divorce were confounding two quite different types of situations: divorces that take place in high-conflict marriages and divorces which take place in other families where family life is not constantly disrupted by arguments and/or violence.

Psychologically, at least, children in very high-conflict marriage families experience their parents' divorce as a relief. When marriages of more middling quality end, however, children experience the family breakup as an unmitigated and inexplicable disaster.

The bad news is that in this country, the majority of divorces involving children apparently are not ending terrible marriages but marriages that are, from a child's point of view, at least "good enough."

"What proportion of divorces are preceded by a long period of overt interparental conflict, and hence, are beneficial to children?" asked Amato and Booth. "From our own data we estimate that less than a third of parental divorces involve highly conflicted marriages."[23] Just 30 percent of divorcing spouses reported more than two serious quarrels in the past month, and less than a quarter said they disagreed "often" or "very often" with their spouses.[24]

This bears repeating: Less than a third of divorces are ending angry high-conflict marriages.

Here's what the best evidence suggests: Most current divorces leave children worse off, educationally and financially, than they would have been if their parents stayed married, and a majority of divorces leave children psychologically worse off as well. Only a minority of divorces in this country are taking place in families where children are likely to benefit in any way from their parents' separation.[25]

The startling results of Amato and Booth's investigation, one of the largest and most well-designed studies of its kind, led these two social scientists to make this unusually firm pronouncement: "Spending one-third of one's life living in a marriage that is less than satisfactory in order to benefit children—children that parents elected to bring into the world—is not an unreasonable expectation." Especially since, as they point out, "Many people who divorce and remarry find that their second marriage is no happier than their first."[26]

Many of the benefits of marriage for adults (with the notable exception of the financial ones) are either far weaker or disappear entirely among the small number of married couples who describe their relationship as less than happy. But is grimly staying in an unhappy but low-conflict marriage parents' only option? While we tend to talk about bad marriages as if they were permanent things, research suggests that marriage is a dynamic relationship; even the unhappiest of couples who grimly stick it out for the sake of the children can find happiness together a few years down the road.

How many unhappy couples turn their marriages around? The truth is shocking: 86 percent of unhappily married people who stick it out find that, five years later, their marriages are happier, according to an analysis of the National Survey of Families and Households done by Linda Waite for this book. Most say they've become very happy indeed. In fact, nearly three-fifths of those who said their marriage was unhappy in the late '80s and who stayed married, rated this same marriage as either "very happy" or "quite happy" when reinterviewed in the early 1990s.

The very worst marriages showed the most dramatic turnarounds: 77 percent of the stably married people who rated their marriage as very unhappy (a one on a scale of one to seven) in the late eighties said that the same marriage was either "very happy" or "quite happy" five years later. Permanent marital unhappiness is surprisingly rare among the couples who stick it out. Five years later, just 15 percent of those who initially said they were very unhappily married (and who stayed married) ranked their marriage as not unhappy at all.

Of course, these impressive statistics don't prove that everyone who divorced during this time period could have forged a happier marriage. But they do prove that the bad marriage is nowhere near as permanent a condition as we sometimes assume. Those unhappily married couples who stick it out don't seem to stay locked together in an angry hell. The good news is that, with time, the marriages of most unhappy couples who stay married get much, much happier.[27]

No one marries hoping it will end in divorce. Clearly, we are losing many marriages that could and should be saved, not only for the sake of the children but for the sake of adult health and happiness, for the sake of the community burdened with the dangerous consequences of unnecessary divorce, and for the sake of our own faith in the possibility of enduring love.

Many now acknowledge marriage's importance for children. But one very big obstacle remains in the minds of many who would otherwise consider support for marriage a matter of common sense: What about domestic violence? Doesn't marriage put women at special risk?

11

IS MARRIAGE
A HITTING LICENSE?

Since the eighties, the focus of our fears for women in marriage shifted from mental to physical damage. From the madeup bruises of Farrah Fawcett in *The Burning Bed,* to the horrifying reality of Nicole Brown Simpson, this new image of a wife—battered by the man who is supposed to love, honor, and cherish her—has become one of the public faces of marriage in America.

Domestic violence is, of course, a serious problem. But is it really true that getting married puts women at special risk for violent assault? Of course, many wives are abused. But so are many live-in lovers and even casual girlfriends. In New York, state and local officials estimate that as many as one-third of crisis cases of domestic violence they handle now involve dating couples.[1] Yet even experts who know better consistently imply that the blame for domestic violence lies not at the feet of violent men but in our ideas about marriage itself.

So two eminent scholars titled their influential essay on rates of domestic violence "The Marriage License as a Hitting License."[2] In their well-regarded 1998 book *When Men Batter Women,* two top researchers Neil Jacobson and John Gottman ask why domestic violence continues. "Perhaps most importantly," they conclude, "marriage as an institution is still structured in such a way as to institutionalize male dominance, and such dominance makes high rates of battering inevitable. . . ."[3]

Even highly respected researchers, well aware that domestic violence is not confined to wives, tend to use *wife abuse* and *domestic violence* interchangeably, a linguistic practice that in itself suggests that marriage puts women at heightened risk." [V]iolent crime against women is largely a matter of husbands assaulting wives," say Jacobson and Gottman flatly. They go on to clarify in the next breath "Women are virtually as likely to be killed by husbands, ex-husbands, boyfriends, and ex-boyfriends as by strangers."[4]

Domestic violence is perhaps the only area in which social scientists casually use the term *husband* to mean any or all of the following: the man one is married to, the man one used to be married to, the man one lives with, the man one is merely having sex with, and/or the man one used to have sex with.

"Is spouse abuse on the increase . . . ?" a reporter asked Dr. Daniel O'Leary, author of a landmark study on marital aggression. Without missing a beat O'Leary replied, "My guess . . . is that it is more common than it was 25 or 50 years ago, partly because aggression is accepted and used so commonly by dating couples, in particular, and by engaged and young marrieds. . . ."[5] In a 1996 article in *Family Relations*, Alfred DeMaris and Steven Swinford come straight out and announce it: "Following others' terminology . . . we have used the terms husband and wife throughout the article to indicate an intimate partner, regardless of official marital status."[6] Researchers routinely compare rates of assault between what they call registered or de facto or common-law marital unions, blurring the profound cultural, legal, and psychological differences between cohabitation and marriage.

The less well-informed lay public, including public officials, are even more likely than experts to talk as if domestic violence and wife-battering are synonymous. So an article in a health magazine about mandatory arrest policies for domestic violence was called "Should Police Officers Be Required to Arrest Abusive Husbands?" as if abusers seldom showed up without wedding rings.[7] When Mayor Giuliani launched a new program to combat domestic violence in 1994, aides described it as a new problem "to track wife-abuse cases" and to train officers "to be more aggressive in arresting violent husbands."[8] When Mario Cuomo passionately denounced domestic violence he automatically spoke with disdain about "husbands hitting wives."[9]

So powerfully entrenched is the idea that marriage aids and abets domestic violence that in several states, legislators have proposed—or actually passed—legislation affixing warning labels about domestic violence to marriage licenses. In Massachusetts Barbara Gray, who drafted warning-label legislation when she was a state representative, described it as a way to warn couples "that one out of two relationships have an element of abuse in them, and that's something they should consider before they get married."[10]

One of the sponsors of warning labels, Washington state senator Margarita Prentice, put it this way: "The origin of the wedding ring represents part of a chain binding the wife to her master. I would say, simply, 'Beware. Stop, look, listen, and be cautious.'"[11] Good advice, perhaps, in general. But when it comes to domestic violence, is it really marriage we need to warn young women against?

No doubt, the only fail-safe method to avoid domestic violence is to avoid intimate relationships altogether. Women who have never married and don't have a boyfriend—or ex-boyfriend—are just about completely safe from domestic violence, although most would consider the price of this "insurance" much too high. But the research clearly shows that, outside of hying thee to a nunnery, the safest place for a woman to be is inside marriage.

Wives, for example, are far less likely than single women to be crime victims overall. When it comes to all crimes of violence (including domestic violence), a 1994 Justice Department report based on the National Crime Victimization Survey showed that single and divorced women were four to five times more likely to be victimized in any given year than married women. (The widowed, however, are the least likely.) Single and divorced women were almost ten times more likely than wives to be raped and about three times more likely to be the victims of aggravated assault than wives.

Interestingly, even though men are more apt to be victims of violent crime than women, marriage protects men from violent crime as well. Bachelors were about four times as likely to be the victims of a violent crime as husbands.[12]

When it comes to domestic disputes, the overwhelming majority of husbands and wives resolve their conflicts peaceably. About 8 percent of wives and 6 percent of husbands in the 1994 survey reported that any of their arguments had become physical in the past year; slightly fewer said that they or their spouse hit, shoved, or threw things during a fight. Just 18 percent of these wives and 7 percent of their husbands (according to the wives' report) were cut, bruised, or seriously injured as a result. Thus when it comes to what we commonly think of as battering—physical violence that results in injuries—only about 1.7 percent of wives and about three-quarters of 1 percent of husbands—are attacked even once each year.[13]

Figures such as these come from surveys that ask men and women to report on arguments that became physical. But data gathered from women's shelters point to families terrorized by much higher levels of systematic male violence. Perhaps, as Michael Johnson argues, two kinds of domestic violence exist: "common couple violence" and "patriarchal terrorism." Common couple violence arises when ordinary arguments get out of hand, involves aggression by both partners, happens relatively infrequently, and does not usually escalate. Patriarchal terrorism, by contrast, is a means by which a small proportion of men control "their" women; the beatings are always initiated by the men; most women do not fight back; and the violence is frequent, severe, and escalates over time. Surveys do a very poor job of catching this type of severe violence, and we know little about the role of marriage in either precipitating it or preventing it.[14]

While men and women are about equally likely to get physical, wives are far more likely to be injured by domestic violence. Data from the National Crime Victimization Survey found that husbands are about thirteen times more likely than wives to commit acts that spouses define as criminal violence.[15]

The fierce academic debate on whether or not women are as likely as men to commit domestic violence probably depends on the definition used. Using the same criteria from large national surveys that lead anti–domestic violence advocates to conclude that, for example, 6 million women are assaulted by a male partner each year, one can reasonably conclude that women are as likely as men to initiate violence at home and family violence is a largely gender-neutral phenomenon.

If we confine our concern to the much smaller pool of women who report being injured by an attack from a partner, battered partners are overwhelmingly female, but there are far fewer of them—according to Murray A. Straus, probably 188,000 women each year.[16] Police, hospital, and family-court records overwhelmingly confirm that while kicking, biting, and scratching one's partner may be gender-neutral, battering is a largely male prerogative.[17]

When it comes to spousal killing, the odds are more equal, at least in America. In the United States, unlike in other countries, wives are almost as likely as husbands to kill their spouses, although not apparently for the same reasons. As Wilson and Daly note, research shows that "men often hunt down and kill spouses who have left them; women hardly ever behave similarly. Men kill wives as part of planned murder-suicides; analogous acts by women are almost unheard of. Men kill in response to revelation of wifely infidelity; women almost never respond similarly, although their mates are more often adulterous. . . . Moreover, it seems clear that a large proportion of the spousal killings perpetrated by wives, but almost none of those perpetrated by husbands, are acts of self-defense."[18]

This is not, as many theorize, a question of guns in the hands of women "neutralizing" men's physical advantages. Gun murders of spouses are actually more likely to be committed by males than other spousal murders.[19] One theory is that historically high rates of divorce and out-of-wedlock childbearing in this country mean that women in America are more likely than women in other countries to, as Wilson and Daly suggest, "feel the need to defend their children of former unions against their current mates."

In any case, the fact that only a tiny fraction of marriages become violent doesn't mean that marital violence is not a serious social problem. Even a tiny fraction of 53 million married couples in America adds up to hundreds of thousands of injured spouses each year. For women in particular (who are much less likely to get in bar fights or gun battles than men), domestic assaults account for a high proportion of violent crimes committed against women each year.[20] But the fact that so few spouses ever hurt each other does make it implausible that the structural conditions or our ideology of marriage are to blame for domestic violence. In fact, the men and women who report physical violence in their marriage have many of the same characteristics that put people at increased risk of interpersonal violence in general.[21] If marriage itself were the root cause of violence against women, we would expect to see that married women were at higher risk of interpersonal violence than other women. We would also expect to see more husbands beating up their wives. Very few do, so some other process must be at work.

In fact, the evidence is overwhelming that being unmarried puts women at special risk for domestic abuse. A large body of research shows, for example, that marriage is much less dangerous for women than cohabitation.[22]

According to the National Crime Victimization Survey, the victimization rate for women separated from their husbands was about three times higher than that of divorced women and about 25 times higher than that of married women. Two-thirds of acts of intimate violence against women were not committed by husbands (and intimate violence in this study's definition excludes violence committed by those casual dating partners a woman considers "friends" or "acquaintances," rather than "boyfriends"). Husbands committed about 5 percent of all rapes against women in 1992–93, compared to 21 percent that were committed by ex-spouses, boyfriends, or ex-boyfriends, and 56 percent that were committed by an acquaintance, friend, or other relative.

Even when it comes to murder, killings are more likely to happen to unmarried cohabitors than spouses.[24] As one scholar sums up the relevant research, "Regardless of methodology, the studies yielded similar results: cohabitors engage in more violence than spouses."[25]

Linda Waite's own analysis of the 1987–88 National Survey of Families and Households for this book shows that married people are much less likely than cohabiting couples to say that arguments between them and their partners had become physical in the past year (4 percent of married people compared to 13 percent of the cohabiting). When it comes to hitting, shoving, and throwing things, cohabiting couples are more than three times more likely than the married to say things get that far out of hand. One reason cohabitors are more violent is that they are, on average, younger and less well-educated than married people. But even after controlling for education, race, age, and gender, people who live together are still three times more likely to report violent arguments than married people.[26]

Contrary to the fears of certain state legislators, something about a marriage license seems to protect married women (and men), to a certain extent, from domestic violence. Nicky Ali Jackson's study, which drew on interviews with more than five thousand married and cohabiting couples who participated in the National Family Violence Resurvey of 1985, found that both men and women who came from violent homes were more likely to have violent relationships. No surprise there. But surprisingly, even among these violence-prone couples, married couples were less likely to engage in violent conflict with their partners than were cohabitors. "Cohabitors with similar teenage victimization experiences," Jackson concluded, "as spouses had higher levels of aggression in their relationships." Even among adults who as children may have witnessed violent marriages, marriage itself provides some protection from domestic violence.[27]

The increased risk of domestic violence faced by unmarried partners is particularly striking because contemporary theories about the origins and nature of domestic violence often describe the problem as one of excessive commitment to traditional family values. One recent college textbook, for example, lists the following among the characteristics of a batterer: "He believes in the traditional home, family and gender-role stereotypes." Also listed prominently under the textbook's heading "Why Women Stay in Violent Relationships," are these factors: "*Religious pressure:* She may feel that the teachings of her religion require her to keep the family together at all costs, to submit to her husband's will, and to try harder" and "*Duty and responsibility:* She feels she must keep her marriage vows till death us do part."[28]

Yet research shows us that men who actually are "heads of households" are less likely than mere boyfriends to become violent and that wives are less likely to be hit than are girlfriends who experience no such religious or moral pressures to stay with their sex partners.

Why are men more likely to attack girlfriends than wives? One simple answer is that boyfriends are less committed than husbands. Jan Stets, one of the researchers who referred to marriage as a hitting license, also confirmed that rates of physical aggression are much higher in cohabiting than married couples. Cohabiting couples, she speculated, are more socially isolated than married couples. They are less integrated into networks of kin and community. The roles of unmarried partners are particularly ill-defined as are social expectations about the nature and purpose of their relationship.

Stets surmised that "the very nature of being in a less committed relationship may create its own dynamic for aggression. Since cohabitors are less likely than married persons to be committed to their relationship . . . it follows that the costs associated with being aggressive are not as great for cohabitors compared to the married. When a conflict arises, cohabitors may be more likely to be aggressive because they do not have much invested in the relationship. If the relationship ends as a result of the aggression, they will not suffer as much as married people, who have a greater long-term interest and may lose more materially, socially, and psychologically if the relationship ends."[29] So boyfriends may be more violent than husbands simply because they have less to lose.

Lower levels of commitment may also raise violence, because they increase sexual jealousy. As we saw in the chapter on sex, cohabiting women are 8 times more likely to be unfaithful than married women (and cohabiting men 4 times as likely as married men to have sex with someone else). Doubts about paternity may trigger violent impulses in men, at least partly explaining the enormously high levels of violence directed at unwed pregnant women by their boyfriends.[30]

Even among the unmarried, the more committed a couple is the less violent they are likely to be. In Linda Waite's analysis of a large, nationally representative sample for this book, cohabiting couples who say they have definite plans to marry are less likely to report physical violence in their relationship than cohabiting couples with no such plans. But engaged cohabiting couples are still much more likely to be violent than otherwise-similar married couples.

Marriage seems to help men desist not just from domestic violence, but all forms of lawbreaking. A study of five hundred chronic juvenile delinquents, which was conducted by researchers who tried to figure out why some youngsters ceased criminal activities and others continued piling up arrests into their early thirties, found that a good marriage made a dramatic difference.

Men who reformed were very similar to men who did not with regard to childhood and family characteristics: They had similar rates of poverty, similar IQs, were rated as equally "difficult" and "aggressive" as children, and were arrested as teens about as frequently. But over time, those who entered a good marriage sharply reduced their criminal activity. A good marriage, the researchers estimated, over time reduced the offense rate by hardcore delinquents by about two-thirds, compared to criminals who did not marry or who did not establish good marriages.[32]

The researchers concluded that "some of the time, some high-rate offenders enter into circumstances like marriage that provide the potential for informal social control. When they do, and in our case when marital unions are cohesive, the investment has a significant preventive effect on offending. 'Good' things sometimes happen to 'bad' actors, and when they do desistance has a chance."[33] The social bonds created by marriage can change the way even hardened criminals behave.

Interestingly, when domestic violence does erupt, marriage makes it easier for the law to contain the behavior. When one scholar looked at the affects of mandatory-arrest policies on future domestic violence, he found striking evidence that marriage matters: Husbands who were arrested became less violent as a result. But boyfriends actually became more violent toward their partners after being arrested for "minor" violent assaults.[34]

Marriage integrates men into the community. Men with a stake in conforming to the social rules are more likely to be deterred from violence when they are shown (by an arrest) how seriously society frowns on domestic violence. Cohabiting men, by contrast, appear to rebel against social control by inflicting more pain on their partners. Cohabiting men have less to lose from being publicly identified as an abuser than do married men.

Similarly, abused women say that the batterer's relatives are among the most effective sources of help in restraining partner violence.[35] Perhaps married women, who are "part of the family," have an easier time soliciting help from in-laws than do women who are more evanescent sex partners and companions. A man's parents and siblings may be more likely to intervene if he is hitting his wife, who has a long-term role in the family and whom they are likely to know better, than if he is abusing a girlfriend.

When researchers at the University of California at Los Angeles's School of Public Health used data from a large national survey to analyze the characteristics of those who experience marital violence, they found in essence that marriage does not beget violence; violence begets violence. The same characteristics that in general put people at increased risk of interpersonal violence also increased the likelihood of violence within marriage. Overall, the young, urban dwellers, the less educated, the poor, and blacks were all more likely to report violence in marriage. Marital violence seems to be part of a larger picture of a culture of risk and aggression, not a distinct problem created by marital mores.[36]

For children, a marriage license may be even more crucial. One study found that a preschooler living with one biological parent and one stepparent was forty times more likely to be sexually abused than one living with two natural parents.[37]

In a University of Iowa study of 2,300 cases of sexual abuse, researchers discovered that nonbiological "father caretakers" were four times as likely to sexually abuse children in their care as we would expect given their numbers.[38] In fact, psychologists Martin Daly and Margo Wilson concluded, "Living with a stepparent has turned out to be the most powerful predictor of severe child abuse risk yet discovered. . . ."[39]

An unmarried mother's boyfriend also appears to pose a particular danger. One study found that although boyfriends contribute less than 2 percent of nonparental child care, they commit almost half of all reported child abuse by nonparents. As researcher Leslie Margolin concluded, "[M]others' boyfriends committed 27 times more child abuse than their hours in child care would lead us to predict . . . a young child left alone with a mother's boyfriend experiences elevated risk of physical abuse."[40]

When violent men batter women or children, the law should vigorously protect them. But blaming marriage as the problem, or seeing high rates of divorce as the solution to domestic violence, misses the point. Many women who are long since legally divorced from abusive husbands can still be, as Nicole Brown Simpson was, at grave risk. So can other women who, like Hedda Nussbaum, are not even married to their abusers. The idea that marriage, rather than violence, is the real problem perpetuates the idea that domestic violence is really a "family matter," somehow fundamentally different in moral character from other violent crimes.

12

IS HER MARRIAGE REALLY
WORSE THAN HIS?

The most powerful and pervasive of the contemporary postmarriage myths is this: His marriage is a lot better than hers. "Guys Wed for Better; Wives for Worse," trumpets one *USA Today* headline (October 11, 1993). "Studies Show Men Do Better in Marriage Than Women," concludes another in *Jet* magazine. "Does Tying the Knot Put Women in a Bind?" asks still another headline for a 1997 *USA Today* story: "Marriage protects men from depression and makes women more vulnerable," one psychology professor tells this article's reporter. "It is the best evidence that marriage is an institution that primarily benefits men." Bowling Green University sociologist Gary Lee tells the reporter, "We have a lot of studies that show, in a variety of different ways, men benefit more from marriage than women."[1]

Until a few generations ago, we viewed marriage as a burden for men and a benefit for women. In the popular legend, men avoided getting "tied down" or "trapped" into marriage by husband-hungry women. Today, in an astonishing reversal of gender stereotypes, marriage is often viewed as suppressing women's very sense of self.

Thus women are described as "casualties of a marital subculture that crushed their emerging identities," to quote the authors of a divorce guide.[2] In the same vein, a review in the *New York Review of Books* approvingly notes that many embrace today's divorce culture as promoting "more freedom for women and less control of children: [M]arriage more often than not spells subordination, while divorce for all its difficulties, brings liberation."[3] *People* magazine tapped into this widespread cultural phenomenon when on January 29, 1996, its editors put a smiling Sally Field on the cover with this tag line: "Free of the need to make a man happy, the newly confident single mom, 49, talks about her divorce, love life, and the hard-won joys of living solo."

Even more remarkably, in academic circles at least, this bleak vision of marriage's gender effects on women can be traced to the work of one woman, sociologist Jesse Bernard, who argued in her influential 1972 book *The Future of Marriage* that each marriage was really two marriages: "his" marriage and "her" marriage. For men, marriage brings health, power, and satisfaction. For women, marriage brings stress, dissatisfaction, and loss of self.

According to Bernard, wives are "anxious, depressed, psychologically distressed," and their emotional health is "dismal."[4] For women, marriage is a kind of psychological torture, gradually debilitating their emotional and mental health. "The poor mental health of wives is like a low-grade infection that shows itself in a number of scattered symptoms . . . ," Bernard wrote, sketching what she saw as the "grim mental-health picture of wives.[5] A happy housewife must be a sick woman: "We do not clip wings or bind feet, but we do make girls sick," Bernard states. "For to be happy in a relationship which imposes so many impediments on her, as traditional marriage does, a woman must be slightly ill mentally."[6]

As the book jacket of the 1982 revised edition of *The Future of Marriage* correctly put it, "The disparity between his and her marriages, hotly debated when it was first proposed, is now a basic assumption in our thinking." Marriage has changed a great deal since Bernard first wrote her book. Many of the changes she advocated, including greater employment opportunities for wives, have since become realities.

Nonetheless, Bernard's basic conclusion—marriage is good for men but bad for women—is still widely repeated not only in popular culture but even in college textbooks used in marriage-and-family courses, as Norval Glenn pointed out in a recent report for the Council on Families. "We do know, for instance, that marriage has an adverse effect on women's mental health," asserts one recent textbook. "Bernard's investigation showed that the psychological costs of marriage were great for women," chimes in another. "If marriage is so difficult for wives," asks a third college textbook, "why do a majority surveyed judge themselves as happy? . . . [S]ince they are conforming to society's expectations, this must be happiness."[7]

But is it true? Is his marriage really so different—and better—than hers? The evidence is in, at least for the ways in which marriage is practiced today: Both men and women gain a great deal from marriage. True, marriage does not affect men and women in exactly the same ways. Both men and women live longer, healthier, and wealthier lives when married, but husbands typically get greater health benefits from marriage than do wives. On the other hand, while both men and women get bigger bank accounts and a higher standard of living in marriage, wives reap even greater financial advantages than do husbands.

Overall, the portrait of marriage that emerges from two generations of increasingly sophisticated empirical research on actual husbands and wives is not one of gender bias, but gender balance: A good marriage enlarges and enriches the lives of both men and women.

How and why did we ever imagine otherwise?

In 1972 the idea that marriage cripples women resonated with feminist concerns about inequality and with promoting career opportunities for women. The arguments in *The Future of Marriage* fit quite neatly with those that Betty Friedan advanced in *The Feminine Mystique;* the two books make many of the same arguments about the destructive effects of the "housewife syndrome" on women's well-being.

The most damning part of Bernard's argument zeroed in on the effect of marriage on women's mental health. For example, one article she relied upon, published in the *American Journal of Psychiatry* in 1966, compared the mental health of men and women using four measures—depression, severe neurotic symptoms, phobic tendency, and passivity. Married men scored better on these four measures of mental health than did single men, while married women scored worse than single women.[8] Bernard concluded from this data that marriage is good for men but "deforms" women's mental health.

Bernard was not the only one to reach this conclusion. In a study published the year after *The Future of Marriage,* Walter Gove found that married women had higher rates of mental illness than did married men, while single men and women had similar rates of mental illness. Echoing Bernard's findings, he concluded that the higher rates of mental illness for women generally were due to higher rates for married women alone.[9]

Almost two generations have passed since Bernard's data were collected, a time during which the world has changed, and social scientists studying marriage have constructed ever more sophisticated models to measure the effects of marriage on men and women. How does Bernard's thesis withstand this onslaught of new evidence?

Not very well, frankly. As we saw in chapter 5, the evidence overwhelmingly suggests that marriage is good for women's mental health. True, by some measures men's physical health benefits are somewhat more than women's, but that is largely because single men, as a group, are so much more prone to antisocial and unhealthy ways of living, which affects single men's mental and physical health. In other words, the reason getting a wife boosts your health more than acquiring a husband is not that marriage warps women, but that single men lead such warped lives.[10]

Bernard concentrated almost exclusively on depression, while the latest research uses broader measures of emotional well-being. There are other forms of mental illness besides depression. Men and women do not necessarily express emotional distress in the same ways. When social scientists use broader measures of mental health, they typically find, as two scholars summarize the evidence, an "equalization of sex difference in overall rates of disorder."[11]

But one of the biggest reasons for the discrepancy in Bernard's findings and our own is that she made no attempt to distinguish between marriage and babies. Of course, in the sixties, the two were more nearly synonymous than they are today, when childless marriages are not uncommon and out-of-wedlock births are quite common.

There is no question that caring for children—especially babies and preschoolers—is stressful for women. Even today, when families are smaller and women are more likely to share caregiving, married mothers with children are more likely than single women to agree that they "sometimes feel overburdened" by "family demands."[12] Time-use studies confirmed that women with children at home were more likely than other women to report feeling a "time crunch," while for men, only teenagers in the home seemed to increase the perceived time crunch.[13] So when Bernard compared married and single women's mental health, she was, to a certain extent, contrasting apples and oranges: married mothers with childless singles.

By contrast, later research that controls for the presence of children finds that marriage protects mothers from depression. For example, in an analysis of 2,300 urban adults, Ronald C. Kessler and Marilyn Essex found that "the presence of a child in the home, especially a preschooler, has a much more seriously depressing effect on single than married people." Even when it comes to housework, married homemakers are less likely to be depressed by comparable levels of housework strains than are unmarried homemakers.[14]

Of course, it is also true that marriage has changed since the early seventies, in the directions Bernard recommended. Women who find staying home with children depressing get more support to keep working, full- or part-time. Working mothers may be somewhat more prone to report feeling stressed than full-time homemakers, but they are less likely to be depressed.[15]

Women are far more prone to depression than men. So it makes sense that married women would be more depressed, on average, than married men. Why did Bernard find that single women were less depressed than single men? The answer is not, as she assumed, that marriage is warping women. Instead, male and female marriage markets operate very differently: Women tend to marry up while men tend to marry down. That means that the unmarried women Bernard studied were, in socioeconomic terms, the cream of the crop: with higher status and high-paying jobs—all factors that protect against depression. By contrast, men who never marry are, on average, less successful than their married counterparts. So once again, without introducing controls for socioeconomic status, Bernard was comparing apples and oranges: high-status women with low-status men. Bernard simply failed to distinguish between the effects of marriage and the effects of high social status on women's depression.

More recent research belies the notion that marriage is a depressing experience for women. Scholars at Rutgers University, for example, actually followed the mental health of almost 1,400 young men and women over a seven-year period as they entered marriages, divorced, or remained single. Marriage, the researchers discovered, boosted both men's and women's mental health. This was not a function of selection—of healthier people marrying while sad sacks stay on the shelf. Instead the Rutgers team found that, even after they took into account the mental health (and other characteristics) of people prior to marriage, ". . . young adults who get and stay married do have higher levels of well-being than those who remain single."[16]

In another recent study, based on three large separate surveys—two national and one concerning people in Illinois—John Mirowsky finds that marriage accounts for none of the well-known "depression gap" between men and women. In fact, for both men and women, the ages at which depression rates are lowest (early forties for women, early fifties for men) are those in which marriage rates are highest.[17]

Social scientists measure depression by asking people questions such as "How many days last week did you feel sad, lonely, have trouble sleeping, or feel everything was an effort, that you couldn't shake the blues?" According to measures such as this women of every age group are more likely to be depressed than men. And the gender gap in depression grows with age. It is smallest for men and women under age thirty and grows with each passing decade. By age sixty and older, women report much higher levels of depression than men the same age. Aha! Proof that marriage depresses women? Unfortunately for advocates of that theory, as women age, the positive effect of marriage on women's mental health also increases.[18]

Linda Waite and Mary Elizabeth Hughes compared depression and emotional well-being in nearly thirteen thousand men and women from ages fifty-one to sixty-one in the early 1990s.[19] After controlling for race, education, family structure, income, and living arrangements, Waite and Hughes determined that married people—with or without children at home—were less depressed and emotionally healthier than comparable singles.[20]

Older unmarried women, whether they lived alone, with their children or with others, were significantly more depressed than older married women. When these women were asked, "How do you rate your emotional health?" the advantage of being married was even clearer: Married women were about one-third more likely to rate their emotional health as "excellent" than unmarried women and only half as likely to rate their emotional health as "poor."[21]

Marriage held a similar advantage for older men. Married men were about a third more likely than single men to say their emotional health was "excellent," and almost two-thirds less likely than men who were not married to rate their own emotional health as "poor."

Finally, when Nadine Marks and James Lambert followed the mental-health characteristics of a nationally representative sample of 13,000 men and women over five years, they too confirmed that marriage for both men and women, staying single was depressing. Overall, after controlling for initial mental-health status and using a variety of measures to gauge emotional well-being, from self-acceptance to hostility, depression, and reported happiness, Marks and Lambert found that the mental health of all categories of singles—never-married, separated, divorced, and widowed—declined over this five-year period, compared to those who remained married for the entire five-year period. Singles who failed to marry became more depressed and less happy over the period, though the declines were sharper for men than for women.

The never-married were also more hostile, had less positive relations with others, and less self-acceptance than the married. The divorced showed lower levels of happiness, personal mastery, positive relations with others, sense of purpose, self-acceptance, and environmental mastery. The widowed became more depressed but did not differ in other ways from the married. Only in two areas—a sense of autonomy and experience of personal growth—did singles outperform the married people.

And in most of these measures, marriage benefited men and women pretty much equally. Men and women who began the study divorced, and remained so, experienced similar declines in well-being over the next five years. Staying widowed had the same negative impact on the mental health of both men and women. Never-married women did somewhat better than married men on one measure of emotional health—happiness—but less well on another—self-acceptance. And both never-married men and women did less well than contemporaries who were married.[22]

The evidence is pretty conclusive: Marriage doesn't boost men's egos while deforming women's souls. Instead, both men and women are psychologically healthier when married. And this is not a case of happy souls finding mates while the sad sacks are left on the shelf. The act of marriage itself leads to better mental health.

But What about Happiness?

When it comes to the relationship between marriage and happiness for both sexes, Bernard's treatment of evidence was even more questionable. As Norval Glenn has pointed out, "First she finds from national surveys that married men report a much higher level of personal happiness than any category of unmarried men. . . . This fact she presents as clear evidence that marriage benefits men. In an appendix, she reports almost identical data on women taken from the same surveys. However, she does not consider these data on women to be evidence that marriage benefits women, because, she reasons, married women only say they are happy because society expects them to say so." Glenn concluded, "To call this reasoning weak would be an understatement."[23]

In fact, virtually every study of happiness that has ever been done has found that married men and women are happier than singles. The happiness advantage of married people is very large and quite similar for men and women and appears in every country on which we have information.[24]

"His" marriage and "her" marriage turn out to be a lot more similar than different. In the most recent surveys, both married men and married women express very high (and very similar) levels of satisfaction with their marriages. Sixty-one percent of husbands and 59 percent of wives say their marriage is "very happy." Thirty-six percent of husbands and wives call their marriage "pretty happy." Just 2 percent of men and 4 percent of women say their marriage is "not too happy."[25]

Using more detailed measures, psychologists Scott Stanley and

Howard Markman reported similar equality between the sexes when it comes to marital bliss. They created a measure of marital quality that included different dimensions, such as satisfaction, dedication, friendship, fun, sensuality. Conversely, they also created a way to measure what they call various danger signs: negative patterns of interaction, loneliness, and thoughts of divorce. Overall, it turned out that his marriage and her marriage were not from different planets. The difference between husbands and wives in marital satisfaction was too small to measure.[26]

Despite the conventional wisdom that women care more about and invest more in personal relationships than men do, husbands and wives also seem to be about equally committed to each other and to marriage. Stanley and Markman also developed a measure for what they call personal dedication: the desire of the spouse to maintain and improve the quality of the relationship. The highly dedicated spouse is willing to sacrifice for the relationship, to invest in it, to strive for his or her partner's welfare, and to link personal goals to it. The dedicated spouse views her- or himself as part of a team, the married partnership as "us" rather than two separate individuals.

To measure personal dedication, Stanley and Markman asked people whether the following statements were true: "My relationship with my partner is more important to me than almost anything else in my life"; "I may not want to be with my partner a few years from now"; "I like to think of my partner and me more in terms of 'us' and 'we' than 'me' and 'him/her'" "I want this relationship to stay strong no matter what rough times we may encounter." Once again, his marriage and her marriage were similar: husbands and wives reported being equally dedicated to their marriages.

And when it comes to evaluating the marriage negatively, men and women also tend to see eye-to-eye. Stanley and Markman found no difference between men and women for the danger signs in marriage— thought of divorce, having little arguments escalate into ugly fights, feeling like one is on the opposite team when it comes to solving problems, and feelings of loneliness. Only one gender difference emerged: Men were far more likely to withdraw when conflict occurred.

The most sophisticated measures of husbands' and wives' happiness, commitment, and dissatisfaction with their spouses reveal remarkably little difference between his marriage and hers.[27]

The Rest of Life

But there is more to life than happiness. What about sex, safety, money, long life, and family satisfaction? How does marriage as an institution stack up for men and women in these other dimensions?

To summarize the story laid out in the previous chapters: Both married men and women live longer, healthier lives, but in this measure men need marriage more. Mortality rates were higher for the unmarried of both sexes, but 50 percent higher among women and 250 percent among men. The relatively unhealthy lives of single men, compared to those of single women, seem to explain the gender gap in marriage benefits here.

When it comes to money, marriage makes both men and women better off. Men get larger gains in earning power than do women, who get only a small marriage premium at most. But then married men, unlike single men, share their incomes with their families, raising the household income of their wives and children. So although both men and women gain from marriage, overall, women gain even more financially from marriage than men do.[28]

When it comes to sex and sexual satisfaction, once again both husbands and wives are better off because they dared to say, "I do." But as for sex, contrary to the popular stereotypes, women seem to benefit even more from marriage itself than men do. Single women are far less likely to have any sex at all, and far less likely to enjoy it when they do, than married women as we saw in chapter 6.

And we saw in chapter 11 that marriage provides some protection for women from domestic violence, at least compared to women in cohabiting relationships. Both husbands and wives are less likely to be victims of criminal violence than unmarried men and women.[29]

So, when we tally our scorecard, on health, wealth, earnings, sex, violence, and happiness, here's what we get: Men, 2; Women, 3; Equal 1. Both men and women get health and earnings benefits from marriage, but men benefit more in physical health and earnings. Both men and women are safer, more sexually satisfied, and wealthier, if married, but women benefit more on sexual satisfaction, financial well-being, and protection from domestic violence, and they benefit about equally on emotional well-being. If you are keeping a gender scorecard, you'd have to call contemporary marriage a pretty good deal for both sexes—both men and women benefit in important ways, sometimes in different amounts. But in most areas of life, marriage makes both men and women better off.

That doesn't mean, of course, that marriage, as we practice it today, is equally fair to both sexes, or no longer in need of reform. In *New Families, No Families* Linda Waite and her coauthor Frances Goldscheider argued that "new families are being formed, in which men and women share economic responsibilities as well as the domestic tasks that ensure that family members go to work or school clean, clothed, fed, and rested, and come home to a place where they provide each other care and comfort."[30] The alternative to "new families," they argue, is likely to be "no families," as women decide that the new marriage bargain—in which they hold a job and remain responsible for all child care and housework—is a bad deal, and as men decide that filling all the requirements of a traditional breadwinner but getting few of the traditional prerogatives or wifely supports is just as unattractive.

The two-earner family, which rose to prominence since Bernard's day, is clearly here to stay. The so-called traditional family is far from extinct, but it is no longer the dominant model of family life either: One child in three has a stay-at-home parent (who isn't also running a business out of the house). The rest live in either dual-earner families (including part-time work) or in single-parent families in which their lone parent is employed.[31]

Two-career families come with gains as well as losses. Even when wives work full-time, they still generally do the majority of the housework; their families gain their income, the connections they make, and the skills they develop at work.[32] Children in dual-worker families get less time from both their mothers and their fathers than children in traditional breadwinner/homemaker families (so do children in single-parent families).[33] Men's health seems to suffer when their wives work more than full-time.[34] The income gains to the family from the wife's income may be balanced by losses in the wage premium earned by husbands.[35]

But wives in new families gain some measure of economic insurance against the risk of divorce. They gain the satisfaction of providing financial support for their families. And if they make career-level incomes, they gain additional help from both their husbands and children in household tasks.[36]

But is the full-time employment of wives in a high-earning job, as Goldscheider and Waite seem to suggest, the only route to a "fair" marriage? Can we have equal marriages with an employed father and a mother who works only in the home or works part-time?

Steven Nock argues that coercion and inequity, not dependency, lie at the heart of the problems of traditional marriage.[37] Dependency is not the enemy. In fact, marriage gets much of its power from the interdependency that allows each spouse to specialize. Marriage works best when husbands and wives need each other. But to achieve this alternative vision of the new family, dependencies must be freely chosen, not coerced. Both partners need to be protected against the risks inherent in even freely chosen dependency.[38] And husband and wife must recognize themselves both as dependents in their joint project, the family—even if they have very different incomes or one has no income at all for a period.

This recognition of marriage as true partnership, an interdependent relationship rather than one of domination and subordination, has implications outside the home as well, affecting, as we shall see, how we treat married couples in the tax code as well as the divorce court.

The world has changed in the three decades since Jesse Bernard concluded that marriage helped men at women's expense. Some of the changes Bernard called for have become a reality: Wives have far more access to higher education and to higher-paying, higher-status jobs. Education and employment give women more say in family decision-making and exert pressure toward equal sharing between husbands and wives.[39] Many more couples today have the kind of marriage Bernard argued would be good for women as well as men.

But as we have acquired a much deeper and more detailed knowledge about the myriad and complex ways in which marriage affects well-being, we can also pronounce Bernard's core thesis just plain wrong or at the very least, outdated. A closer look, a broader view, and several decades of new research show that her influential conclusion that marriage is good for men's mental health but bad for women's is not true. On average, his marriage and her marriage are equally committed, equally happy, and equally psychologically healthy.

13

WHY IS MARRIAGE IN TROUBLE?

If marriage is so great, why is it in so much trouble? If marriage is so wonderful, why do about half of all recent marriages now end in divorce? Why are about a third of our babies born to unmarried women? Why would anybody voluntarily dissolve (or fail to form) a relationship that helps them live longer, healthier, happier, sexier, and more affluent lives? Good questions. In social science, explanations are always more elusive than descriptions. The whys are harder, and less certain, than the whats.

But one thing we do know: the answer is not, as we have seen, that Americans no longer value marriage. Americans of all ethnic and class backgrounds place a good marriage high on their lists of personal and social ideals. So something in the larger social climate and arrangements must have changed that makes it harder for us to achieve our own self-declared goal. What might that something, or somethings, be?

No doubt, as many experts counsel, some of the trends weakening marriage are long-standing and irreversible, part of the very fabric of contemporary life. As society moves away from an agrarian economy to first an industrial and then to a postindustrial economy governed by a modern welfare state, marriage becomes less indispensable; individuals can count on others to provide what used to be strictly family matters.

We don't produce most of our own food on small farms, with husbands doing the plowing and wives minding the chickens and milking the cows. We don't need wives to make butter or sew our clothes, much less weave the cloth from which they are made. We have the Gap,

7-Eleven, and McDonald's on every corner to supply our basic needs. We don't depend as much on our children to support us in retirement. We don't count on family members alone to take care of us if disaster strikes: We have insurance, Social Security, unemployment compensation, pensions, and 401(k)s.

Three hundred years ago, the conventional wisdom was "You can tell a bachelor by his smell." Just maintaining the basic decencies of life was a two-person job. Today, by contrast, even single mothers with small children can usually ensure the basics: food, clean clothes, a school, a roof overhead with heat and sanitary running water underneath, and basic medical care. A market economy, combined with the rise in government programs (not just welfare and Medicaid but everything from public sanitation and building codes to guaranteed public education), along with more recent sweeping improvements in women's job opportunities, make marriage less strictly necessary for survival than it once was. Nobody we know would want to change that, even if we could.

But does that mean a 50 percent divorce rate is inevitable? We don't think so. For in addition to these long-term structural forces, there have been a whole range of more recent, potentially reversible social changes: some large, some small, some governmental or economic, many more strictly cultural, all tugging in the same direction—weakening public support for the marriage vow.

The forces of the market, of government, and of public opinion have all, in a wide variety of ways, shifted in the direction of parceling out to the unmarried many of the rights and benefits previously reserved to the married. Cohabitors began demanding the sexual and social rights of the married, for example, and courts became increasingly sympathetic to the view that it is unconstitutional discrimination to treat married and unmarried couples differently. Landlords and school districts, among others, are forbidden by federal law to make distinctions between married and unmarried individuals. Welfare and public-housing policy created marriage penalties for low-income and working-class couples.[1]

Spouses, significant others, professionals, and wider social institutions have all increased their approval of divorce dramatically. That means, though we seldom realize it, that support for the marriage commitment has concomitantly declined. A simple but, we believe, true answer to the question of why marriage is in trouble is that Americans have invested less moral, spiritual, cultural, political, and legal energy into supporting the marriage vow. This reduced support for marriage expresses itself in a wide variety of relationships and institutions that touch the lives of married couples.

Americans, for example, while no less eager for marriage, have become notably more enthusiastic about divorce and about other alternatives to marriage, from cohabitation to unwed childbearing. In 1962, 51 percent of young mothers agreed that "divorce is usually the best solution" when parents can't seem to work out their marriage problems. When these same (now middle-aged) women were interviewed in 1977, 80 percent saw divorce as the best solution to persistent marital problems.[2] By the mid-1990s, only a small minority of American women (17 percent) now think that parents should stay together even if they don't get along.[3]

In 1996, when asked, "How wrong do you personally think it is when people divorce?" a quarter of Americans took the strongly permissive attitude toward divorce, going so far as to say either that divorce was right for everybody or that it was not a moral issue at all.[4]

The flip side of the "liberalization" of attitudes toward divorce, cohabitation, and unwed childbearing is the privatization of marriage. We are no longer certain how much marriage matters, and therefore we've become increasingly reluctant to help married couples stay together, since rooting for the success of the marriage has been redefined an "interference" with the personal choices of others. Besides, who is to say what is really for the best?

Most of the professional "custodians of the family"—clergy, counselors, psychologists, educators, and even family scholars—have promoted and approved of this new view of marriage as a private, even an individual decision. In particular, such experts have helped redefine how we decide whether or not to divorce. The overarching message coming from the helping professions is that the main question to ask in deciding whether or not to divorce is, What would make me happy? In this way, family experts have reinforced for struggling couples and the broader culture the idea that emotional gratification is the main purpose and benefit of marriage.

For example, here is how Richard Gardner, a respected clinical psychiatrist, a professor at the College of Physicians and Surgeons at Columbia University, and an author both of manuals for therapeutic professionals and popular guides for divorcing parents, summed up the range of professional opinion on the subject in 1982: "There are those who recommend that parents not consider the divorce's effects on the children in making their decision. . . . They consider the children's welfare to be a contaminant to such decision making. My own belief is that the effects on the children should be one of the considerations, albeit minor. The major determinants should be whether or not the parents feel that there is enough pain in their relationship to warrant its being broken."[5]

In her popular 1996 guide for people considering divorce, psychotherapist Mira Kirshenbaum, clinical director of the Chestnut Hill Institute in Massachusetts, gave much the same advice when it comes to staying together for the kids' sake: "[C]hildren aren't glue and shotgun weddings don't work out . . . if you want to look for a sign of life you've got to look beyond the children for it."[6]

Like many in her profession, Kirshenbaum believes there may be too few divorces, not too many. One of her clients, she chides, stayed married for years just because "only a bad person, he thought, would walk out on a partner and all the hopes they'd had for the future, to say nothing of what this would do to their children. . . . [F]or every divorce brought about by people who should feel more responsible to themselves and their partners, there's a relationship not ending because someone feels too responsible."[7]

These types of family professionals have enormous influence not only on their own clients but on the culture at large. As Barbara Dafoe Whitehead has pointed out, such experts "drawn from the ranks of sociology, psychology, and the therapeutic professions" are "treated as authoritative by media and policy elites. Even religious opinion increasingly draws upon social scientific teachings and insights. Talk of 'roles and relationships,' 'singlehood,' and 'gender identities' not only fills the pages of the *New York Times;* they are also the stuff of Sunday sermons and inspirational bestsellers." After reading through the literature written by family experts in the seventies, Whitehead observed, "One can't help but note the dwindling use of the word 'marriage.' Marriage becomes just one form of 'coupling and uncoupling' or one possible 'intimate lifestyle.'"[8]

At the same time that marriage counselors and clergy were rethinking their attitudes toward divorce, another influential group of professionals was doing the same: family lawyers. No-fault divorce, a revolution in family law that swept the country over a ten-year period, was primarily the brainchild of the professional bar. In 1968 more than 60 percent of the country felt divorce should be more difficult to obtain.[9] Family lawyers on the front line of the divorce courts felt otherwise, and bar associations quietly lobbied state legislatures for changes that would make divorce a cleaner, faster, and less judgmental legal process. Liberals and feminists have sometimes been blamed for the "divorce revolution," but in reality it was the legal profession that pushed hardest for no-fault divorce, and it is family lawyers and judges who remain its most satisfied customers.[10]

Lawyers tend to focus on divorce law as they experience it: a mechanistic procedure for putting an official end to relationships that are already, from their point of view, dead. With the advent of no-fault, family lawyers became important cultural carriers of the new vision of marriage as a contingent relationship, no longer all that different, in the eyes of the law, from living together. Thanks to no-fault, the marriage contract is no longer enforceable. It takes two to marry but only one to divorce at any time, for any reason, as fast as the courts can sort out property and custody issues.

Under no-fault, family lawyers are the ones who explain to the wife who marches in saying, "I'm not giving him a divorce" that she has no choice in the matter. Vows of permanent obligation, they warn misguided men and women, are just hopeful words not reasonable expectations. The law will always side with the one person who wants out. The court's job is to do the divorce as fairly, quickly, and painlessly as possible, which to many couples still may not be that fair, quick, or painless at all.

The law doesn't care who wants a divorce or why. This is not how married couples naturally think about their shared commitment. Even today, after thirty years of no-fault, there are still spouses who express surprise at how little power they are given in the courts over the fate of their own marriage. Sometimes even lawyers skirt the issue, leaving it up to the judge to do the explaining. Maggie Gallagher recently interviewed an Iowa woman—whose husband left her after he had an affair—who testified in court that she didn't believe the marriage was irretrievably broken down. The surprised judge flipped through the legal books to show her he had to grant the divorce, even if she objected. "I thought maybe he could delay the divorce, order counseling or something," she related afterward.

If much of the magic that marriage works stems from its ability to give men and women a sense of security that their partnership will last, the sharp decline in the law's willingness to enforce the terms of the marriage contract has reduced the benefits of marriage for everyone. Everyone's marriage is profoundly affected by the presence (or absence) of social and legal supports.

Two out of three brides who married as recently as the 1960s could expect to be married until death ended the union.[11] The permanent marriage contract was supported in the past by religious and moral proscriptions on divorce and by a legal system that often allowed divorce only for cause or required extensive waiting periods in the case of contested divorces. When spouses understood their contract was both enforceable and difficult to break, each could invest in the marriage with greater assurance. Women at home raising children, or putting their husbands through law school, had more confidence that they would share in the financial rewards of their husbands' success.

But in the seventies, most states changed their divorce laws, giving one spouse the unilateral power to declare the marriage over. Many people, especially family lawyers, believe that no-fault divorce has no effect on the divorce rate. But the best new research shows that the shift to unilateral divorce by itself raised divorce rates (about 6.5 percent, accounting for 17 percent of the increase in divorce rates between 1968 and 1988).[12]

Under a unilateral divorce regime, even husbands and wives who are personally committed to marriage understand that they have no control at all over the ultimate outcome. Law and society will not support, and may even ridicule, efforts to keep the marriage together after one partner declares his or her desire to leave.

For many, if not most, couples, divorce now hovers at the edge of the marital consciousness, a disaster that one has to prepare for, and defend against, simply because the costs of divorce—a financial setback for men, a financial disaster for women and children, an emotional trauma for all involved—are so high.[13]

Unilateral divorce affects even those married couples that don't end up in divorce court. By discouraging investments in marriage, these new divorce laws also lower the returns to marriage even in marriages that remain stable. For example, two researchers found that the move to unilateral divorce alone lowered husbands' wage premium by three percentage points.[14] Many wives are also working longer hours or having fewer children than they want in order to protect themselves from the consequences of divorce.[15] In a divorce-prone society, men and women become afraid to specialize—especially women—in home and family.

There is evidence, for example, that the powerful wage premium men get from marriage declines sharply as their statistical risk of divorce rises. Jeffrey S. Gray and Michael J. Vanderhart found that "the marriage premium was nearly 26 percent for husbands who did not divorce, and whose wives specialized in home productions; the marriage wage premium is only 3 percent for husbands who subsequently divorce and whose wives worked 40 hours per week in the labor force." Even after the researchers control for wives' work hours, a 10 percent increase in a husband's probability of divorce lowers his marriage wage premium by 8 percent.[16]

Meanwhile, in 1997, 51 percent of mothers worked full-time, even though just 30 percent agreed that full-time work was "the ideal situation for you."[17] There is considerable evidence that fear of divorce prevents many women from reaping one of the prime traditional benefits of marriage for mothers: the chance to spend more time with their kids.[18]

The more uncertain people are that any partnership will last, the more they act as individuals and the less they act as permanent partners. But the more spouses act as separate individuals, the less they get from the marriage partnership, and the more likely the marriage will fail. Fear of divorce can thus become a self-fulfilling prophecy.

Married couples in the midst of interpersonal struggles experience this new detachment of significant others as a loss of support. When your clergyman, your counselor, and your lawyer all advise you that divorce is an acceptable solution, even a preferable one, to your own personal dissatisfaction with your marriage—that the only question you have to face is, What do you really want?—you will have a harder time sustaining any faith at all in the idea that the marriage vow is important for its own sake, that your marriage could be worth fighting to save. If you get the idea from the media, your therapist, or friends that staying in an unsatisfying marriage makes you a coward, or worse, a bad role model for your kids, you will have an even harder time believing that staying married makes sense.

And of course this loss of support for the marriage vow happened just as sex roles within marriage were changing, producing confusion, turmoil, and inequity within millions of American homes. As more wives entered the workplace, out of personal desire or personal fear or both, the gender balance within marriage shifted. The traditional marriage bargain was fair in the sense that it distributed family labor reasonably equally between men and women. Married men's total work hours (inside and outside the home) were about the same as those for married women, except when the family included children too young to go to school, when wives often put in more hours.[19]

During the last two generations, the terms of the traditional bargain shifted—at least temporarily—in a way that made marriage less fair for women. Married mothers moved into the labor force, but continued to perform all their traditional tasks in the home, working, as it were, a "second shift."[20] (The most recent time-use studies, though, show the gender scales are getting closer in balance once again: Women are spending less time in housework, and men are spending a bit more, making the effort each puts into the family more nearly equal.)[21]

But permissive divorce attitudes do more than encourage divorce. They actually make happy marriage less likely. Culture matters. Scholarly research confirms what ordinary people assume: Those of us with more favorable attitudes toward divorce are more likely to end their marriages than people with less favorable attitudes towards divorce.[22] But the latest research reveals something less obvious: adopting favorable ideas about divorce actually tends to lower the quality of a person's marriage.[23]

Using data from a survey of almost 1,300 married couples, two scholars found that "those who adopted less supportive attitudes toward divorce reported a decline in marital conflict between 1983 and 1988, whereas those who adopted more supportive attitudes toward divorce reported an increase in marital conflict."[24] Couples who embraced the idea of divorce also experienced larger drops in marital happiness and in marital togetherness than couples who adopted less favorable attitudes toward divorce. So even as divorce became an easier, more common, and more acceptable outlet for marital unhappiness, marriages became unhappier. Husbands and wives married in the '80s report more problems, conflicts, and less togetherness than those married in the '70s did.[25]

The dynamic that builds a happy marriage is not just, as so many in the therapeutic professions assume, a personal and individual one. Our attitude toward marriage and not just about our partners in particular, either nurture marital success or inhibit it. To put it in plain English, for many people, commitment produces contentment; uncertainty creates agony. Some couples undoubtedly move toward the closure of divorce simply to escape the emotional hell of perpetual ambivalence.

When people aren't certain their marriage will last, they invest less time in the relationship and take fewer steps to resolve disagreements. "Ironically," these researchers conclude, "by adopting attitudes that provide greater freedom to leave unsatisfying marriages, people may be increasing the likelihood that their marriage will become unsatisfying in the long run."[26]

Ideas and ideals are powerful forces. Sociologists know this, and so do ordinary people who struggle with questions about whether and how much their marriage vows ought to constrain their behavior. Our ideas about divorce are really only the flip side of our ideals of marriage. Just as laws regulating divorce are laws shaping the marriage contract, so too, our attitudes about what is a good enough reason for divorce help define what the marriage commitment is. We cannot embrace no-fault divorce as a new social ideal without fundamentally changing the way we think about marriage in ways that turn out to be deeply hostile to our goal of building a happy marriage.

The effects of this tug-of-war between hope and fear, between the desire for marriage and the broad cultural and legal permissiveness toward divorce, are particularly on display in the attitudes of young adults, the next generation of married couples and the first raised in a divorce culture.

Marriage remains a strong, personal goal. Ninety-four percent of college freshmen in one 1997 survey said they personally hoped to get married. Just 3 percent didn't hope to marry. And young people had very negative attitudes about divorce, with more than 70 percent of young adults, men and women, agreeing that "children do better with both parents." And more than two out three agreed that "when parents divorce, children develop permanent emotional problems." Only 23 percent believed that divorcing couples try hard to save their marriages. Seventy-six percent of teens believed divorce laws are too lax.[27]

Yet young Americans increasingly view marriage as just one of many equally acceptable relationship alternatives. At the same time, perhaps because they no longer see marriage as necessarily permanent, less than one in twenty young Americans are strongly committed to the idea that "single women should not have children, even if they want to." A majority of teens agreed that a man and woman who decide to raise a child out of wedlock are either "doing their own thing and not affecting anyone else" or even "experimenting with a worthwhile alternative lifestyle." They strongly endorse cohabitation, perhaps in the mistaken belief that it will provide divorce insurance. Between 1975 and 1995, the proportion of high-school seniors agreeing that "it is usually a good idea for a couple to live together before getting married in order to find out whether they really get along" skyrocketed from 35 percent to 59 percent.[28]

The portrait of the next generation that emerges is one in which young men and women long for stable marriage but increasingly are worried and anxious about their ability to achieve it. As marriages become less certain and stable, alternatives to marriage appear more reasonable and attractive. When asked whether they themselves would consider having an out-of-wedlock child, only 48 percent of American girls in the high-school class of '92 said no firmly. By the late nineties, the Census Bureau reported that 40 percent of women under thirty who became mothers for the first time were not married.[29] "Generally speaking," report two sociologists who, in 1998, conducted focus-group interviews in northern New Jersey with single, childless young adults who didn't have college degrees, "these young women seem to trust in the permanence of two family bonds: the mother-child bond and the parent-daughter bond . . . some women say they may have children even if they cannot be married; and second, most of the women expect to take care of themselves economically but also look to their parents as a safety net."[30]

Rising divorce creates its own downward social momentum. Daughters of divorced parents are more likely to divorce themselves and are three times as likely to become unmarried mothers. Meanwhile, having a child born out of wedlock reduces the chances that an unwed mother (or unwed father) will marry and increases the risk that a future marriage will fail.

Women who have an out-of-wedlock child, for example, are only about one-half to one-third as likely to marry as women who don't. This is not because unwed mothers don't value marriage. Three scholars using a large nationally representative sample discovered that unwed mothers were not any less likely to plan to marry in the near future than women who did not have out-of-wedlock births. But having a baby outside of marriage did reduce a young woman's chances of achieving her dream: 45 percent of single women who expected to marry within five years did so; but only 28 percent of unwed mothers who expected to marry within five years achieved their goal.[31]

And when women with children do marry, as Linda Waite put it in an essay with Lee Lillard, "a feedback effect" can be seen "in which divorces increase the number of marriages that include stepchildren, and in which the presence of these stepchildren, in turn, both heightens the risk that the new marriage will end and lowers the chances that the couple will have a child of their own—a birth that would have made their marriage more stable."[32]

The divorce culture thus sets in motion changes that affect even those spouses who don't split up. When people perceive their own divorce risk as high, they become afraid to invest in their own marriage; they hedge their bets, financially and emotionally. They think and act more like singles than spouses who have confidence in the institution of marriage. Divorce anxiety not only produces more divorce, but it creates less happiness in marriage, even in those unions that do survive. Marriage can become just a piece of paper if you are always wondering in the back of your mind whether or not your partner might walk.

Why is marriage in trouble? We want marriage, but we are afraid to discourage divorce or unwed childbearing. The marriage vow thus receives less support from families, society, experts, government, and the law. Important changes in sex roles have challenged married couples to make new adjustments at the very time the social prestige of marriage as a uniquely favored union has declined, and divorce as a solution to emotional difficulties is more widely approved than ever before. Marriage is more often described as just one of an array of personal lifestyles, no one of which is intrinsically preferable to any other, one "style" of intimate relationship about which others important to you, from your lawyer to your therapist to your own best friend, are obliged to remain agnostic.

But the more we treat marriage just like other relationships, the more ghostly and insubstantial the marriage relation becomes. In order to have the option to marry, to make a permanent, public commitment to one other human being, we have to first, as a society, create the marriage option—to make it something different, bigger, and firmer than merely living together. The alternative is to allow marriage to wither into a mere piece of paper, which changes or adds nothing to the way a couple is viewed or treated.

In such a society, the choice to cohabit might become even easier than it is today. But the choice to marry would be stripped from us. If we cannot "go back" to the ways of the past, how do we move forward to a better future? How do we restore young Americans' faith in their capacity to create lasting love? What can we do to renew marriage so that not only we but our children and our children's children can continue to experience the transforming power of the marriage vow?

14

RENEWING MARRIAGE

The scientific evidence is now overwhelming: Marriage is not just one of a wide variety of alternate family forms or intimate relations, each of which are equally good at promoting the well-being of children or adults. Marriage is not merely a private taste or a private relation; it is an important public good. As marriage weakens, the costs are borne not only by individual children or families but by all of us taxpayers, citizens, and neighbors. We all incur the costs of higher crime, welfare, education and health-care expenditures, and in reduced security for our own marriage investments. Simply as a matter of public health alone, to take just one public consequence of marriage's decline, a new campaign to reduce marriage failure is as important as the campaign to reduce smoking.

As Linda Waite put it to her fellow scholars in her presidential address to the Population Association of America, "Social scientists have a responsibility to weigh the evidence on the consequences of social behaviors in the same way as medical researchers evaluate the evidence of the consequences of, say, cigarette smoking or exercise. . . . I think social scientists have an obligation to point out the benefits of marriage beyond the mostly emotional ones, which tend to push people toward marriage but may not sustain them when the honeymoon is over. We have an equally strong obligation to make policymakers aware of the stakes when they pull the policy levers that discourage marriage."[1]

When society as a whole helps support marriage as an institution, we are all better off. Cohabitation is something that individuals can create for themselves, by themselves. The decision to marry, as we have seen, is a choice to enter into a larger, more durable bond, which requires social, moral, and legal support. By recognizing the public union of men and women, the larger society helps individuals achieve the goals and gains marriage represents: a supportive partner one can trust, a safe place for raising children.

These profound benefits of marriage do not come only with a traditional division of labor, in which the wife takes primary responsibility for home and family and the husband takes responsibility for supporting them. Couples may decide on a wide variety of ways to divide family labor, to assign household tasks, to share responsibility for earning what the family needs to live on, and to care for children. They may change their bargain as their situation changes. They should still get substantial benefits from marriage, with its long-term commitment and teamwork, provided society supports the essence of the marital vow: permanence, mutual support, sexual fidelity.

But because marriage is not merely a private, emotional relationship, strengthening marriage requires more than private, emotional efforts. If the private inner meaning of marriage—a lifelong commitment to form a new family—is to be maintained, then its larger public role must be acknowledged and supported by the larger society and its institutions, including (but not limited to) the government.

A roughly 50 percent divorce rate and a 33 percent out-of-wedlock birthrate are not inevitabilities. In fact, the United States stands alone even among industrialized nations in the rate at which we change partners and form families that consist of one adult and children. Our fragile families are at least partly the consequence of a certain set of interrelated cultural ideas—about the importance of fathers, the nature of sex and commitment, the obligations of parents to each other and to their children—that are relatively recent and hardly inevitable. We can change our minds if we choose.

And our high rates of divorce and unwed childbearing also respond to the public policies our governments promote in divorce law, welfare reform, family-tax policy, and even statements from leaders—cumulative decisions that can (at the margin) make it easier or more difficult for people to form lasting, satisfying marriages.

Already there are signs that the new public respect for marriage and fatherhood are changing people's behavior. A recent Census Bureau report concluded that, after tumultuous rises for two decades, our rates of family fragmentation may finally be bottoming out. Since 1990, for the first time in two generations, the divorce rates appear to have declined slightly; the out-of-wedlock childbirth rate has stopped rising; teen pregnancies are falling.[2]

How can we build on such recent, modest, but encouraging success? What more can we do to restore marriage as the normal, stable context for raising children? How can we help more men and women succeed in their quest for enduring, loving marriages?

There are no magic bullets that will renew marriage overnight. But there are steps that we can and should take to support marriage as a public promise, a moral ideal, and as a social institution. Here are nine steps to building a marriage-friendly America:[3]

1. Get the Message Out

We need to place marriage in a prominent place on the public agenda. We need to discuss the foundational importance of marriage to family life, its importance to society as a whole, and its importance to individuals. We need to debate and discuss the ways that we as a nation support—or undermine—marriage as an institution, through tax policy, government assistance, legislation and the courts, school policies and programs, the messages sent by the media, as well as state and local programs and policies.

Social scientists and other experts in academia and government—whose views reverberate throughout the culture—have a particular responsibility to let the public know about the large and compelling body of scientific evidence that marriage matters. This is not just an issue of morality but of public health.

Among most first-rate family scholars, the "Murphy Brown debate" is over. The research has been done; the results are in: Our extraordinarily high rates of divorce and out-of-wedlock childbearing are damaging too many of our children. And as Linda Waite's and others' research detailed in this book has shown, the rates threaten the health, wealth, and well-being of adults as well.

This does not mean, of course, that divorce or separation is never justified. But individuals who make the decision to divorce need to be well-informed about its potential costs to themselves, their partners, and their children. When spouses are preoccupied with their own immediate frustrations and disappointment, family experts have a responsibility to remind them of the long-term investment they have in each other and in their children. People struggling in their marriage also need to know that feelings change: Troubled marriages can and probably will get better.

Family experts, in other words, have an obligation to let the public know: Sure smoking kills, but so does divorce. Yes, a college education boosts a man's earnings, but so does getting and keeping a wife. Of course children need parental attention, but they do best if they get it from both a mother and a father.

The academics who are the professional custodians of the family—who train the next generation of social workers, reporters, women's-magazine editors, teachers, marriage counselors, psychiatrists, family lawyers, and even the clergy—have a particular obligation to call their students' attention to the research pointing to the powerful importance of enduring marriage for both adults and children. As Professor Norval Glenn pointed out, "[W]hat good scholars do is for naught . . . if their findings, theories, and insights are not relayed accurately to those who may base decisions upon them."[4]

So, too, family experts in academia and elsewhere should put a high priority on improving the training of counselors, social workers, judges, teachers, religious workers—including priests, ministers, and rabbis—and other professional service providers of the family, making them aware of the importance of marriage not only to children but to adults and the wider society.

Children of single parents need to know that they, too, can succeed. But they also need teachers, schools, counselors, and other caring adults to acknowledge, rather than deny, their suffering. As future fathers and mothers, husbands and wives, they, too, need to know that marriage is an important and achievable goal. There is help available for building the intact family they were denied as children; we suspect that children of single parents would be especially interested in new training in couples and relationship skills offered in many cities through a variety of marriage-preparation, education, and encounter programs.[5] And adult authority figures need to give young people, especially boys, the motivation to grow up to become responsible, committed fathers and husbands and to help them develop the skills to carry through with this commitment. It would be a grave mistake, arising out of a misguided sense of compassion, to give boys or girls the impression that marriage doesn't matter.

Divinity schools and other institutes that train clergy should incorporate the latest research news into their training programs, reassuring clergy and lay counselors that a renewed emphasis on marriage is not old-fashioned or overly moralistic but simple common sense, ratified by the best scientific research.

As sociology teaches us, parents, family, and friends have an even more important role in getting the message out, for you are the true custodians of what really counts as a "social norm." What parents and other family members and close friends say to couples living together without commitment or to married couples tempted to break their vows has an even more powerful impact on how people act.

If we value marriage, there are two key values to communicate as well as live by. If marriage matters, we need to make a distinction between marriage and other forms of relationships. This does not mean branding anyone with a scarlet letter. But it does mean, at least, gently resisting demands to treat cohabiting couples exactly like married couples.

Parents, in particular, should urge their adult children to make the commitment of marriage to the loves of their lives—assuming that the partners are mature and responsible. Despite what popular culture (or rebellious teens) may tell you, as a parent, you have an enormous influence over even your adult child. One study found that adult children whose mothers are strongly opposed to cohabitation marry at a rate nearly five times higher than young adults whose mothers strongly approve of cohabitation.[6]

If you want your kids to value marriage, do not treat girlfriends or boyfriends exactly the same as spouses. And do offer to help support your children while they get settled if they get married. Encourage pregnant couples who love each other to marry before the child is born, and help them form a strong foundation for a new family as well.

If your children, siblings, or friends are struggling in a marriage, lend them your faith as well as your ear. Tell them the marriage bond is worth fighting for. Remind them that divorce brings as many problems as it solves. Offer them the gift of hope: Tell them that almost nine out of ten very unhappy couples who do stick it out manage to make their marriage happier, and most are very happy indeed. Point them toward pro-marriage resources—books, clergy, marriage-education courses, and counselors—so they don't have to fight the good fight alone. Buy them a copy of this book and highlight the parts on sex, health, wealth, or children, depending on the situation. There are many new resources to help unhappy couples stay together and love each other better. (See the appendix for a list of community resources and organizations offering couple-skills training.)

2. Get the Facts

Part of getting the message out is getting the facts straight. The low priority that federal and state governments place on gathering information on marriage and divorce is a national disgrace. Can we imagine the response if we suggested cutting the monthly government survey of unemployment or the number of jobs added to the economy? Our society can no more afford to ignore basic statistics on marriage and divorce than to ignore basic statistics on employment or job creation.

If we don't know the characteristics of people who are marrying or divorcing, we can't know, for instance, if long-running marriages are breaking up at an increasing rate or if more children are seeing their parents divorce. We can't know if black and white people show the same rates of marriage or find out the divorce rate of highly educated or less-educated men or women.

National data on marriage and divorce come from marriage licenses and divorce registration certificates collected by county officials and reported to state vital statistics offices in state health departments. We get information on births and deaths in much the same way—from certificates collected by county officials, which they report to state governments, which then report them on a voluntary basis to the federal government. The National Center for Health Statistics then compiles these figures for the nation as a whole. But state governments do a much better job of collecting information on births and deaths than they do of keeping track of marriages and divorces that occur in their jurisdiction.

In fact, information from states got so bad that in 1995 the federal government discontinued its contractual arrangement to obtain any data on marriage and divorce of individuals from state health departments. State health departments continue to count the number of marriages and divorces but no longer report any information about the kinds of people getting married or divorced; they now just tell the federal government how many marriages and divorces occurred in their state during a given period. Since 1990, the federal government has produced no detailed information on marriages and divorces for the nation. According to officials at the National Center for Health Statistics, states give information on marriage and divorce "very, very low priority."[7] And many states report only some of the information requested by the federal government, making it difficult to compare information for different states or to combine these numbers into information on the whole country. A lack of resources at the federal and state level has precluded any effort to rebuild and invest in the collection of marriage-and-divorce data.

The increasingly dismal state of our marriage statistics results in part from the fact that the state health departments responsible for collecting marriage and divorce data don't see marriage and divorce as "health" issues. The federal government has also abdicated its responsibility in this regard, allowing our national statistical system to fall into disrepair. We hope that this book will help responsible officials get the message: marriage is not just a moral issue; it's a public-health issue.

Fortunately, incentives for states to improve their handling of marriage-and-divorce statistics may be changing. Recent federal legislation that mandates welfare reform contains a provision that states should reduce childbearing by unmarried women. States that show the largest reduction in the percentage of births to unmarried women will receive a "bonus" from the federal government of up to $25 million per year. Although the information that states need is already available on birth certificates, this incentive makes marriage itself much more relevant to states and may make states more willing to collect data on marriage and divorce.[8] If not, Congress should provide new incentives for states to collect accurate family data.

The lack of information on people who get married or divorced keeps us from understanding much at all about what is happening to families. All future research into the benefits of marriage—or the effects of efforts to stem divorce—will be hampered by the government's failure to take marriage data seriously. The neglect of marriage by the states has been more than matched by the federal government under Democrats and Republicans alike. No federal agency or research office has the general responsibility for the data on marriage and divorce. Perhaps as a result, there are no government-sponsored reports that synthesize available information about marriage, cohabitation, and divorce, which are comparable to the recent report *To Have and To Hold: Strategies to Strengthen Marriage and Relationships* authorized by the Australian parliament.

We urge both federal and state governments to put a renewed emphasis on the collection and dissemination of timely information on marriage and divorce. This effort should include both complete vital registration of marriages and divorces by all states—using a common reporting format—and compilation and dissemination of family-related facts and figures for the nation as a whole. Congress or the president should direct all government-funded and government-administered surveys of individuals to include detailed information about marital and cohabitation status. More research should be directed at estimating the true public costs of marital failure in taxpayer dollars spent on welfare, child-support collections, juvenile delinquency and other crime prevention, mental health and other medical costs in order to help put the public costs of supporting marriage in perspective.

Similarly, when reporting on issues ranging from teen pregnancy to domestic violence, government agencies should routinely gather and present data on trends for married and unmarried couples (or single women and men) separately.

Especially as more states experiment with ways to discourage divorce, an accurate picture of marriage, divorce, and out-of-wedlock birth trends is important. Moreover, if we as a society fail to monitor these crucial indicators of family life, we may be blinded to important trends and asleep to developing dangers.

3. Create a Tax and Welfare Policy That Is Promarriage

Over time, largely through neglect, the tax code has become significantly less supportive of both marriage and family. Restoring the value of the dependent allowance for children, eliminating penalties for marriage in the tax code, and structuring child-care benefits so that they do not punish specialization in home and family are just a few examples of how federal tax policy can support or undermine marriage. We should, for instance, increase the new "child credit," so that it more adequately reflects the true out-of-pocket costs of raising children and protects more of the income families need to raise children.[9] Married couples, in particular (because the majority of single mothers do not make enough money to pay income taxes, and even receive tax subsidies through the Earned Income Tax Credit or EITC), feel the bite of increased taxation and have economized by drastically cutting back on childbearing to the point that the average married woman has significantly less than two children during marriage. One way to ensure that more of our children are born inside marriage is to stop the tax raid on family income.

Other penalties for marriage appear in the tax code and in public-assistance programs such as public housing and food stamps that serve the economically disadvantaged. Supporting marriage among the poor and working class, without punishing single parents (who are already under enormous economic stress), can be tricky. Early efforts in Congress to eliminate the marriage penalty for two-income couples, for example, would have inadvertently created a "homemaker penalty" for one-earner married couples.

Perhaps the best way to repair the middle-class marriage penalties in the tax code is to reinstate "income-splitting." But the middle-class marriage penalty pales beside the huge marriage penalty federal policy imposes on low-income workers, especially through the Earned Income Tax Credit. Most poverty benefits have an income limit—and the limit for married couples is seldom twice the limit for single parents. Thus, when two low-income workers marry, their new joint income often disqualifies them for the Earned Income Tax Credit and other benefits, so marriage often makes them significantly poorer—perhaps one reason that marriage is so relatively uncommon in poor neighborhoods. For example, if a single mother of two children, working full-time at the minimum wage, marries a single man earning $8 an hour, the couple could lose as much as $8,000 per year in reduced benefits and higher taxes.[10]

One way to eliminate this enormous, unintended marriage penalty, would be to allow low-income married couples to "split" their income for the purposes of qualifying for welfare, child care, Medicaid, and the Earned Income Tax Credit. We could make subsidies for children available to parents without regard to their income. And we could take a complete and thorough review of the tax code and government benefits that carry marriage penalties.[11]

4. Change Laws to Strengthen Marriage

Let's begin by reforming no-fault divorce, especially for couples with children who are minors. The legal story of marriage is now directly at odds with social purposes and cultural meaning of the marriage vow. Thanks to pure no-fault statutes, the law now sends the message to couples that marriage is a temporary commitment that can be abrogated unilaterally by either partner at any time and for any reason. All people who marry are seeking to do something other than merely live together until one of them spots a better deal elsewhere. The law should find new ways to support and affirm the importance of a permanent, binding marriage commitment.

And the law is a power tool. A recent study found that the move to no-fault divorce by itself caused a 6 percent increase in divorce when it was implemented by states; the move to unilateral divorce accounted for 17 percent of the overall increase in divorce rates between 1968 and 1988.[12]

We are not advocating a return to the same fault-based system that used to exist. We do think it is important to slow the rush to divorce and to restore some power to the spouse who wants to keep the marriage together. One option worth considering is to place long waiting periods on contested no-fault divorces, especially for couples with children who are minors or establish long-term financial dependency of one spouse, usually the wife. Before no-fault, waiting periods of two to three years were common in the United States and five- to seven-year waiting periods were typical in Europe. Now, a few states, such as Pennsylvania and Utah, have a three-year separation requirement for no-fault divorces, but most states have no waiting period at all.[13] Amazingly, the New Jersey state legislature actually voted last summer to slash that state's eighteen-month waiting period for divorce.

Such waiting periods accomplish a number of useful goals: First, they give some weight to the marriage vow, acknowledging that divorce is not a simple individual "right." Second, they slow the rush to divorce, giving some spouses a chance to fully consider counseling and reconciliation before becoming entangled in new relationships. Third, they give the spouse who is being left a "breathing spell" in which to emotionally recover before facing the extensive and complicated legal decision that divorce entails.

The Louisiana Covenant Marriage Act, passed into law in August 1997, includes a number of ideas for reform, including restricting allowable grounds for divorce, lengthening waiting periods, and requiring counseling before a divorce is granted. But the Covenant Marriage Act is best known for providing couples who wish to marry with a choice between the existing law, permitting unilateral divorce, or the new covenant contract, which allows divorce on a limited number of serious grounds. Arizona passed a similar law in May 1998.

We should reinstate long-run financial support of spouses who have put the needs of their families over the demands of their own career. The current, shockingly poor financial situation facing women and children after divorce effectively pushes many wives away from investments in their families and toward investments in their own earning power—as a kind of insurance against divorce. Some of these spouses—usually but not exclusively women—would choose to work less if they were insured somehow so that they would not bear all the financial costs of a divorce. Both spouses in such marriages should share the costs—if there are any—

of the lower earning power of the spouse who cared for home and family at the expense of her or his own career.

5. Restore the Special Legal Status of Marriage
Our courts and legal system need to develop a new model of the rights and responsibilities that come with marriage—and those that don't come without it. This new model of marriage as a distinct social and legal status should be based on shared norms of responsibility. It should recognize that individuals do not pass into and out of a marriage unaltered. It should recognize that the longer people have been married, the more interdependent their lives have become and the more damage is done by separating those lives legally. And it should recognize that rights and responsibilities in marriage change in fundamental ways when the couple has children who have not reached adulthood.

Considering what steps to take in this direction, family law scholar Milton Regan Jr. argues that we should consider reinstating fault grounds for divorce alongside no-fault divorce. Fault, in Regan's conception, would be limited to behavior that violates general and strongly held norms about appropriate behavior of spouses. Misconduct of this type might include abuse or promiscuous sexual infidelity. Regan thinks that fault should be considered in financial and custody determinations, even in states that offer only no-fault divorce, because ignoring serious misconduct "sends the message that those who abuse the marital relationship ought to share in its fruits equally with those whom they have abused."[14]

A few states, such as Michigan and Florida, are experimenting with new approaches, focused less on preventing divorce than on strengthening new marriages. In May 1998, Florida passed the Marriage Preparation and Preservation Act of 1998. Under the Florida law, engaged couples who complete a marriage-preparation course pay reduced marriage-license fees. Each courthouse will have listings of approved courses sponsored by religious and secular organizations. This law also mandates that high-school students complete a course in marriage and relationship skills. Couples applying for a marriage license will receive a handbook prepared by the Florida Bar Association that lays out their legal rights and responsibilities to each other and to their children both during the marriage and in the event of dissolution. Finally, like many other states, Florida will require couples who have children and file for divorce to take a course specifically designed for such families.

6. Enlist Religious and Other Community Support

The vast majority of people in America marry in a religious ceremony. This gives religious leaders and institutions both a privileged role in and special responsibilities toward marriage. The Community Marriage Policy (CMP) builds on this special relationship in a program to strengthen marriage. The Community Marriage Policy has been developed and promoted by Michael McManus, a syndicated religious journalist and the author of *Marriage Savers*.

In a CMP initiative, clergy and congregations in a community get together and decide on guidelines for requiring marriage preparation and community support for all marriages that take place in their congregation. This includes, at a minimum, that the couple take a premarital inventory and discuss the results with a trained mentoring couple or counselor. The couple also attends several weeks of educational group sessions. Churches and synagogues are encouraged to offer a larger set of marriage services, including ministries to troubled marriages and marriage enrichment. The Community Marriage Policy has been adopted by eighty cities to date, with much anticipation but little information on the impact to date.[15]

A few communities have broadened the ideas in the Community Marriage Policy to include secular leaders and organizations. Among these, the Greater Grand Rapids Community Marriage Policy is the best known. In 1996 Grand Rapids (Michigan) launched an ambitious community-wide mobilization of religious and civic leaders as well as health professionals and their organizations to facilitate a program designed to support children through strengthening marriage. This effort has some core funding, an able executive leader, and institutional support from a prominent Christian community mental-health center. This effort has enlisted a wide range and sizable number of community leaders who have made tremendous efforts to be inclusive of many different views on marriage.

As part of the Greater Grand Rapids Community Marriage Policy, the business sector, health and legal professions, and many other organizations are being asked to find ways that they can strengthen and support marriages at all ages and stages. After more than a year of careful planning, the initiative began offering training to ministers and courses to couples. It has set a goal of reducing the divorce rate by 25 percent by the year 2010 and will measure interim benchmarks of progress toward this goal.

7. Scrutinize Other Policies for Unintended Antimarriage Consequences

Governments should consider, when drafting policies on health insurance, the potential effect on unwed childbearing. Couples who expect a birth but don't have health insurance may delay or forgo marriage to become eligible for Medicaid funding of the costs of delivery or because private-insurance plans refuse to cover pregnancy as a "pre-existing condition." Consider the case of one real-life couple: Debbie and George had been planning to marry and have children eventually, when Debbie became pregnant. She works part-time and does not have health insurance. George is a highly paid state employee with good health benefits. If they marry now, George's insurance won't cover the birth because the pregnancy is a "pre-existing condition." If they don't get married, Medicaid will pay the costs of prenatal care and delivery. So, they won't marry until after the birth. And what happens if the baby is born with health problems that require extensive and expensive treatment? Probably no marriage then, either, with costs of health care for mother and child shifted to the state. Clearly, we need to look at the incentives for unmarried childbearing and divorce embedded within a variety of public policies.

8. Discourage Unmarried Pregnancy and Childbearing

Schools, media, sports figures, magazines, and models should stop glorifying and supporting unmarried pregnancy and childbearing. The consequences of single parenthood for teens are especially worrisome.

Having a baby outside marriage makes getting married later much more difficult and much less likely.[16] Having a baby before finishing high school makes both parenthood and education a bigger challenge. Although many children raised by a single parent do well, the chances that children will have happy, successful lives are substantially higher if they grow up with two married parents. Television programs and movies that make unmarried pregnancy and childbearing seem like a morally superior choice, sex-education programs focused on the "mechanics" to the exclusion of the social and moral implications of various choices, and parents and friends who fail to point out the costs to all involved if parents don't marry and don't do their best to build a successful happy marriage all undermine marriage.

The challenge for our society lies in encouraging and supporting marriage without punishing those—especially children—who might be affected by our actions. We have to walk this delicate line in designing programs for pregnant teens and in altering the tax code or public-assistance programs.

9. Rethink Domestic-Partnership Legislation

What about other contentious issues, such as gay marriage or domestic-partnership legislation? As private citizens, the authors have reached different conclusions, with Linda Waite tending to favor and Maggie Gallagher tending to oppose extending marriage to same-sex couples. The state of social-science research, as it now stands, sheds little light on the question: Would gay couples (and their children) reap the same benefits from legal marriage that men and women who marry do? As social scientists, the most we can conclude is, Maybe, maybe not.

The answer depends in part on the extent to which gender matters. A family consisting of two mothers would undoubtedly be better off financially than the average single-mother family. But would one of the two women reap the breadwinner's bonus married men get? Or would they both be "married mothers," cutting back on earnings to care for kids? Would two bachelors who "married" settle down to an orderly life together, reaping the health advantages men get from marriage? Or would they barhop in tandem? Again, we suspect, but do not know, that adults in such same-sex couples would reap some, but not all, the benefits of marriage. The benefits afforded same-sex couples by marriage would also depend on the extent to which family, friends, and other social institutions supported these unions.

As for children, the intergenerational effects of deciding, in effect, that gender is irrelevant to the public project of marriage are, frankly, unknown and unknowable—to us or anyone else as social scientists, unless and until some jurisdiction permits gay marriages and we start following the development of children of same-sex couples to see how they do. We, as a society, have to decide whether to take the leap of faith required to legalize gay marriage, but we need to make that decision based on other discourses—on religious and moral views about social justice and sexual morality—but not on the basis of scientific knowledge about the consequences for individuals of these unions.

We can say, however, that the recent public arguments made for extending "domestic partnership" benefits to all cohabiting couples are based on a myth. Extending marriage benefits to cohabiting men and women who have refused to marry sends a message social scientists now know to be dangerously false—that cohabitation is the functional equivalent of marriage. Cohabitation is not just like marriage. On average, cohabiting couples are less sexually faithful, lead less settled lives, are less likely to have children, are more likely to be violent, make less money, and are less happy—and less committed—than married couples. Ironically, this negative characterization applies primarily to cohabiting couples who have no definite plans to get married, those who live with children of only one of the partners, and those who have been married before. Engaged cohabiting couples without children seem more like married couples in their attitudes and behaviors.[17]

If, out of a sense of fairness to gays, local governments or businesses do choose to create domestic-partnership benefits, they should (also out of fairness) restrict the benefits to couples who are not legally able to marry. Domestic partners who want partnership benefits have only to marry to get them. Giving the benefits of marriage to people who have refused its responsibilities is neither fair nor wise.

Bring Men Back In

As Frances Goldscheider said in a letter to *The Nation*, "If men come to realize the economic and sexual bargain they are getting from marriage and family, they might be prepared to offer more to their potential or actual spouses to encourage them to join with them or stay with them." Many women find a marriage bargain unappealing if it requires them to share in supporting the family financially and to run the house and take primary responsibility for children. Goldscheider argues that a "new bargain" should be struck, one that calls on men whose wives work to share the responsibility for caring for a home and family. In that case, the advantages of marriage could flow at least as readily from an egalitarian family as a traditional one, and certainly beat living alone.[18]

The social changes that have led to declines in marriage, increases in cohabitation, divorce, and childbearing by unmarried women are inextricably intertwined. They are part of a wider web of social change that include shifts in our views of appropriate roles for men and women, increasing and increasingly prolonged education, the rush of women toward demanding and rewarding careers, and changing views of sex outside of marriage. These changes are powerful, pervasive, popular, and probably permanent, leading many to simply counsel despair: "[T]he changes in the structure of the family are probably the result of some sizeable and largely unstoppable changes in social and economic patterns," concludes David Ellwood in *Poor Support*. "[T]here is no way of going back to where we were before," agrees family scholar Arlene Skolnick.[19]

By contrast, we think that the fact that there is no going backward makes it doubly important to move forward. We think that moving forward requires that all of us—parents, clergy, educators, experts, policymakers, and concerned Americans—put the problem of marriage on the front burner and come up with new strategies to reward and strengthen the marital commitment.

For although marriage as an institution has been weakened by societal change, broad and compelling evidence suggests that it is vitally important: Adults no less than children require rooted relationships to flourish.

No social institution other than marriage consistently and dependably provides them.

In spite of the breakneck pace of social and economic transformation, the basic human needs for trust, love, loyalty, fidelity, commitment, and meaning are part of our nature as Homo sapiens. As a species, we have developed social institutions over eons to get the most out of these creatures that we are. The family, focused around the married couple, forms the keystone of these universal social institutions.

As the traditional Protestant marriage ceremony puts it: "To have and to hold from this day forward, for better, for worse, for richer, for poorer, in sickness and in health, to love and to cherish, till death do us part." This is the extraordinary vow that ordinary men and women dare to take every day.

Decades of social-science research have confirmed the deepest intuitions of the human heart: As frightening, exhilarating, and improbable as this wild vow of constancy may seem, there is no substitute. When love seeks permanence, a safe home for children who long for both parents, when men and women look for someone they can count on, there are no substitutes. The word for what we want is *marriage*.

Appendix: Resources for a Marriage Movement

Note: What follows is a diverse group of Web sites, individuals, and organizations dedicated to strengthening marriage and/or discouraging divorce and unwed child-bearing, which we think may be useful to couples, parents, citizens, policymakers, legislators, faith communities, and other community groups interested in ideas, programs, and policies to strengthen marriage as well as to the media covering marriage and family issues. We do not necessarily endorse all of the ideas, agendas, or proposals these groups promote.

For information on marriage preparation and marriage education:

> The Coalition for Marriage, Family and Couples Education (CMFCE)
> Diane Sollee, Director
> 5310 Belt Road, NW
> Washington, D.C. 20015–1961
> Phone: (202) 362–3332
> E-mail: *CMFCE@smartmarriages.com*
> Web site: *www.smartmarriages.com*

For information on Community Marriage Policies, and faith-based "marriage savers" strategies:

> Marriage Savers
> Mike and Harriet McManus, co-directors
> 9311 Harrington Drive
> Potomac, MD 20854
> Phone: (301) 469–5873
> Web site: *www.marriagesavers.org*

For information on supporting marriage and fatherhood in low-income and welfare communities:

Resource Center on Couples and Marriage Policy Center on Law and Social Policy
Theodora Ooms, Executive Director
1616 P. Street, NW, Suite 150
Washington, D.C. 20036
Phone: (202) 328–5163
E-mail: *Tooms@clasp.org*
Web site: *www.clasp.org*

For information on divorce law reforms intended to reduce divorce:

Americans for Divorce Reform
John Crouch, Executive Director
2111 Wilson Boulevard, Suite 550
Arlington, VA 22201–3057
E-mail: *divorcereform@usa.net*
Web site: *www.divorcereform.org*

For information on the marriage penalty, tax reform, and other public-policy issues relating to marriage, see:

The Institute for American Values
David Blankenhorn, President
1841 Broadway, Suite 211
New York, NY 10023–7603
Phone: (212) 246–3942
E-mail: *IAV@worldnet.att.net*
Web site: *www.americanvalues.org*

The Howard Center for Family, Religion and Society
Allan C. Carlson, President
934 North Main Street
Rockford, IL 61103
Phone: (815) 964–5819
E-mail: *howdctr@bossnt.com*

The Urban Institute
C. Eugene Steuerle, Senior Fellow
2106 M Street, NW
Washington, D.C. 20037
Phone: (202) 833–7200
E-mail: *paffairs@ui.urban.org*
Web site: *www.urban.org*

Notes

Chapter 1: The Marriage Wars

1. Steven Mintz and Susan Kellogg, *Domestic Revolutions: A Social History of American Family Life* (New York: The Free Press, 1988), 206–207. (All three previous quotes come from this source.)
2. Randall Collins and Scott Coltrane, *Sociology of Marriage and the Family: Gender, Love and Property,* 4th ed. (Chicago: Nelson-Hall, 1995) 372.
3. Norval Glenn, David Popenoe, Jean Bethke Elshtain, and David Blankenhorn eds. "Values, Attitudes, and the State of American Marriage," in *Promises to Keep: Decline and Renewal of Marriage in America* (Lanham, Md.: Rowman and Littlefield, 1996), 28.
4. Danielle Crittenden, *What Our Mothers Didn't Tell Us: Why Happiness Eludes the Modern Woman* (New York: Simon & Schuster, 1999), 60.
5. Alan W. Petrucelli, "Mel Harris: We Are Not the Waltons," *Working Mother,* December 1996, 21.
6. Glenn, "Values, Attitudes," 20–21.
7. Dennis K. Orthner, David Blankenhorn, Steven Bayme, and Jean Bethke Elshtain eds. "The Family in Transition" in *Rebuilding the Nest: A New Commitment to the American Family* (Milwaukee: Family Service America, 1990), 95.
8. Glenn, "Values, Attitudes," 15.
9. Arthur Levine and Jeanette S. Cureton, *When Hope and Fear Collide: A Portrait of Today's College Student* (San Francisco: Jossey-Bass, 1998), 95.
10. Mel Krantzler and Pat Krantzler, *The New Creative Divorce: How to Create a Happier, More Rewarding Life, During—and After—Your Divorce* (Holbrook, Mass.: Adams Media Corp, 1998), 3.
11. Judy Root Aulette, *Changing Families* (Belmont, Calif.: Wadsworth, 1994), 278.
12. Scott Coltrane, "Family Policy Wonderland," *Contemporary Sociology* 27(3): 230 (1998).
13. Karen S. Peterson, "Does Tying the Knot Put Women in a Bind?" *USA Today,* 22 April 1997.
14. Nena O'Neill and George O'Neill, *Open Marriage: A New Life Style for Couples* (New York: M. Evans and Company, 1972), 43, quoted in Barbara Dafoe Whitehead, "The Experts' Story of Marriage," Council on Families Working Paper WP14 (New York: Institute for American Values, 1992), 1.

15. Andrew Cherlin, *Marriage, Divorce, Remarriage* (Cambridge, Mass.: Harvard University Press, 1992), 71.

16. "Experts Disagree over Benefits, Harm Divorce Can Hold for Kids." *Jackson (Miss.) Clarion Star-Ledger,* 2 September 1992, A5.

17. Richard A. Gardner, *Psychotherapy with Children of Divorce* (New York: Jason Aronson, 1982), 11–12.

18. Arland Thornton, "Reciprocal Influences of Family and Religion in a Changing World," *Journal of Marriage and Family* (1985): 47; Karen S. Peterson, "Opinions Split Over Avoiding Divorce," *USA Today,* 25 July 1998.

19. "Single Parent Issue Touches Sensitive Nerve," *Los Angeles Times,* 22 July 1993, E1–2, quoted in Barbara Dafoe Whitehead, "The Decline of Marriage as the Social Basis of Childrearing" in *Promises to Keep,* 5.

20. Linda J. Waite's tabulations from the National Education Longitudinal Survey (NELS:88) files, first follow-up.

21. Whitehead, "The Decline of Marriage," 5.

22. Jane R. Eisner, "It's Perfectly Normal for Parents to Control What Their Kids Read," *Philadelphia Sun,* 20 October 1996.

23. David Blankenhorn, *Fatherless America: Confronting Our Most Urgent Social Problem* (New York: Basic Books, 1995), 314.

24. Barbara Dafoe Whitehead, "The Experts' Story of Marriage," Council on Families Working Paper WP14 (New York: Institute for American Values, August 1992), 6–7.

25. David Knox and Caroline Schacht, eds. 1991. *Choices in Relationships: An Introduction to Marriage and the Family,* 3d. ed. (St. Paul, Minn.: West Publishing Co., 1991), 124, 142.

26. Blankenhorn, *Fatherless America,* 314.

27. Kathleen Kiernan, "Family Change: Issues and Implications," in *The Fragmenting Family: Does it Matter?* ed. Mirian E. David (London: Institute of Economic Affairs, 1998), 64.

28. William Damon, "The Path to a Civil Society Goes through the University," *The Chronicle of Higher Education,* 16 October 1998, B4.

29. For a discussion of these legal changes, see Maggie Gallagher, *The Abolition of Marriage: How We Destroy Lasting Love.* (Washington, D.C.: Regnery Publishing, 1996), chapter 10.

30. David Blankenhorn, "Separation of Marriage and State," *Propositions* 2, (1998), 11.

31. Drucilla Cornell, "Fatherhood and Its Discontents: Men, Patriarchy, and Freedom" in *Lost Fathers: The Politics of Fatherlessness in America,* ed. Cynthia R. Daniels (New York: St. Martin's Press, 1998), 199–200.

32. Gallagher, *The Abolition of Marriage,* 42.

33. Richard Cohen, "Critic at Large: Significant Mothers," *Washington Post,* 30 August 1987, p. 3.

34. David Blankenhom, "I Want What I Want," *Propositions* (Spring 1998): 10.

Chapter 2: The Marriage Bargain

1. As Donald Hernandez (with David E. Myers, *America's Children: Resources from Family, Government and the Economy* [New York: Russell Sage Foundation, 1993], 134–35, points out, even at the height of the breadwinner-homemaker family's prevalence, the proportion of children living in these families never reached 60 percent; many families lived in different arrangements.

2. Jill Abramson, "Still Playing Key Role on a Most Painful Day," *The New York Times*, 18 August 1998, 15.

3. For an excellent discussion of changes in family law as they affect marriage, see Milton C. Regan Jr., "Postmodern Family Law: Toward a New Model of Status," in *Promises to Keep*, 157–85.

4. C. Eugene Steuerle, Edward M. Gramlich, Hugh Heclo, and Demetra Nightingale, *The Government We Deserve* (Washington, D.C.: Urban Institute Press, 1998).

5. Andrew M. Greeley, *Religious Change in America* (Cambridge, Mass.: Harvard University Press, 1989).

6. See Arland Thornton, "Reciprocal Influences of Family and Religion in a Changing World," *Journal of Marriage and the Family* 47 (1985): 381–94.

7. Joan Aldous, "Problematic Elements in the Relationship Between Churches and Families," in *Families and Religions: Conflict and Change in Modern Society*, eds. William D'Antonio and Joan Aldous (Beverly Hills, Calif.: Sage, 1983), 67–80.

8. Dennis K. Orthner, "The Family in Transition," 98.

9. For the case of gains in specialization and trade for countries, see Robert L. Heilbroner, ed., *The Essential Adam Smith* (New York: W. W. Norton & Co., 1986), 161–68. See Gary S. Becker, *A Treatise on the Family* (Cambridge, Mass.: Harvard University Press, 1991), 57–61, for an application of specialization within marriage.

10. See Frances K. Goldscheider and Linda J. Waite, "Sex Differences in Entry into Marriage," *American Journal of Sociology* 92 (1986): 91–109, for results on higher marriage rates of men with high incomes. See Andrew J. Cherlin, "The Effect of Children on Marital Dissolution," *Demography* 14(3): 265–72 (1977), for results on men's failure to support the family as a predictor of divorce.

11. Micaela DiLeonardo, "The Female World of Cards and Holidays: Women, Families and the Work of Kinship," *Signs* 12 (1987): 440–53.

12. Linda J. Waite and Mark R. Nielsen, "The Rise of the Dual-career Family," in *Work and Family: Today's Realities and Tomorrow's Visions*, eds. R. Hertz and N. Marshall (University of California Press, forthcoming. These figures apply to women ages twenty-five to fifty-five in 1997.

13. This argument is made by Gerald Marwell, "Why Ascription? Parts of a More or Less Formal Theory of the Functions and Dysfunctions of Sex Roles," *American Sociological Review* 40 (1975): 445–55.

14. Hernandez and Myers, *American's Children*, 285–87.

15. The arguments about the situation faced by single men and women are summarized in Lee A. Lillard and Linda J. Waite, "'Til Death Do Us Part: Marital Disruption and Mortality," *American Journal of Sociology* 100 (1995): 1131–56.

16. Steven L. Nock, *Marriage in Men's Lives* (New York: Oxford University Press, 1998), 6–7.

17. George A. Akerlof, "Men without Children," *The Economic Journal* 108 (1998): 287–309. Quote on p. 290.

18. Steven L. Nock, "The Consequences of Premarital Fatherhood," *American Sociological Review* 63(1998): 250–63.

19. National Research Council, *Measuring Poverty: A New Approach*, eds. Constance F. Citro and Robert T. Michael (Washington, D.C.: National Academy Press, 1995).

20. Some research suggests that sick wives get less care from their husbands than sick husbands get from their wives. See S. M. Allen, "Gender differences in spousal caregiving and unmet need for care," *Journal of Gerontology: Social Sciences* 49(4): S187–S195 (1994).

21. Lois M. Verbrugge, "Marital Status and Health," *Journal of Marriage and the Family* 41(1979): 267–85.

22. This research is reviewed in James S. House, Debra Umberson, and Karl Landis, "Structures and Processes of Social Support," *Annual Review of Sociology* 14 (1988): 293–318.

23. Diane C. Elvenstar, *First Comes Love: Deciding Whether or Not to Get Married* (Indianapolis/New York: The Bobbs-Merrill Co., 1983), 28.

24. Becker, *Treatise on Family*, 48–49.

25. Elvenstar, 1983.

26. Ibid.

Chapter 3: The Cohabitation Deal

1. U. S. Bureau of the Census, *Marital Status and Living Arrangements, March 1997*, Current Population Reports, Series P20, No. 506 (Washington, D.C., 1998).

2. Oropesa finds that non-Latino whites are most negative toward cohabitation, regardless of the couple's plans to marry. Mexican Americans and Puerto Ricans are more accepting but, on average, are neutral toward living together by an unmarried couple. The question on which this analysis is based asks an individual to agree or disagree with the statement "It is all right for an unmarried couple to live together even if they have no interest in considering marriage" or a variant that states that they have plans to marry. Agreement with this statement does not imply endorsement of cohabitation, just lack of condemnation. See R. S. Oropesa, "Normative Beliefs about Marriage and Cohabitation: A Comparison of Non-Latino Whites, Mexican Americans, and Puerto Ricans," *Journal of Marriage and the Family* 58 (February 1996): 49–62.

3. Larry L. Bumpass, "The Declining Significance of Marriage: Changing Family Life in the United States" (paper presented at the Potsdam International Conference, "Changing Families and Childhood," December 1994).

4. Susan L. Brown and Alan Booth, "Cohabitation Versus Marriage: A Comparison of Relationship Quality," *Journal of Marriage and the Family* 58 (1996): 668–78.

5. Christine Bachrach, "Cohabitation and Reproductive Behavior in the U. S." *Demography* 24(4): 623–37 (1987).

6. Joseph Hopper, "The Symbolic Origins of Conflict in Divorce" (paper presented at the meetings of the American Sociological Association, 1998).

7. Dennis K. Orthner, "The Family in Transition," 93–118.

8. At least in the United States. Larry L. Bumpass and James A. Sweet, "National Estimates of Cohabitation," *Demography* 26 (1989): 615–25. See also Bumpass, "Declining Significance of Marriage," 1994. In the Nordic countries cohabitation is somewhat different.

9. Larry L. Bumpass, R. Kelly Raley, and James A. Sweet. "The Changing Character of Stepfamilies: Implications of Cohabitation and Nonmarital Childbearing," *Demography* 32: 425–36.

10. Ibid., 425.

11. Lingxin Hao, "Family Structure, Private Transfers, and the Economic Well-being of Families with Children," *Social Forces* 75(1996): 269–92. Lingxin Hao, "Family Structure, Parental Input, and Child Development" (paper presented at the meetings of the Population Association of America, Washington, D.C., March 1997). Braver makes the point (in Sanford L. Braver and Diane O'Connell, *Divorced Dads: Shattering the Myths*

[New York: Jeremy P. Tarcher/Putnam, 1998]) that unilateral divorce and the fact that mothers almost always get custody of the children makes fatherhood much riskier for men today than it was for their fathers. Remarriage poses many of the same threats as cohabitation does, except that remarriages are more stable.

12. Philip Blumstein and Pepper Schwartz, *American Couples: Money, Work, Sex* (New York: William Morrow, 1983), 437.

13. Ibid, 432.

14. Ibid.: Marin Clarkberg, Ross M. Stolzenberg, and Linda J. Waite, "Attitudes, Values and Entrance into Cohabitational Versus Marital Unions," *Social Forces* 74 (1995): 609–32.

15. Blumstein and Schwartz, *American Couples,* 428–29.

16. Ibid., 432.

17. Ibid., 341.

18. Judith Treas, "Money in the Bank: Transaction Costs and the Economic Organization of Marriage," *American Sociological Review* 58 (5): 723–34 (1993).

19. Nicole Marwell, "Meanings of Marriage and Cohabitation: A Qualitative Study of Puerto Rican Women" (master's thesis, the University of Chicago, 1994).

20. Catherine E. Ross, "Reconceptualizing Marital Status as a Continuum of Social Attachment," *Journal of Marriage and the Family* 57 (1995): 129–40.

21. Blumstein and Schwartz, *American Couples,* 424.

22. Clarkberg, Stolzenberg, and Waite, "Attitudes, Values and Entrance," 623.

23. Blumstein and Schwartz, *American Couples,* 431.

24. Alan Booth and David Johnson, "Premarital Cohabitation and Marital Success," *Journal of Family Issues* 9 (1988): 255–72.

25. Clarkberg, Stolzenberg, and Waite, "Attitudes, Values and Entrance," 624.

26. Scott J. South and Glenna D. Spitze, "Housework in Marital and Nonmarital Households," *American Sociological Review* 59 (1994): 327–47.

27. Clarkberg, Stolzenberg, and Waite, "Attitudes, Values and Entrance," 621.

28. Ibid. See pp. 610–611 for literature review.

29. Beth Anne Shelton, *Women, Men, and Time: Gender Differences in Paid Work, Housework, and Leisure* (Westport, Conn.: Greenwood, 1992)

30. Blumstein and Schwartz, *American Couples,* 364–65.

31. Ibid., 445–46.

32. Clarkberg, Stolzenberg, and Waite, "Attitudes, Values and Entrance," 622.

33. Ibid., 623.

34. Blumstein and Schwartz, *American Couples,* 422.

35. Ibid., 445.

36. Ibid., 446.

37. Lee A. Lillard, Michael J. Brien, and Linda J. Waite, "Pre-Marital Cohabitation and Subsequent Marital Dissolution: Is It Self-selection?" *Demography* 32 (1995): 437–58; Elizabeth Thomson and Ugo Collela, "Cohabitation and Marital Stability: Quality or Commitment?," *Journal of Marriage and the Family* 54 (1992): 259–68.

Chapter 4: In Sickness and in Health

1. Glenn Stanton, *Why Marriage Matters: Reasons to Believe in Marriage in a Post-modern Society* (Colorado Springs, Colo.: Pinon Press, 1997), 81. Stanton cites Harold J. Morowitz, "Hiding in the Hammond Report," *Hospital Practice* 10 (1975): 35, 39; the 70 percent

figure is calculated from the table on age-standardized death rates for men age forty to sixty-nine, broken down by marital categories and smoking status.

2. Catherine E. Ross, John Mirowsky, and Karen Goldsteen, "The Impact of the Family on Health: Decade in Review," *Journal of Marriage and the Family* 52 (1990): 1061.

3. Ibid.

4. See Bernard L. Cohen and I-Sing Lee, "A Catalog of Risks," *Health Physics* 36 (1979): 707–22. Keep in mind that some of the lower death rates of the married may result from the selection of healthy people into marriage.

5. Michael F. Roizen, *RealAge: Are You as Young as You Can Be?* (New York: Cliff Street Books, 1999).

6. James S. Goodwin, William C. Hunt, Charles R. Key, and Jonathan M. Samet, "The Effect of Marital Status on Stage, Treatment, and Survival of Cancer Patients," *Journal of the American Medical Association* 258 (1987): 3125–30. (Marriage did not seem to affect the in-hospital death rates for patients seeking nonsurgical treatment.)

7. Howard S. Gordon and Gary E. Rosenthal, "Impact of Marital Status on Hospital Outcomes: Evidence from an Academic Medical Center," *Archives of Internal Medicine* 155(Dec. 11/25): 2465–71.

8. Yuanreng Hu and Noreen Goldman, "Mortality Differentials by Marital Status: An International Comparison," *Demography* 27(2): 233–50 (1990).

9. J. M. Mossey and E. Shapiro, "Self-Rated Health: A Predictor of Mortality among the Elderly," *American Journal of Public Health* 72 (1982): 800–808.

10. Walter R. Gove, "Sex, Marital Status, and Mortality," *American Journal of Sociology* 79 (1973): 45–67. See also Beth A. Hahn, "Marital Status and Women's Health: The Effect of Economic Marital Acquisitions," *Journal of Marriage and the Family* 55 (1993):495–504.

11. Specifically, 49 percent of married women versus 38 percent of unmarried women rated their health as excellent or very good; meanwhile, 17 percent of married women, compared to 28 percent of unmarried women, rated their health as fair or poor. The comparable figures for men were 53 percent versus 42 percent (for excellent or very good health) and 14 percent versus 27 percent (for fair or poor health). Linda J. Waite's tabulations from the Health and Retirement Survey, wave 1. See Thomas F. Juster and Richard Suzman, "An Overview of the Health and Retirement Survey," *Journal of Human Resources* 30 (1995): S7–S56.

12. Mike Murphy, Karen Glaser, and Emily Grundy, "Marital Status and Long-term Illness in Great Britain," *Journal of Marriage and the Family* 59 (1997): 156–64. The authors point out that figures from the population of those in private households show better health for single adults beyond age seventy-five, but this is due entirely to the higher probability that ill single adults will enter institutions. When institutionalized adults are included, the health advantage of the married reappears.

13. These findings come from simulations done using the results in Lillard and Waite, " 'Til Death Do Us Part," 1131–56.

14. The percentages living to age sixty-five are 88 percent of married men versus 69 percent of widowed men, 65 percent of divorced men, and 63 percent of never-married men. For women, 92 percent of forty-eight-year-old married women lived to age sixty-five, compared to 81 percent of never-married women, 82 percent of divorced women, and 90 percent of widows.

15. Lee A. Lillard and Constantijn Panis, "Marital Status and Mortality: The Role of Health," *Demography* 33 (1996): 313–27. The authors found evidence of both

adverse selection into marriage on health *and* positive selection on unmeasured characteristics.

16. Ibid.

17. Debra Umberson, "Family Status and Health Behaviors: Social Control as a Dimension of Social Integration," *Journal of Health and Social Behavior* 28 (1987): 306–19.

18. Jack C. Smith, James A. Mercy, and Judith M. Conn, "Marital Status and the Risk of Suicide," *American Journal of Public Health* 78 (1988): 78–80.

19. Lillard and Waite, " 'Til Death Do Us Part," 1147. Frances E. Kobrin and Gerry L. Hendershot, "Do Families Ties Reduce Mortality? Evidence from the United States: 1966–1968," *Journal of Marriage and the Family* 39 (1977): 737–45. Kobrin and Hendershot show that single adults who are living in someone else's home do particularly poorly.

20. Blumstein and Schwartz, *American Couples,* 334–42.

21. Carol Miller-Tutzauer, Kenneth E. Leonard, and Michael Windle, "Marriage and Alcohol Use: A Longitudinal Study of 'Maturing Out,'" *Journal of Studies on Alcohol* 52 (1991): 434–40.

22. Umberson, "Family Status and Health Behaviors," 316.

23. Ross et al., "The Impact of the Family," 1061. See also Umberson, "Family Status and Health Behaviors," 316.

24. Oakley Stern Ray, *Drugs, Society and Human Behavior* (St. Louis: C.V. Mosby, 1978), referenced in Umberson, "Family Status and Health Behaviors," 319.

25. Miller-Tutzauer et al., "Marriage and Alcohol Use," 437–38. See Jerald G. Bachman, Katherine N. Wadsworth, Patrick M. O'Malley, Lloyd D. Johnson, and John E. Schulenberg, *Smoking, Drinking, and Drug Use in Young Adulthood* (Mahwah, N.J.: Lawrence Erlbaum Associates, 1997).

26. Bachman et al., *Smoking, Drinking, Drug Use,* 3–9.

27. Debra Umberson, "Gender, Marital Status and the Social Control of Health Behavior," *Social Science and Medicine* 34 (1992): 907–17.

28. Lillard and Waite, " 'Til Death Do Us Part," 1149.

29. In Lillard and Panis, "Marital Status and Mortality," the authors find that the health benefit of marriage for men depends on the circumstances. They find that the net health benefit for men of entering a first marriage is zero but that divorced men who remarry get a significant health gain. Compare these results to Lillard and Waite's findings on mortality in " 'Til Death Do Us Part," 1131–56.

30. Blumstein and Schwartz, *American Couples,* 336.

31. Eugene Litwak and Peter Messeri, in collaboration with Samuel Wolfe, Sheila Gorman, Merril Silverstein, and Miguelo Guilarte, "Organizational Theory, Social Supports, and Mortality Rates: A Theoretical Convergence," *American Sociological Review* 54(1): 49–66 (1989).

32. Umberson, "Gender, Marital Status," 907–17.

33. Ross et al., "The Impact of the Family," 1064. Umberson, "Gender, Marital Status," 907–17.

34. See, for example, Sheldon Cohen, William J. Doyle, David P. Skoner, Bruce S. Rabin, Jack M. Gwaltney Jr., "Social Ties and Susceptibility to the Common Cold," *Journal of the American Medical Association* 277 (1997): 1940–44.; Tracy Bennett Herbert and Sheldon Cohen, "Depression and Immunity: A Meta-analytic Review," *Psychological Bulletin* 113 (1993): 472–86.

35. Martha Livingston Bruce and Philip J. Leaf, "Psychiatric Disorders and 15-Month Mor-

tality in a Community Sample of Older Adults," *American Journal of Public Health* 79:727–30; Ross et al., "The Impact of the Family," 1063.

36. Debra Umberson, Meichu D. Chen, James S. House, Kristine Hopkins; and Ellen Slaten, "The Effect of Social Relationships on Psychological Well-being: Are Men and Women Really So Different?" *American Sociological Review* 61 (1996): 837–57.

37. K.A.S. Wickrama, Frederck O. Lorenz, Rand D. Conger, and Glen H. Elder Jr., "Marital Quality and Physical Illness: A Latent Growth Curve Analysis," *Journal of Marriage and the Family* 59 (1997): 143–55.

38. Janice K. Kiecolt-Glaser, Ronald Glaser, John T. Cacioppo, Robert C. MacCallum, Mary Syndersmith, Cheongtag Kim, and William B. Malarkey, "Marital Conflict in Older Adults: Endocrinological and Immunological Correlates," *Psychosomatic Medicine* 59 (1997): 339–49.

39. Janice K. Kiecolt-Glaser, William B. Malarkey, MaryAnn Chee, Tamara Newton, John T. Cacioppo, Hsiao-Yin Mao, and Ronald Glaser, "Negative Behavior During Marital Conflict Is Associated with Immunological Down-Regulation," *Psychosomatic Medicine* 55 (1993): 395–409.

40. Janice K. Kiecolt-Glaser, Laura D. Fisher, Paula Ogrocki, Julie C. Stout, Carl E. Speicher, and Ronald Glaser, "Marital Quality, Marital Disruption, and Immune Function," *Psychosomatic Medicine* 49 (1987): 13–34.

41. James W. Pennebaker, "Writing about Emotional Experiences as a Therapeutic Process," *Psychological Science* 8 (1997): 162–66.

42. David M. Schnarch, *Constructing the Sexual Crucible: An Integration of Sexual and Marital Therapy* (New York: W. W. Norton & Co., 1991), chap. 12.

43. Umberson, "Family Status and Health Behaviors," 314.

44. Bachman et al., "Smoking, Drinking, and Drug Use," 172–73.

45. Umberson, "Family Status and Health Behaviors," 315.

46. Lillard and Waite, " 'Til Death Do Us Part," 1149.

47. Ross et al., "The Impact of the Family," 1064–65.

48. Hahn, "Marital Status and Women's Health," 500–502.

49. Ibid.

50. See, for example, Ross et al., "The Impact of the Family" 1065.

51. Having a wife offers slightly more protection than having a husband, however. See Kenneth G. Manton, E. Stallard, and Max A. Woodbury, "Longitudinal Models of Disability Changes and Active Life Expectancy in Elderly Populations: The Interaction of Sex, Age and Marital Status," *Modeling Noncommunicable Diseases,* eds. W. Morgenstern et. al., (Berlin: Springer-Verlag, 1995) 113–30. See also Vicki A. Freedman, "Family Structure and the Risk of Nursing Home Admission," *Journal of Gerontology: Social Sciences* 51B(2): S61–S69 (1996).

52. Litwak et al., "Organizational Theory, Social Supports," 61.

53. Umberson, "Gender, Marital Status," 907–17.

54. Lisa F. Berkman and Lester Breslow, "Social Networks and Mortality Risk," chap. 4 in *Health and Ways of Living: The Alameda County Study* (New York: Oxford University Press, 1983).

55. Clarkberg, Stolzenberg, and Waite, "Attitudes, Values and Entrance," 609–34.

56. Bachman et al., "Smoking, Drinking, and Drug Use," 173–74.

1. Robert S. Weiss, *Staying the Course: The Emotional and Social Lives of Men Who Do Well at Work* (New York: Fawcett Columbine, 1990), 113.

2. Christopher Hayes, Deborah Anderson, and Melina Blau, *Our Turn: Women Who Triumph in the Face of Divorce* (New York: Pocket Books, 1993), 70, quoted in Barbara Dafoe Whitehead, *The Divorce Culture: How Divorce Became an Entitlement and How It Is Blighting the Lives of Our Children* (New York: Alfred A. Knopf, 1997), 60.

3. John Mirowsky and Catherine E. Ross, *Social Causes of Psychological Distress* (New York: Aldine De Gruyter, 1989).

4. Ibid., 90–92.

5. Arne Mastekaasa, "The Subjective Well-being of the Previously Married: The Importance of Unmarried Cohabitation and Time Since Widowhood or Divorce," *Social Forces* 73 (1994): 665.

6. Jack C. Smith, Mercy, and Conn, "Marital Status and the Risk," 78–80.

7. Ibid.

8. James A. Davis, "New Money, an Old Man/Lady, and 'Two's Company': Subjective Welfare in the NORC General Social Surveys, 1972–1982," *Social Indicators Research* 15 (1984): 319–50. Davis also found that race and recent financial change predicted happiness.

9. Seven percent of spouses versus 13 percent of singles said they were "not too happy." Twenty percent of the widowed were "not too happy," as were 18 percent of the divorced and 27 percent of the separated. Tabulations by Linda J. Waite from the General Social Survey, 1990–1996 waves.

10. Tabulations by Linda J. Waite from the General Social Survey, 1990–1996 waves.

11. Judith S. Wallerstein and Sandra Blakeslee, *The Good Marriage: How and Why Love Lasts* (Boston: Houghton Mifflin, 1995), 85.

12. Ibid., 45.

13. Ibid., 115.

14. Ibid., 139.

15. Ibid., 219.

16. For a detailed discussion of these measures, see Carol D. Ryff and Corey Lee M. Keyes, "The Structure of Psychological Well-being Revisited," *Journal of Personality and Social Psychology* 69 (1995): 719–27.

17. Nadine F. Marks and James D. Lambert, "Marital Status Continuity and Change among Young and Midlife Adults: Longitudinal Effects on Psychological Well-being." *Journal of Family Issues* 19 (1998): 652–86.

18. Allan V. Horwitz, Helene Raskin White, and Sandra Howell-White, "Becoming Married and Mental Health: A Longitudinal Study of a Cohort of Young Adults," *Journal of Marriage and the Family* 58 (1996): 895–907. Once the authors take into account age, income, and social support, the impact of marriage on problem drinking becomes statistically insignificant for men but remains significant for women.

19. For women, Horwitz et al. ("Becoming Married and Mental Health," 895–907) find that depression in the later year depends *only* on depression at the beginning of the study.

20. Horwitz et al., "Becoming Married and Mental Health," 904.

21. Ibid., 901. See also Marks and Lambert, "Marital Status Continuity," 652–86.

22. Walter R. Gove and Michael Hughes, "Possible Causes of the Apparent Sex Differences in Physical Health: An Empirical Investigation," *American Sociological Review* 44 (1979): 126–46.

23. Tabulations done for this book by Linda J. Waite from the Health and Retirement Survey. See Juster, Thomas F., and Richard Suzman, "An Overview of the Health and Retirement Survey," *Journal of Human Resources* 30 (1995): S7–S56. See also Linda J. Waite and Mary Elizabeth Hughes, "At Risk on the Cusp of Old Age: Living Arrangements and Functional Status among Black, White, and Hispanic Adults in the Health and Retirement Survey," *Journal of Gerontology: Social Sciences* 54B (1998): S136–S144.

24. Blumstein and Schwartz, *American Couples,* 186–87; Clarkberg, Stolzenberg, and Waite, "Attitudes, Values and Entrance," 609–34.

25. Mastekaasa, "Subjective Well-being," 682.

26. Bumpass and Sweet, "National Estimates of Cohabitation," 615–25.

27. Horwitz et al., "Becoming Married and Mental Health," 903.

28. Ross, "Reconceptualizing Marital Status," 129–40.

29. Horwitz et al., "Becoming Married and Mental Health," 903.

30. Ross, "Reconceptualizing Marital Status," 137.

31. Linda J. Waite's tabulations from the 1972–1994 General Social Survey. Although we might suspect that many more people are unhappy in their marriage than will admit this to a survey interviewer, responses on marital happiness are closely related to reports of overall happiness. We might also suspect that in an era of easy divorce, unhappily married people divorce, leaving only the happily married. In fact, we see no evidence that this has occurred. See Norval D. Glenn, "Values, Attitudes," 15–33.

32. Linda J. Waite's tabulations from the National Survey of Families and Households, 1987/88 and 1992/94.

33. Peter Berger and Hansfried Kellner, "Marriage and the Construction of Reality: An Exercise in the Microsociology of Knowledge," *Diogenes* 46 (1964): 1–25.

34. Émile Durkheim, *Suicide* (1897; reprint, New York: Free Press, 1951).

35. Russell P. D. Burton, "Global Integrative Meaning as a Mediating Factor in the Relationship between Social Roles and Psychological Distress," *Journal of Health and Social Behavior* 39 (1998): 201–15. See also Mirowsky and Ross, *Social Causes,* 25.

36. Ibid., 209. Burton also found that men who were employed but neither married nor parents were less distressed than the comparison group—men who were unemployed, single, and not parents.

37. Ibid, 210–13.

38. J. Kenneth Davidson Sr., and Nelwyn B. Moore, *Marriage and Family: Change and Continuity* (Boston: Allyn and Bacon, 1996) 322.

39. Norval Glenn, *Closed Hearts, Closed Minds: The Textbook Story of Marriage* (New York: Institute for American Values 1997), 11.

Chapter 6: With My Body I Thee Worship

1. Dalma Heyn, *Marriage Shock: The Transformation of Women into Wives* (New York: Villard, 1997), 163.

2. Ashton Applewhite, *Cutting Loose: Why Women Who Leave Their Marriages Do So Well* (New York: HarperCollins, 1997), 216.

3. The data that follows is (unless otherwise noted) based on one of these surveys: The National Health and Social Life Survey, designed and carried out at the University of Chicago by Edward Laumann, John Gagnon, Robert Michael, and Stuart Michaels, referred to here as "The National Sex Study." The study was based on interviews in 1992 with 3,500 men

and women between the ages of eighteen and fifty-nine. We use the information directly in statistical analyses and we also make use of findings reported by Laumann et al. in their book *The Social Organization of Sexuality* (Edward O. Laumann, John H. Gagnon, Robert T. Michael, and Stuart Michaels, *The Social Organization of Sexuality: Sexual Practices in the United States* [Chicago: University of Chicago Press, 1994.]

4. Scott Stanley and Howard Markman, *Marriage in the '90s: A Nationwide Random Phone Survey* (Denver, Colo.: PREP Inc., 1997).

5. The National Sex Survey identified those unmarried men and women who were living with someone in a sexual relationship. We refer to these people as cohabiting, and to un-married people who are not living with someone in a sexual relationship as single. Single people could be never-married, or they could be separated, divorced or widowed. The National Sex Survey does not differentiate between those cohabitors who are en-gaged from those who are not. Stanley and Markman distinguish people who are mar-ried, those who are engaged and not living together, those who are engaged and living together, and those who are cohabiting but not engaged.

6. Laumann et al., *Social Organization of Sexuality*, Table 3.4. "Previously married" men and women include those who are divorced, separated, or widowed. Steven Stack and James Gundlach also find high levels of sexual inactivity among divorced adults in a national survey; 16 percent of divorced men and 34 percent of divorced women in their study had no sex partners in the past year. Steven Stack and James H. Gundlach, "Divorce and Sex," *Archives of Sexual Behavior* 21(4): 359–67 (1992).

7. Laumann et al., *Social Organization of Sexuality*, Table 3.4, 88–89.

8. If they were married, the "primary partner" was always the spouse. If they were living with someone, their "primary partner" was always the live-in lover.

9. Linda J. Waite and Kara Joyner, "Emotional and Physical Satisfaction in Married, Cohab-iting and Dating Sexual Unions: Do Men and Women Differ?" in *Studies on Sex*, eds. Ed-ward O. Laumann and Robert Michael (Chicago: University of Chicago Press, forthcoming).

10. For evidence supporting the sociobiological perspective, see, for example: David Buss, *The Evolution of Desire: Strategies of Human Mating* (New York: Basic Books, 1994); John Marshall Townsend, "Sex without Emotional Involvement: An Evolutionary Interpre-tation of Sex Differences," *Archives of Sexual Behavior* 24 (1995): 173–206; John De-Lamater, "Gender Differences in Sexual Scenarios," in *Females, Males and Sexuality*, ed. Kathryn Kelley (Albany: SUNY Press, 1987), 127–40.

11. Waite and Joyner, "Emotional and Physical Satisfaction," Appendix Table A.

12. Scott M. Stanley and Howard J. Markman, "Assessing Commitment in Personal Rela-tionships," *Journal of Marriage and the Family* 54 (1992): 595–608.

13. Waite and Joyner, "Emotional and Physical Satisfaction," Table 1.

14. Wallerstein and Blakeslee, *The Good Marriage*, 173.

15. Blumstein and Schwartz, *American Couples*, 383–84.

16. Wallerstein and Blakeslee, *The Good Marriage*, 33.

17. Ibid., 50.

18. Buss, *Evolution of Desire*, 173–75.

19. Wallerstein and Blakeslee, *The Good Marriage*, 183.

20 Laumann et al., *Social Organization of Sexuality*, Table 11.12.

21. Tabulations by Linda J. Waite and Kara Joyner, from the National Health and Social Life Survey.

22. Ibid.

23. Robert G. Bringle and Bram P. Buunk, "Extradyadic Relationships and Sexual Jealousy," in *Sexuality in Close Relationships*, eds. K. McKinney and S. Sprecher (Hillsdale, N.J.: Lawrence Erlbaum Associates, 1991), 135–53.

24. Blumstein and Schwartz, *American Couples*, 424–25.

25. Renata Forste and Koray Tanfer, "Sexual Exclusivity among Dating, Cohabiting, and Married Women," *Journal of Marriage and the Family* 58 (1996): 33–47.

26. Tabulations by Linda J. Waite and Kara Joyner, from the National Health and Social Life Survey.

27. William R. Mattox Jr, "What's Marriage Got to Do with It: Good Sex Comes to Those Who Wait," *Family Policy* (February, 1994), 1–7. The Family Research Council, which sponsored this research, is an activist not a scholarly organization. It would be useful if the academic community would investigate and confirm (or disprove) this tantalizing but tentative research.

Chapter 7: The Wages of Wedlock

1. U.S. Bureau of the Census, *Statistical Abstract of the United States: 1997*, 117th edition (Washington, D.C., 1997), Table 719, p. 466.

2. These are sample means for white men age twenty-four to thirty-one, in 1989 dollars. See Jeffrey S. Gray, "The Fall in Men's Return to Marriage." *Journal of Human Resources* 32 (1997): 481–503.

3. Robin L. Bartlett and Charles Callahan III, "Wage Determination and Marital Status: Another Look," *Industrial Relations* 23 (1984): 90–96. These findings refer to the decade from 1966 to 1976. See also Shoshana A. Grossbard-Shechtman and Shoshana Neuman, "Cross-productivity Effects of Education and Origin on Earnings: Are They Really Reflecting Productivity?" in *Handbook of Behavioral Economics*, vol. 2A, *Behavioral Environments*, Stanley Kaish, Benjamin Gilad, Roger Frantz, Harinder Singh, and James Gerber (Greenwich, Conn.: JAI Press, 1991), 125–45.

4. Robert F. Schoeni, "Marital Status and Earnings in Developed Countries," *Journal of Population Economics* 8 (1995): 351–59.

5. Bartlett and Callahan, "Wage Determination," 94–96. See also Sanders Korenman and David Neumark, "Does Marriage Really Make Men More Productive?" *Journal of Human Resources* 26 (1991): 282–307. We are not arguing that *no* selection of high-earning men or men with steep earnings trajectories into marriages occurs. We argue that selection does not account for *all* the higher earnings of married men; marriage itself leads to about half.

6. Kermit Daniel, "The Marriage Premium," in *The New Economics of Human Behavior*, eds. Mariano Tommasi and Kathryn Ierulli (Cambridge, England: Cambridge University Press, 1995), 113–25.

7. Ibid. Some occupations presume that the person officially holding the job has the unpaid assistance of his wife in carrying out job tasks. Ministers whose wives run the Sunday school, executives in large corporations whose wives organize social events, doctors or plumbers whose wives keep the books and schedule the work are all participating in two-person careers. See Hannah Papanek, "Men, Women, and Work: Reflections on the Two-Person Career," *American Journal of Sociology* 78 (1973): 852–72. See also Amyra Grossbard-Shechtman, "Marriage and Productivity: An In-

terdisciplinary Analysis" in *Handbook of Behavioral Economics,* vol. A, *Behavioral Micro-economics,* eds. Benjamin Gilad and Stanley Kaish (Greenwich, Conn.: JAI Press, 1986), 289–302.

8. Korenman and Neumark, "Does Marriage Really Make," 296.

9. Daniel estimates that men in their twenties and early thirties make between 4.5 percent to 6.3 percent more than those same men would make if they hadn't married. Daniel, "The Marriage Premium," 121. See also simulations by Daniel presented in Linda J. Waite, "Does Marriage Matter?" *Demography* 32 (1995): 483–507, 495–96.

10. Bartlett and Callahan, "Wage Determination," 94–96. See also Korenman and Neumark, "Does Marriage Really Make," 293–94.

11. Greg J. Duncan and Bertil Holmlund, "Was Adam Smith Right After All?: Another Test of the Theory of Compensating Differentials," *Journal of Labor Economics* 1 (1983): 366–79.

12. Jeffrey S. Gray and Michael J. Vanderhart, "The Determinants of Wages: Does Marriage Matter?" in *Ties that Bind: Perspectives on Marriage and Cohabitation,* eds. Linda Waite, Christine Bachrach, Michelle Hindin, Elizabeth Thomson, and Arland Thornton (Aldine de Gruyter, forthcoming).

13. Joni Hersch, "Male-Female Differences in Hourly Wages: The Role of Human Capital, Working Conditions, and Housework," *Industrial Labor Relations Review* 44 (1991): 746–59.

14. Frances K. Goldscheider and Linda J. Waite, *New Families, No Families?: The Transformation of the American Home* (Berkeley, Calif.: University of California Press, 1991). See also Micaela DiLeonardo, "The Female World of Cards," 440–53.

15. Gary S. Becker, "Human Capital, Effort, and the Sexual Division of Labor," *Journal of Labor Economics* 3(1), part 2:S33–S58 (1985).

16. Shoshana Grossbard-Shechtman, *On the Economics of Marriage: A Theory of Marriage, Labor, and Divorce* (Boulder, Colo.: Westview Press, 1993).

17. Joni Hersch, "Effects of Housework on Earnings of Husbands and Wives: Evidence from Full-Time Piece Rate Workers," *Social Science Quarterly* 66 (1985): 210–17; Hersch, "Male-Female Differences," 752. Waite's own research, with Gus Haggstrom and David Kanouse, found that married men who become parents for the first time work more hours than married men who do not, but earnings for husbands are about the same, whether or not they have children. See Linda J. Waite, Gus W. Haggstrom, and David E. Kanouse, "Changes in the Employment Activities of New Parents," *American Sociological Review* 50 (1985): 263–72; and Linda J. Waite, Gus W. Haggstrom, and David E. Kanouse, "The Effects of Parenthood on the Career Orientation and Job Characteristics of Young Adults," *Social Forces* 65 (1986): 43–73. But see Daniel, "The Marriage Premium," 121, who reports a negative effect of children on white men's marriage premium.

18. South and Spitze, "Housework," 327–47.

19. See Peter Kostiuk and Dean Follmann, "Learning Curves, Personal Characteristics, and Job Performance," *Journal of Labor Economics* 7 (1989): 126–49; Kathryn Shaw, "The Quit Propensity of Married Men," *Journal of Labor Economics* 5 (1987): 533–60.

20. Eng Seng Loh, "Productivity Differences and the Marriage Wage Premium for White Males," *Journal of Human Resources* 31 (1996): 566–89.

21. Grossbard-Shechtman, *Economics of Marriage,* 243–56. See also Grossbard-Shechtman and Neuman, "Cross-Productivity Effects," 136.

22. Philip Blumstein and Pepper Schwartz. Personal communication with Maggie Gallagher July 1998.

23. See estimates by Daniel, presented in Waite, "Does Marriage Matter?" 495–96.

24. Andrea H. Beller and John W. Graham, *Small Change: The Economics of Child Support* (New Haven: Yale University Press, 1993).

25. South and Spitze, "Housework," 327–47. These are unadjusted figures but Table 2 (p. 338) shows similar gaps after adjusting for presence, gender, and ages of children and other factors. See also Goldscheider and Waite, *New Families, No Families?* 142–71.

26. Grossbard-Shechtman, *Economics of Marriage*, chapter 14.

27. Ibid.

28. Jane Waldfogel, "The Effect of Children on Women's Wages," *American Sociological Review* 62 (1997): 209–17.

29. Ibid.

30. Waite, Haggstrom, and Kanouse, "Changes in the Employment," 263–72. See also Sonalde Desai and Linda J. Waite, "Women's Employment During Pregnancy and after the First Birth: Occupational Characteristics and Work Commitment," *American Sociological Review* 56 (1991): 551–66.

31. Hersch, "Effects of Housework on Earnings", 210–17.

32. Shelley Coverman, "Gender, Domestic Labor Time, and Wage Inequality," *American Sociological Review* 48 (1983): 623–37. Note that Coverman and Hersch ("Male-Female Differences," 746–59) use the same measures of housework with different data and reach different conclusions about effects on wages. Coverman examines weekly earnings for currently married, currently employed men and women. Hersch looks at hourly earnings for employees at eighteen Oregon firms.

33. Saul D. Hoffman and Greg J. Duncan, "What Are the Economic Consequences of Divorce?," *Demography* 25 (1988): 641–45. See also Karen C. Holden and Pamela J. Smock, "The Economic Consequences of Marital Dissolution: Why Do Women Bear a Disproportionate Cost?," *Annual Review of Sociology* 17 (1991): 51–78; and Richard R. Peterson, "A Re-evaluation of the Economics Consequences of Divorce," *American Sociological Review* 61 (1996): 528–36.

34. Suzanne M. Bianchi, "The Changing Economic Roles of Women and Men," in *State of the Union: America in the 1990s, Vol. One: Economic Trends,* ed. Reynolds Farley (New York: Russell Sage Foundation, 1995), 107–54.

35. Grossbard-Shechtman, *Economics of Marriage,* 254.

36. Hernandez with Myers, *America's Children,* 417–47. See Lee A. Lillard, Michael J. Brien, and Linda J. Waite, "A Joint Model of Marital Childbearing and Marital Disruption," *Demography* 30 (1993): 653–82. This article shows that women who face higher chances of divorce are less likely to have a child or an additional child than are women who face lower chances of divorce.

Chapter 8: For Richer or for Poorer

1. Dirk Johnson, "Uncertain Future, on Their Own, Awaits," *New York Times,* 16 March 1997, 1.

2. Blumstein and Schwartz, *American Couples,* 341.

3. Stephanie Coontz and Donna Franklin, "When the Marriage Penalty is Marriage," *New York Times,* 28 October 1997, A23.

4. Lingxin Hao, "Family Structure," 269–92.

5. Joseph Lupton and James P. Smith, "Marriage, Assets, and Savings." In Shoshana Gross-

bard-Schechtman (ed.), *Marriage and the Economy*. Cambridge, England: Cambridge University Press.

6. Ibid., Table 5.

7. Ibid., conclusions.

8. Ibid., Table 3, p. 11.

9. Hao, "Family Structure," 269–92.

10. Blumstein and Schwartz, *American Couples,* 341.

11. Ibid., 70.

12. Ibid., 81.

13. Laurence J. Kotlikoff and Avia Spivak, "The Family as an Incomplete Annuities Market," *Journal of Political Economy* 89 (1981): 372–91.

14. Hao, "Family Structure," (269–92); Ronald R. Rindfuss and Audrey VandenHeuvel, "Cohabitation: Precursor to Marriage or Alternative to Being Single?" *Population and Development Review* 16 (1990): 703–26.

15. Blumstein and Schwartz, *American Couples,* 62.

16. Ibid., 102.

17. Hao, "Family Structure," 283.

18. Blumstein and Schwartz, *American Couples,* 103–105. Quote is on p. 105.

19. Hao, "Family Structure," Table 2, p. 282.

20. Lynn. A. Karoly, "Anatomy of the U.S. Income Distribution: Two Decades of Change," *Oxford Review of Economic Policy* 12 (1): 76–95 (1996).

21. Annemette Sørensen, "Women's Economic Risk and the Economic Position of Single Mothers," *European Sociological Review* 10 (1994): 173–88.

22. Daniel, "The Marriage Premium," 113–25.

23. Blumstein and Schwartz, *American Couples,* 87.

24. Andrea H. Beller and John W. Graham, *Small Change: The Economics of Child Support* (New Haven: Yale University Press, 1993), 82. Figures for child support due are from 1985.

25. Ibid.

26. Richard R. Peterson, "Re-evaluation," 528–36.

27. Sara McLanahan and Gary Sandefur, *Growing Up with a Single Parent: What Hurts, What Helps* (Cambridge, Mass: Harvard University Press, 1994), 24.

28. Ibid., Table 5, p. 87

29. Janet Wilmoth, "The Timing of Marital Events over the Life Course and Pre-Retirement Wealth Outcomes" (paper presented at meetings of the Population Association of America, Chicago, April 1998).

30. Karen C. Holden, "The Transition from Wife to Widow: Data Issues in Measuring First-Period Income Effects in SIPP and the RHS," in Bureau of the Census, *Individuals and Families in Transition Understanding Change through Longitudinal Data,* comps. Hazel V. Benton, Debra A. Ganni, and Delma T. Frankel (Washington, D.C., 1989) 23–32. See also Holden and Smock, "The Economic Costs," 51–78.

31. Cathleen D. Zick and Ken R. Smith, "Immediate and Delayed Effects of Widowhood on Poverty: Patterns from the 1970s," *The Gerontologist* 26 (1986): 669–75.

32. Richard V. Burkhauser, J. S. Butler, and Karen C. Holden, "How the Death of a Spouse Affects Economic Well-being after Retirement: A Hazard Model Approach, *Social Science Quarterly* 72 (1991): 504–19.

33. Holden and Smock, "The Economic Costs," 51–78.

34. Richard V. Burkhauser, "Protecting the Most Vulnerable: A Proposal to Improve Social Security Insurance for Older Women," *The Gerontologist* 34, (1994): 148–49.

35. Leatha Lamison-White, "Poverty in the United States: 1996" in Bureau of the Census, Current Population Reports, Series P60-198 (Washington, D. C., September 1997), 60–198.

36. Ibid. See Table D.

37. Christopher Jencks, *The Homeless* (Cambridge, Mass.: Harvard University Press, 1994), 58.

38. McLanahan and Sandefur, *Growing Up with a Single Parent*, 83.

39. Ibid., 84.

40. National Research Council, *Measuring Poverty: A New Approach,* eds. Constance F. Citro and Robert T. Michael (Washington, D.C.: National Academy Press). See also Bureau of the Census, *Measuring the Effect of Benefits and Taxes on Income and Poverty: 1992,* Current Population Reports, Series P-60, Consumer Income; no. 186-RD (Washington, D.C., 1993).

41. Kathleen Mullan Harris, *Teen Mothers and the Revolving Welfare Door* (Philadelphia: Temple University Press, 1997), 80–94.

42. Mary Jo Bane and David T. Ellwood, "Slipping into and out of Poverty: The Dynamics of Spells," *Journal of Human Resources* 21(1): 1–23.

Chapter 9: Being Fruitful

1. Judith S. Wallerstein (speech before the Second Annual Congress of American Family and Conciliation Courts, June 6, 1997). Text supplied by the author.

2. See, for example, McLanahan and Sandefur *Growing Up with a Single Parent*, 39–63. See also Paul R. Amato and Alan Booth, *A Generation at Risk: Growing Up in an Era of Family Upheaval* (Cambridge, Mass.: Harvard University Press, 1997).

3. Andrew J. Cherlin, P. Lindsay Chase-Lansdale, and Christine McRae, "Effects of Parental Divorce on Mental Health throughout the Life Course," *American Sociological Review* 63 (1998): 239.

4. McLanahan and Sandefur, *Growing up with a Single Parent,* 167–68.

5. Ibid., 24.

6. Beller and Graham, *Small Change,* 16–54.

7. Bureau of the Census, *Statistical Abstract of the United States: 1996,* 116th ed. (Washington, D.C., 1996), Table 720, p. 467.

8. McLanahan and Sandefur, *Growing Up with a Single Parent,* 82. See also Hernandez with Myers, *America's Children,* chap. 10, 385–416.

9. Jane D. McLeod and Michael J. Shanahan, "Poverty, Parenting, and Children's Mental Health," *American Sociological Review* 58 (1993): 351–66. See also Susan E. Mayer, *What Money Can't Buy: Family Income and Children's Life Chances,* Cambridge, Mass.: Harvard University Press).

10. Mayer, *What Money Can't Buy,* 113.

11. Harriet B. Presser, "Shift Work and Child Care among Young Dual-Earner American Parents," *Journal of Marriage and the Family* 50 (1998): 133–48.

12. McLanahan and Sandefur, *Growing Up with a Single Parent,* 95–115.

13. Ibid., 105.

14. P. Lindsay Chase-Lansdale, Lauren S. Wakschlag, and Jeanne Brooks-Gunn, "A Psychological Perspective on the Development of Caring in Children and Youth: The Role of the Family," *Journal of Adolescence* 18 (1995): 515–56.

15. Diane N. Lye, Daniel H. Klepinger, Patricia Davis Hyle, and Anjanette Nelson, "Childhood Living Arrangements and Adult Children's Relations with their Parents," *Demography* 32 (1995): 261–80.

16. James S. Coleman, "Social Capital in the Creation of Human Capital," *American Journal of Sociology* 94 (Supplement): S95–S120 (1988).

17. Robert J. Sampson, "Urban Black Violence: The Effect of Male Joblessness and Family Disruption," *American Journal of Sociology* 93 (1987): 348–82. See also Bernard L. Bloom, "A Census Tract Analysis of Socially Deviant Behaviors," *Multivariate Behavioral Research* 1 (1966): 307–20; and Shepard G. Kellam, Rebecca G. Adams, C. Hendricks Brown, and Margaret E. Ensminger, "The Long-term Evolution of the Family Structure of Teens and Older Mothers," *Journal of Marriage and the Family* 44 (1982): 539–54.

18. Nan Marie Astone and Sara S. McLanahan, "Family Structure, Residential Mobility, and School Dropout: A Research Note," *Demography* 31 (1994): 575–84.

19. Carol S. Aneshensel and Clea A. Sucoff, "The Neighborhood Context of Adolescent Mental Health," *Journal of Health and Social Behavior* 37 (1996): 293–310.

20. Jane Mauldon, "The Effects of Marital Disruption on Children's Health, *Demography* 27 (1990): 431–46.

21. Ronald Angel and Jacqueline Lowe Worobey, "Single Motherhood and Children's Health," *Journal of Health and Social Behavior* 29 (1988): 38–52. Note that the group of married mothers includes stepfamilies.

22. Trude Bennett, Paula Braveman, Susan Egerter, and John L. Kiely, "Maternal Marital Status as a Risk Factor for Infant Mortality," *Family Planning Perspectives* 26 (1994): 252–56.

23. Nina Oyen, Trond Markestad, Rolv Skjaerven, Lorentz M. Irgens, Karin Helweg-Larsen, Bernt Alm, Gunnar Norvenius, and Goran Wennergren, "Combined Effects of Sleeping Position and Prenatal Risk Factors in Sudden Infant Death Syndrome: The Nordic Epidemiological SIDS Study," *Pediatrics* 100 (1997): 613–20.

24. Jerald G. Bachman et al., *Smoking, Drinking, and Drug Use,* 172–73.

25. Ian Roberts, "Sole Parenthood and the Risk of Child Pedestrian Injury," *Journal of Pediatric Health* 30 (1994): 530–32.

26. Angel and Worobey, "Single Motherhood," 38–52.

27. Joan S. Tucker, Howard S. Friedman, Joseph E. Schwartz, Michael H. Criqui et al., "Parental Divorce: Effects on Individual Behavior and Longevity," *Journal of Personality and Social Psychology* 73 (1997): 381–91.

28. Olle Lundberg, "The Impact of Childhood Living Conditions on Illness and Mortality in Adulthood," *Social Science and Medicine* 36 (1993): 1047–52.

29. P. Lindsay Chase-Lansdale and Mavis Heatherington, "The Impact of Divorce on Lifespan Development: Short and Long-term Effects," eds. Paul B. Baltes, David L. Featherman, and Richard M. Lerner *Life Span Development and Behavior,* vol. 10 (Hillsdale, N.J.: Lawrence Erlbaum Associates, 1990) 105–50.

30. P. Lindsay Chase-Lansdale, Andrew J. Cherlin, and Kathleen E. Kiernan, "The Longterm Effects of Parental Divorce on the Mental Health of Young Adults: A Developmental Perspective," *Child Development* 66 (1995): 1614–34.

31. Hao, "Family Structure, Parental Input" (paper presented at the meetings of the Population Association of America, Washington D.C., March, 1997).

32. Amato and Booth, *A Generation at Risk,* chap. seven, 182–208.

33. Ibid., 204.

34. Nicholas Zill, "Understanding Why Children in Stepfamilies Have More Learning and

Behavior Problems Than Children in Nuclear Families," in *Stepfamilies: Who Benefits, Who Does Not?* eds. Alan Booth and Judy Dunn (Hillsdale, N.J.: Lawrence Erlbaum Associates, 1994), 97–106.

35. McLanahan and Sandefur, *Growing Up with a Single Parent.* See Figure 2.

36. Astone and McLanahan, "Family Structure, Residential Mobility," 575–84.

37. Cynthia Harper and Sara McLanahan, "Father Absence and Youth Incarceration" (paper presented at the annual meetings of the American Sociological Association, San Francisco, August 1998).

38. Ross L. Matsueda and Karen Heimer, "Race, Family Structure, and Delinquency: A Test of Differential Association and Social Control Theories," *American Sociological Review* 52 (1987): 826–40.

39. Robert L. Flewelling and Karl E. Bauman, "Family Structure as a Predictor of Initial Substance Use and Sexual Intercourse in Early Adolescence," *Journal of Marriage and the Family* 52 (1990): 171–81.

40. Martin Daly and Margo Wilson, "Evolutionary Psychology and Marital Conflict: The Relevance of Stepchildren," in *Sex, Power, Conflict: Evolutionary and Feminist Perspectives,* eds. David M. Buss and Neil M. Malamuth (Oxford: Oxford University Press, 1996), 9–28.

41. Amato and Booth, *A Generation at Risk,* 147–81.

42. McLanahan and Sandefur, *Growing Up with a Single Parent,* 39–63.

43. Amato and Booth, *A Generation at Risk,* 84–119, Flewelling and Bauman, "Family Structure as a Predictor," 171–81.

44. Andrew J. Cherlin, Kathleen E. Kiernan, and P. Lindsay Chase-Landsdale, "Parental Divorce in Childhood and Demographic Outcomes in Young Adulthood," *Demography* 32 (1995): 299–318.

45. Ibid.

46. Flewelling and Bauman, "Family Structure as a Predictor," 176.

47. Judith S. Musick, *Young, Poor and Pregnant: The Psychology of Teenage Motherhood* (New Haven: Yale University Press, 1993).

48. See, for example, Judith Rich Harris, *The Nurture Assumption: Why Children Turn Out the Way They Do* (New York: The Free Press, 1998).

49. Arlene S. Skolnick, *The Intimate Environment: Exploring Marriage and the Family* 6th ed. (New York: HarperCollins, 1996), 343–44.

50. Amato and Booth, *A Generation at Risk,* 77–78.

51. McLanahan and Sandefur, *Growing Up with a Single Parent,* 5.

Chapter 10: When Should Parents Part?

1. Tamara Jones, "The Commitment," *Washington Post,* 10 May 1998, Magazine Section, 9.

2. Roper Center Data Review, "The Family: Marriage: Highly Valued," *The Public Perspective* 9(8) February/March 1998: 17. See also Glenn, "Values, Attitudes," 15–33.

3. Orthner, "The Family in Transition," 98.

4. Roper Center Data Review, "Why Is Divorce So Common?" *The Public Perspective* 9(8) February/March 1998: 19.

5. John H. Grych and Frank D. Fincham, "Marital Conflict and Children's Adjustment: A Cognitive-Contextual Framework," *Psychological Bulletin* 108 (1990): 267–90.

6. Rex Forehand, Gene Brody, Nichola Long, Jerry Slotkin, and Robert Fauber, "Di-

vorce/Divorce Potential and Interparental Conflict: The Relationship to Early Adolescent Social and Cognitive Functioning," *Journal of Adolescent Research* 1 (1986): 389–97.

7. "Sociologists Differ about Family Textbooks' Message," *Footnotes* 26(1): 7, 10 (1998).

8. Karen S. Peterson, "Opinions Split over Avoiding Divorce," *USA Today*, 25 July 1998.

9. Wayne Mitchell and Tamara Mitchell, "When You Marry for a Reason Other Than Love," *Bonkers*, March/April 1999: 22.

10. Naomi Miller, *Single Parents by Choice: A Growing Trend in Family Life* (New York: Insight Books, 1992), 38.

11. Peterson, "Opinions Split," *USA Today*.

12. Philip A. Cowan and Carolyn P. Cowan, "Marriage Isn't Answer to Family Poverty," *New York Times*, 5 November 1997, Letters to the Editor, A26.

13. "Experts Disagree Over Benefits," *Jackson (Miss.) Clarion-Ledger*, 2 September 1992, A5.

14. Grych and Fincham, "Marital Conflict," 267–90.

15. Forehand et al., "Divorce/Divorce Potential," 389–97.

16. Carolyn Webster-Stratton, "The Relationship of Marital Support, Conflict and Divorce to Parent Perceptions, Behaviors, and Childhood Conduct Problems," *Journal of Marriage and the Family* 51 (1989): 417–30.

17. Ed Spruijt and Martijn de Goede, "Transition in Family Structure and Adolescent Well-being," *Adolescence* 32 (Winter 1997): 897–911.

18. Andrew J. Cherlin, Frank F. Furstenberg Jr., P. Lindsay Chase-Lansdale, Kathleen E. Kiernan, Philip K. Robins, Donna Ruane Morrison, and Julien O. Teitler, "Longitudinal Studies of Effects of Divorce on Children in Great Britain and the United States," *Science* 252 (1991): 1386–89.

19. Chase-Lansdale, Cherlin, and Kiernan, "The Long-term Effects," 1614–34.

20. Cherlin, Chase-Lansdale, and McRae, "Effects of Parental Divorce," 239.

21. Amato and Booth, *A Generation at Risk,* 219.

22. Ibid., 222.

23. Ibid., 220.

24. Ibid., 220.

25. Ibid., 204.

26. Ibid., 238.

27. Linda J. Waite's tabulations from waves 1 and 2 of the National Survey of Families and Households, based only on respondents who were married in 1987/88 and still married to the same people in 1992/94.

Chapter 11: Is Marriage a Hitting License?

1. Diane Sierpina, "Putting an End to a Loved One's Violence," *New York Times*, 9 June 1996, Connecticut Weekly, Section 13, 1, 12–13.

2. Jan E. Stets and Murray A. Straus, "The Marriage License as a Hitting License: A Comparison of Assaults in Dating, Cohabiting, and Married Couples," in *Physical Violence in American Families: Risk Factors and Adaptations to Violence in 8,145 Families,* eds. Murray A. Straus and Richard J. Gelles (New Brunswick, N.J.: Transaction, 1990), 227–44.

3. Neil Jacobson and John Gottman, *When Men Batter Women: New Insights into Ending Abusive Relationships* (New York: Simon & Schuster, 1998), 268.

4. Jacobson and Gottman, *When Men Batter Women,* 269.

5. Vivien Kellerman, "Long Island Q & A: Daniel O'Leary; A Researcher Looks into the Problem of Spousal Abuse," *New York Times*, 7 August 1994, Long Island Weekly, Section 13, 2.

6. Alfred DeMaris and Steven Swinford, "Female Victims of Spousal Violence: Factors Influencing Their Level of Fearfulness," *Family Relations* 45, (1996): 98–106.

7. Even Stark and Lawrence Sherman, "Should Police Officers Be Required to Arrest Abusive Husbands?" *Health* 8(5): 32 (1994).

8. James C. McKinley Jr., "Giuliani to Combat Domestic Violence with Police and Computers," *New York Times*, 26 April 1994, Metro Section, B3.

9. Ron Rosenbaum, "Staring into the Heart of the Heart of Darkness," *New York Times*, 4 June 1995, Magazine Section, 36–45, 50, 58, 61, 72.

10. "The Marriage Warnings," *New York Times*, 30 November 1995, Metro Section, B15.

11. "Warning: Marriage Could Be Hazardous," *New York Times*, 19 February 1995, Section 1, 40.

12. Ronet Bachman, "Violence Against Women," *A National Crime Victimization Survey Report*, Jan., NCJ–145325 (Washington, D.C.: U.S. Department of Justice, Office of Justice Programs, Bureau of Justice Statistics, 1994). See Tables 2 and 3. Note that these figures do not take into account age, education, race, or other characteristics that affect risk of victimization.

13. Linda J. Waite's tabulations from the National Survey of Families and Households, 1987/88.

14. Michael P. Johnson, "Patriarchal Terrorism and Common Couple Violence: Two Forms of Violence against Women," *Journal of Marriage and the Family* 57 (1995): 283–94.

15. Murray A. Straus, "Physical Assaults by Wives: A Major Social Problem," in *Current Controversies on Family Violence,* eds. Richard J. Gelles and D. R. Loseke (Newbury Park, Calif.: Sage, 1993), 67–87.

16. Ibid.

17. See also Russell P. Dobash, R. Emerson Dobash, Margo Wilson, and Martin Daly, "The Myth of Sexual Symmetry in Marital Violence," *Social Problems* 39(1): 71–91 (1992); and Johnson, "Patriarchal Terrorism," 283–94.

18. Margo Wilson and Martin Daly, "Who Kills Whom in Spouse Killings?: On the Exceptional Sex Ratio of Spousal Homicides in the United States" *Criminology* 30 (1992): 189–215.

19. Ibid.

20. Susan B. Sorenson, Dawn M. Upchurch, and Haikang Shen, "Violence and Injury in Marital Arguments: Risk Patterns and Gender Differences," *American Journal of Public Health* 86(1): 35–40 (1996).

21. Ibid.

22. Higher rates of domestic violence among cohabiting than married couples may be the result—at least in part—of selection of those with personality problems, problems getting along with others, or problems with drugs or alcohol into cohabitation. See Alan Booth and David R. Johnson, "Premarital Cohabitation and Marital Success," *Journal of Family Issues* 9 (1992): 255–72. See also Kazuo Yamaguchi and Denise B. Kandel, "Dynamic Relationships between Premarital Cohabitation and Illicit Drug Use: An Event-History Analysis of Role Selection and Role Socialization," *American Sociological Review* 50 (1985): 530–46.

23. Ronet Bachman and Linda E. Saltzman, "Violence against Women: Estimates from the

Redesigned Survey," *National Crime Victimization Survey Special Report*, August, 96–0029-P (Washington, D.C: U.S. Department of Justice, Office of Justice Programs, Bureau of Justice Statistics, 1995). 4, Table 4.

24. Wilson and Daly, "Who Kills Whom," 197–99.

25. Nicky Ali Jackson, "Observational Experiences of Intrapersonal Conflict and Teenage Victimization: A Comparative Study among Spouses and Cohabitors," *Journal of Family Violence* 11 (1996): 191–203.

26. Linda J. Waite's analyses, using the 1987–1988 waves of the National Survey of Families and Households.

27. Jackson, "Observational Experiences," 200.

28. Bryan Strong and Christine DeVault, eds, *The Marriage and Family Experience* (Minneapolis/St. Paul, Minn.: West Publishing, 1995), 494–502.

29. Jan E. Stets, "Cohabiting and Marital Aggression: The Role of Social Isolation," *Journal of Marriage and the Family* 53 (1991): 669–80.

30. Buss, *The Evolution of Desire*, 129–31.

31. Linda J. Waite's analysis on the National Survey of Families and Households, 1987–88. These differences are the net of race, gender, education, and age.

32. John H. Laub, Daniel S. Nagin, and Robert J. Sampson, "Trajectories of Change in Criminal Offending: Good Marriages and the Desistance Process," *American Sociological Review* 63 (1998): 225–38. Quote on p. 237.

33. Ibid.; see also Daniel S. Nagin and Ray Paternoster, "Personal Capital and Social Control: The Deterrence Implications of Individual Differences in Criminal Offending," *Criminology* 32 (1994): 581–606.

34. Lawrence Sherman, Janell D. Schmidt, and Dennis P. Rogan, *Policing Domestic Violence: Experiments and Dilemmas* (New York: The Free Press, 1992) chap. 7, cited in Richard J. Gelles, *Intimate Violence in Families,* 3d. (Thousand Oaks, Calif.: Sage, 1997), 138.

35. Richard J. Gelles and Murray A. Straus, *Intimate Violence* (New York: Simon & Schuster, 1998). See also DeMaris and Swinford, "Female Victims," 98–106.

36. Sorenson, Upchurch, and Shen, "Violence and Injury," 39.

37. Martin Daly and Margo Wilson, "Child Abuse and Other Risks of Not Living with Both Parents," *Ethology and Sociobiology* 6 (1985): 197–210.

38. Leslie Margolin and John L. Craft, "Child Sexual Abuse by Caretakers," *Family Relations* 38 (1989): 450–55

39. Daly and Wilson, "Evolutionary Psychology," 9–28.

40. Leslie Margolin, "Child Abuse by Mothers' Boyfriends: Why the Overrepresentation?," *Child Abuse & Neglect* 16 (1992): 541–51. Quote on p. 546.

Chapter 12: Is Her Marriage Really Worse Than His?

1. Karen S. Peterson, "Does Tying the Knot Put Women in a Bind?" *USA Today,* 22 April 1997.

2. Hayes, Anderson, and Blau, *Our Turn,* 35.

3. Andrew Hacker, "The War over the Family," *The New York Review of Books* 44(19): 34–38, (1997).

4. Jesse Bernard, *The Future of Marriage,* (New York: Bantam Books, 1972). See p. 29.

5. Jesse Bernard, *The Future of Marriage,* 2d. (New Haven: Yale University Press, 1982, 36–37.

6. Ibid., 51.

7. Glenn, *Closed Hearts, Closed Minds,* 9.

8. Bernard, *Future of Marriage,* 2d. ed., Tables 2, 11, and 14. Bernard took these figures from Genevieve Kaupfer, Walter Clark, and Robin Room, "The Mental Health of the Unmarried," *American Journal of Psychiatry* 122 (1966): 841–51.

9. Gove, "Sex, Marital Status, and Mortality," 45–67.

10. George Akerlof makes the same argument. See Akerlof, "Men without Children," 287–309.

11. Allan V. Horwitz and Helene Raskin White, "Becoming Married, Depression, and Alcohol Problems among Young Adults," *Journal of Health and Social Behavior* 32 (1991): 221–37.

12. John R. Logan and Glenna D. Spitze, *Family Ties: Enduring Relations between Parents and Children* (Philadelphia: Temple University Press, 1996).

13. John P. Robinson and Geoffrey Godbey, *Time for Life: The Surprising Ways Americans Use Their Time* (University Park, Pa.: Pennsylvania State University Press, 1997). See pp. 130–31 and p. 237.

14. Ronald C. Kessler and Marilyn Essex, "Marital Status and Depression: The Importance of Coping Resources," *Social Forces* 61 (1982): 484–507. In this sample, the unmarried homemakers are primarily widows; these results take into account presence of children, race, age, education, family income, and strain.

15. At least if they have no difficulty arranging for child care and if their husbands share child care. Catherine Ross and John Mirowsky, "Child Care and Emotional Adjustment to Wives' Employment," *Journal of Health and Social Behavior* 29(2): 127–38 (1988).

16. Horwitz, White, and Howell-White, "Becoming Married and Mental Health," 895.

17. John Mirowsky, "Age and the Gender Gap in Depression," *Journal of Health and Social Behavior* 37 (1996): 362–80.

18. Ibid.

19. The Health and Retirement Survey, funded by the National Institute on Aging, conducted baseline interviews with 12,654 men and women age fifty-one to sixty-one in 1992. See Thomas F. Juster and Richard Suzman, "Overview of the Health and Retirement Survey," S7–S56.

20. Linda J. Waite and Mary Elizabeth Hughes, "At Risk on the Cusp of Old Age: Living Arrangements and Functional Status among Black, White and Hispanic Adults," *Journal of Gerontology: Social Sciences* 54B: S136–S144.

21. In these comparisons the category *single* includes those who never married and the separated, divorced, and widowed.

22. Marks and Lambert, "Marital Status Continuity," 652–86.

23. Glenn, *Closed Hearts, Closed Minds,* 8.

24. Steven Stack and J. Ross Eshleman, "Marital Status and Happiness: A 17-Nation Study," *Journal of Marriage and the Family* 60 (1998): 527–36. See also Davis, "New Money, An Old Man/Lady," 319–50.

25. Susan Mitchell, *The Official Guide to American Attitudes: Who Thinks What about the Issues That Shape Our Lives* (Ithaca, N.Y.: New Strategist Publications, 1996), 248.

26. Stanley and Markman, *Marriage in the '90s,* 23. The authors report a "non-statistically significant trend for men to report being a bit happier in their marriages."

27. Ibid.

28. No analyses have ever tried to balance the earnings premium that men get from mar-

riage against the share of husbands' typically higher earnings that wives get in order to see which spouse benefits more financially.

29. In analyses done for this book, Waite finds that after she took into account the net of age, education, and race, the likelihood of male-to-female violence was 3.5 percent, 11.6 percent, and 14.5 percent for married, committed cohabiting, and uncommitted cohabiting couples, respectively. The likelihood of female-to-male violence was 3.9 percent, 11.0 percent, and 13.1 percent, respectively. Note that the gap in the sex of the aggressor was greatest for uncommitted cohabiting couples.

30. Goldscheider and Waite, *New Families, No Families?,* xiii.

31. Waite and Nielsen, "The Rise of the Dual-career Family," (in press) 192–209.

32. Toby L. Parcel and Elizabeth G. Menaghan, *Parents' Jobs and Children's Lives* (New York: Aldine de Gruyter, 1994).

33. Sandra L. Hofferth, "Women's Employment and Care of Children in the United States," New York: Aldine de Gruyter, in press 2001.

34. Ross M. Stolzenberg, "What is the Effect of One Spouse's Employment on the Other Spouse's Health?" (Working Paper 99–15, Alfred P. Sloan Center on Parents, Children, and Work, University of Chicago, 1999).

35. Gray and Vanderhart, "The Determinants of Wages," (forthcoming).

36. Goldscheider and Waite, *New Families, No Families?,* 192–209.

37. Nock, Steven L., *Marriage in Men's Lives* (New York: Oxford University Press, 1998).

38. Especially financial dependency for the spouse who puts family ahead of career.

39. Goldscheider and Waite, *New Families, No Families?,* 124–41.

Chapter 13: Why Is Marriage in Trouble?

1. For a discussion of these changes see Maggie Gallagher, *The Abolition of Marriage,* 131–52.

2. Arland Thornton, "Changing Attitudes Toward Family Issues in the United States," *Journal of Marriage and the Family* 51 (1989): 873–93.

3. William G. Axinn and Arland Thornton, "The Transformation in the Meaning of Marriage," in *Ties that Bind: Perspectives on Marriage and Cohabitation,* eds. Linda Waite, Christine Bachrach, Michelle Hindin, Elizabeth Thomson, and Arland Thornton (forthcoming).

4. Roper Center Data Review, "Americans Rate Their Society and Chart Its Values: A Roper Center Review of Findings of the General Social Survey and the 1996 Survey of American Political Culture," *The Public Perspective* 8(2): 1–27, 16 (1997).

5. Gardner, *Psychotherapy with Children of Divorce,* 12.

6. Mira Kirshenbaum, *Too Good to Leave, Too Bad to Stay: A Step-by-Step Guide to Help You Decide Whether to Stay in or Get out of Your Relationship* (New York: Plume Books, 1996), 56–57.

7. Ibid., 50.

8. Whitehead, "The Experts' Story of Marriage," 16.

9. Andrew Cherlin, *Marriage, Divorce, Remarriage* (Cambridge, Mass.: Harvard University Press, 1992), 47.

10. Herbert Jacob, *Silent Revolution: The Transformation of Divorce Law in the United States* (Chicago: The University of Chicago Press, 1988).

11. Samuel H. Preston and John McDonald, "The Incidence of Divorce within Cohorts of American Marriages Contracted Since the Civil War," *Demography* 16 (1979): 1–26, Table 2.

12. Leora Friedberg, "Did Unilateral Divorce Raise Divorce Rates?: Evidence from Panel Data," *American Economic Review* 88 (1998): 608–27.

13. See Peterson, "A Re-evaluation," 528–36. See also Sanford L. Braver and Diane O'Connell, *Divorced Dads: Shattering the Myths* (New York: Jeremy P. Tarcher/Putnam, 1998).

14. Gray and Vanderhart, "The Determinants of Wages," (forthcoming).

15. For evidence on the effect of risk of divorce on childbearing, see Lee A. Lillard, and Linda J. Waite, "A Joint Model of Marital Childbearing and Marital Disruption," *Demography* 30 (1993): 653–82.

16. Gray and Vanderhart, "The Determinants of Wages," (forthcoming).

17. Karlyn Bowman, "Opinion Pulse," *The American Enterprise* 9(3): 90 (1998).

18. Alan Parkman, "Why are Married Women Working So Hard?" *International Review of Law and Economics* 18(1): 41–49 (1998).

19. Thomas F. Juster and Frank P. Stafford, eds., *Time, Goods and Well-being* (Ann Arbor, Mich.: Institute for Social Research, 1985).

20. Arlie Hochschild, *The Second Shift: Working Parents and the Revolution at Home* (New York: Viking, 1989).

21. Robinson and Godbey, *Time for Life,* 104.

22. See, for example, Paul R. Amato, "Explaining the Intergenerational Transmission of Divorce," *Journal of Marriage and the Family* 58 (1996): 628–40; Alan Booth, David R. Johnson, Lynn K. White, and John Edwards, "Predicting Divorce and Permanent Separation," *Journal of Family Issues* 6 (1985): 331–46.

23. Paul R. Amato and Stacy J. Rogers, "Do Attitudes Toward Divorce Affect Marital Quality?," *Journal of Family Issues* 20 (1999): 69–86.

24. Ibid., 83.

25. Stacy J. Rogers, and Paul R. Amato, "Is Marital Quality Declining? Evidence from Two Generations," *Social Forces* 75 (1997): 1089–1100.

26. Amato and Rogers, "Do Attitudes Toward Divorce," 85.

27. Louis Harris and Associates, Generation 2001: A Survey of the First College Graduating Class of the New Millennium, 8 (February 1998).

28. David Popenoe, *Changes in Teen Attitudes Toward Marriage, Cohabitation and Children, 1975–1995* (New Brunswick, N.J.: National Marriage Project, 1999), 1–10.

29. Linda J. Waite's tabulations from the National Education Longitudinal Survey (NELS:88, Wave 3, 1992); percentage of mothers unmarried at first birth from Amara Bachu, "Trends in Marital Status of U.S. Women at First Birth: 1930 to 1994," Bureau of the Census Population Division Working Paper No. 20 (Washington, D.C., 1998). *www.census.gov/population/www/documentation/twps0020/twps0020.html*

30. Barbara Dafoe Whitehead and David Popenoe, *Why Wed?: Young Adults Talk about Sex, Love, and First Unions* (New Brunswick, N.J.: The National Marriage Project, 1999), 17.

31. Neil G. Bennett, David E. Bloom, and Cynthia K. Miller, "The Influence of Nonmarital Childbearing on the Formation of First Marriages," *Demography* 32 (1995): 56.

32. Lillard, and Waite, "Joint Model of Marital," 679; See also Linda J. Waite and Lee A. Lillard, "Children and Marital Disruption," *American Journal of Sociology* 96 (1991): 930–53.

Chapter 14: Renewing Marriage

1. Waite, "Does Marriage Matter?" 483–508.

2. Stephanie J. Ventura, Joyce A. Martin, Sally C. Curtin, and T. J. Matthews, "Report of

Final Natality Statistics, 1996," *Monthly Vital Statistics Report* 46(11), supp. (Hyattsville, Md.: National Center for Health Statistics, 1998). For divorce rate see Bureau of the Census, *Statistical Abstract of the United States: 1997,* 117th ed. (Washington, D.C., 1997), Table 145.

3. We have drawn liberally here on Theodora Ooms, *Toward More Prefect Unions: Putting Marriage on the Public Agenda* (Washington, D.C.: Family Impact Seminar, 1998).

4. Glenn, *Closed Hearts, Closed Minds,* 18.

5. For a list of marriage-preparation and couples-training programs in your area, contact the Coalition for Marriage, Family and Couples Education, 5310 Belt Rd., NW, Washington, D.C., 20015–1961. You can visit their website at *www.smartmarriages.com*; send E-mail to *cmfce@smartmarriages.com,* or call (202)362–3332. Most churches and synagogues run couples programs or can refer you to programs in your area.

6. William G. Axinn and Arland Thornton, "Mothers, Children, and Cohabitation: The Intergenerational Effects of Attitudes and Behavior," *American Sociological Review* 58 (1993): 240.

7. Stephanie Ventura, National Center for Health Statistics, personal communication with Linda J. Waite, July 24, 1998.

8. Ventura, personal communication.

9. Steuerle et al., *The Government We Deserve.* See also C. Eugene Steuerle, "A Comprehensive Approach to Removing Marriage Penalties" in *Strengthening American Marriages: A Communitarian Perspective,* ed. M. K. Whyte, with contributions by D. Browning and W. Doherty (forthcoming, Rowman and Littlefield).

10. C. Eugene Steuerle, "The Effects of Tax and Welfare Policies on Family Formation," in *Strategies for Strengthening Marriage: What Do We Know? What Do We Need to Know?* (Washington, D.C.: Family Impact Seminar, 1998) 153–62.

11. Ibid.

12. Friedberg, "Did Unilateral Divorce Raise Divorce Rates?" 608–27.

13. Ibid., Table 1.

14. Regan, "Postmodern Family Law," 157–85.

15. Michael J. McManus, *Marriage Savers: Helping Your Friends and Family Avoid Divorce* (Grand Rapids, Mich.: Zondervan Publishing House, 1995). We have taken many of the ideas here, with permission, from Ooms, *Toward More Perfect Unions,* 36–37.

16. Bennett, Bloom, and Miller, "The Influence of Nonmarital Childbearing," 47–62.

17. Susan L. Brown and Alan Booth, "Cohabitation Versus Marriage: A Comparison of Relationship Quality," *Journal of Marriage and the Family* 58 (1996): 668–78; Susan Brown, "Cohabitation as Marriage Prelude Versus Marriage Alternative: The Significance for Psychological Well-being" (paper presented at the meetings of the American Sociological Association, San Francisco, August 1998).

18. Frances Goldscheider, "Wedded—Bliss," *The Nation,* Letters, 26 June 1995; 906. See also Valerie Kincade Oppeheimer. "The Role of Economic Factors in Union Formation," in *Ties That Bind: Perspectives on Marriage and Cohabitation,* eds. Linda Waite, Christine Bachrach, Michelle Hindin, Elizabeth Thomson, and Arland Thornton (Aldine de Gruyter, forthcoming).

19. David Ellwood, *Poor Support: Poverty and the American Faámily* (New York: Basic Books, 1988), 46; Arlene Skolnick, *Embattled Paradise: The American Family in an Age of Uncertainty* (New York: Basic Books, 1991), 18.

Bibliography

Abramson, Jill. "Still Playing Key Role on a Most Painful Day." *New York Times,* 18 August 1998.

Akerlof, George A. "Men Without Children." *The Economic Journal* 108 (1998): 287–309.

Aldous, Joan. "Problematic Elements in the Relationship Between Churches and Families." In *Families and Religions: Conflict and Change in Modern Society.* Beverly Hills, Calif.: Sage, 1983.

Allen, S. M. "Gender differences in spousal caregiving and unmet need for care." *Journal of Gerontology: Social Sciences,* 49(1994): S187–S195.

Amato, Paul R. "Explaining the Intergenerational Transmission of Divorce." *Journal of Marriage and the Family.* 58 (1996): 628–40.

Amato, Paul R., and Alan Booth. *A Generation at Risk: Growing Up in an Era of Family Upheaval.* Cambridge, Mass.: Harvard University Press, 1997.

Amato, Paul R., and Stacy J. Rogers. "Do Attitudes Toward Divorce Affect Marital Quality?" *Journal of Family Issues* 20 (1999): 69–86.

Aneshensel, Carol S., and Clea A. Sucoff. "The Neighborhood Context of Adolescent Mental Health." *Journal of Health and Social Behavior* 37 (1996): 293–310.

Angel, Ronald, and Jacqueline Lowe Worobey. "Single Motherhood and Children's Health." *Journal of Health and Social Behavior* 29 (1988): 38–52.

Applewhite, Ashton. *Cutting Loose: Why Women Who Leave Their Marriages Do So Well.* New York: HarperCollins, 1997.

Astone, Nan Marie, and Sara S. McLanahan. "Family Structure, Residential Mobility, and School Dropout: A Research Note." *Demography* 31 (1994): 575–84.

Aulette, Judy Root. *Changing Families.* Belmont, Calif.: Wadsworth Publishing, 1994.

Axinn, William G., and Arland Thornton. "Mothers, Children, and Cohabitation: The Intergenerational Effects of Attitudes and Behavior." *American Sociological Review* 58 (1993): 233–46.

———. "The Transformation in the Meaning of Marriage." In *Ties That Bind: Perspectives on Marriage and Cohabitation,* edited by Linda Waite, Christine Bachrach, Michelle Hindin, Elizabeth Thomson, and Arland Thornton. Forthcoming.

Bachman, Jerald G., Katherine N. Wadsworth, Patrick M. O'Malley, Lloyd D. Johnson, and John E. Schulenberg. *Smoking, Drinking, and Drug Use in Young Adulthood.* Mahwah, N.J.: Lawrence Erlbaum Associates, 1997.

Bachman, Ronet. "Violence Against Women." *A National Crime Victimization Survey Report.*

January NCJ-145325. Washington, D.C.: U.S. Department of Justice, Office of Justice Programs, Bureau of Justice Statistics, 1994.

Bachman, Ronet, and Linda E. Saltzman. "Violence against Women: Estimates from the Redesigned Survey." *National Crime Victimization Survey Special Report.* August, 96–0029-P. Washington, D.C.: U.S. Department of Justice, Office of Justice Programs, Bureau of Justice Statistics, 1995.

Bachrach, Christine. "Cohabitation and Reproductive Behavior in the U.S." *Demography* 24 (1987): 623–37.

Bachu, Amara. "Trends in Marital Status of U.S. Women at First Birth: 1930 to 1994." U.S. Bureau of the Census Population Division Working Paper No. 20, 1998. http://www.census.gov/population/www/documentation/twps0020/twps0020.html

Bane, Mary Jo, and David T. Ellwood. "Slipping into and out of Poverty: The Dynamics of Spells." *Journal of Human Resources* 21 (1986): 1–23.

Bartlett, Robin L., and Charles Callahan III. "Wage Determination and Marital Status: Another Look." *Industrial Relations* 23 (1984): 90–96.

Becker, Gary S. *A Treatise on the Family.* Cambridge, Mass.: Harvard University Press, 1991.

———. "Human Capital, Effort, and the Sexual Division of Labor." *Journal of Labor Economics* 3, no. 1, part 2 (1985): S33–S58.

Beller, Andrea H., and John W. Graham. *Small Change: The Economics of Child Support.* New Haven: Yale University Press, 1993.

Bennett, Neil G., David E. Bloom, and Cynthia K. Miller. "The Influence of Nonmarital Childbearing on the Formation of First Marriages." *Demography* 32 (1995): 47–62.

Bennett, Trude, Paula Braveman, Susan Egerter, and John L. Kiely. "Maternal Marital Status as a Risk Factor for Infant Mortality." *Family Planning Perspectives* 26 (1994): 252–56.

Berger, Peter, and Hansfried Kellner. "Marriage and the Construction of Reality: An Exercise in the Microsociology of Knowledge." *Diogenes* 46 (1964): 1–25.

Berkman, Lisa F., and Lester Breslow. "Social Networks and Mortality Risk." Chap. 4 in *Health and Ways of Living: The Alameda County Study.* New York: Oxford University Press, 1983.

Bernard, Jesse. *The Future of Marriage.* New York: Bantam Books, 1972.

———. *The Future of Marriage,* 2nd ed. New Haven: Yale University Press, 1982.

Bianchi, Suzanne M. "The Changing Economic Roles of Women and Men." In *Economic Trends,* edited by Reynolds Farley, 107–54. Vol. 1 of *State of the Union: America in the 1990s.* New York: Russell Sage, 1995.

Blankenhorn, David, "Normalizing Divorce," *Propostions* 2 (1998): 9.

Bloom, Bernard L. "A Census Tract Analysis of Socially Deviant Behaviors." *Multivariate Behavioral Research* 1 (1966): 307–20.

Blumstein, Philip, and Pepper Schwartz. *American Couples: Money, Work, Sex.* New York: William Morrow, 1983.

Booth, Alan, and David R. Johnson. "Premarital Cohabitation and Marital Success." *Journal of Family Issues* 9 (1988): 255–72.

Booth, Alan, David R. Johnson, Lynn K. White, and John Edwards. "Predicting Divorce and Permanent Separation." *Journal of Family Issues* 6 (1985): 331–46.

Bowman, Karlyn. "Opinion Pulse." *The American Enterprise* 9 (1998): 90–93.

Braver, Sanford L., and Diane O'Connell. *Divorced Dads: Shattering the Myths.* New York: Jeremy P. Tarcher/Putnam, 1998.

Bringle, Robert G., and Bram P. Buunk. "Extradyadic Relationships and Sexual Jealousy." In

Sexuality in Close Relationships, edited by Kathleen McKinney and Susan Sprecher, 135–53. Hillsdale, N.J.: Lawrence Erlbaum Associates, 1991.

Brown, Susan. "Cohabitation as Marriage Prelude Versus Marriage Alternative: The Significance for Psychological Well-being." Paper presented at the meetings of the American Sociological Association, San Francisco, August 1998.

Brown, Susan L., and Alan Booth. "Cohabitation Versus Marriage: A Comparison of Relationship Quality." *Journal of Marriage and the Family* 58 (1996): 668–78.

Bruce, Martha Livingston, and Philip J. Leaf. "Psychiatric Disorders and 15-Month Mortality in a Community Sample of Older Adults." *American Journal of Public Health* 79 (1989): 727–30.

Bumpass, Larry L. "The Declining Significance of Marriage: Changing Family Life in the United States." Paper presented at the Potsdam International Conference, "Changing Families and Childhood," December 14–17, 1994.

Bumpass, Larry L., and James A. Sweet. "National Estimates of Cohabitation." *Demography* 26 (1989): 615–25.

Bumpass, Larry L., R. Kelly Raley, and James A. Sweet. "The Changing Character of Stepfamilies: Implications of Cohabitation and Nonmarital Childbearing." *Demography* 32 (1995): 425–36.

Burkhauser, Richard V. "Protecting the Most Vulnerable: A Proposal to Improve Social Security Insurance for Older Women." *The Gerontologist* 34 (1994): 148–49.

Burkhauser, Richard V., J. S. Butler, and Karen C. Holden. "How the Death of a Spouse Affects Economic Well-being after Retirement: A Hazard Model Approach." *Social Science Quarterly* 72 (1991): 504–19.

Burton, Russell P. D. "Global Integrative Meaning as a Mediating Factor in the Relationship Between Social Roles and Psychological Distress." *Journal of Health and Social Behavior* 39 (1998): 201–15.

Buss, David M. *The Evolution of Desire: Strategies of Human Mating.* New York: Basic Books, 1994.

Chase-Lansdale, P. Lindsay, and Mavis Heatherington. "The Impact of Divorce on Life-span Development: Short and Long-term Effects." In *Life Span Development and Behavior,* edited by Paul B. Baltes, David L. Featherman, and Richard M. Lerner, 105–50. Vol. 10. Hillsdale, N.J.: Lawrence Erlbaum Associates, 1990.

Chase-Lansdale, P. Lindsay, Andrew J. Cherlin, and Kathleen E. Kiernan. "The Long-term Effects of Parental Divorce on the Mental Health of Young Adults: A Developmental Perspective." *Child Development* 66 (1995): 1614–34.

Chase-Lansdale, P. Lindsay, Lauren S. Wakschlag, and Jeanne Brooks-Gunn. "A Psychological Perspective on the Development of Caring in Children and Youth: The Role of Family." *Journal of Adolescence* 18 (1995): 515–56.

Cherlin, Andrew J. "The Effect of Children on Marital Dissolution." *Demography* 14, (1997): 265–72.

———. *Marriage, Divorce, Remarriage.* Cambridge, Mass.: Harvard University Press, 1992.

Cherlin, Andrew J., Frank F. Furstenberg Jr., P. Lindsay Chase-Lansdale, Kathleen E. Kiernan, Philip K. Robins, Donna Ruane Morrison, and Julien O. Teitler. "Longitudinal Studies of Effects of Divorce on Children in Great Britain and the United States." *Science* 252 (1991): 1386–89.

Cherlin, Andrew J., Kathleen E. Kiernan, and P. Lindsay Chase-Lansdale. "Parental Divorce in Childhood and Demographic Outcomes in Young Adulthood." *Demography* 32 (1995): 299–318.

Cherlin, Andrew J., P. Lindsay Chase-Lansdale, and Christine McRae. "Effects of Parental Divorce on Mental Health Throughout the Life Course." *American Sociological Review* 63 (1998): 239–49.

Clarkberg, Marin, Ross M. Stolzenberg, and Linda J. Waite. "Attitudes, Values and Entrance into Cohabitational Versus Marital Unions." *Social Forces.* 74 (1995): 609–32.

Cohen, Bernard L., and I-Sing Lee. "A Catalog of Risks." *Health Physics* 36 (1979): 707–22.

Cohen, Sheldon, William J. Doyle, David P. Skoner, Bruce S. Rabin, and Jack M. Gwaltney Jr. "Social Ties and Susceptibility to the Common Cold." *Journal of the American Medical Association* 277 (1997): 1940–44.

Coleman, James S. "Social Capital in the Creation of Human Capital." *American Journal of Sociology* 94, supplement (1988): S95–S120.

Coltrane, Scott. "Family Policy Wonderland." *Contemporary Sociology* 27(3) (1998): 230–33.

Collins, Randall, and Scott Coltrane. *Sociology of Marriage and the Family: Gender, Love, and Property,* 4th ed. Chicago: Nelson-Hall, 1995.

Coontz, Stephanie, and Donna Franklin. "When the Marriage Penalty is Marriage." *New York Times,* 28 October 1997, A23.

Coverman, Shelley. "Gender, Domestic Labor Time, and Wage Inequality." *American Sociological Review* 48 (1983): 623–37.

Cowan, Philip A., and Carolyn P. Cowan. "Marriage Isn't Answer to Family Poverty." *New York Times,* 5 November 1997, Letters to the Editor, p. A26.

Crittenden, Danielle. *What Our Mothers Didn't Tell Us: Why Happiness Eludes the Modern Woman.* New York: Simon & Schuster, 1999.

Daly, Martin, and Margo Wilson. "Child Abuse and Other Risks of Not Living with Both Parents." *Ethology and Sociobiology* 6 (1985): 197–210.

———. "Evolutionary Psychology and Marital Conflict: The Relevance of Stepchildren." In *Sex, Power, Conflict: Evolutionary and Feminist Perspectives,* edited by David M. Buss and Neil M. Malamuth, 9–28. Oxford: Oxford University Press, 1996.

Daniel, Kermit. "The Marriage Premium." In *The New Economics of Human Behavior,* edited by Mariano Tommasi and Kathryn Ierulli, 113–25. Cambridge: Cambridge University Press, 1995.

Davidson, J. Kenneth Sr., and Nelwyn B. Moore. *Marriage and Family: Change and Continuity.* Boston: Allyn and Bacon, 1996.

Davis, James A. "New Money, An Old Man/Lady, and 'Two's Company': Subjective Welfare in the NORC General Social Surveys, 1972–1982." *Social Indicators Research* 15 (1984): 319–50.

DeLamater, John. "Gender Differences in Sexual Scenarios." In *Females, Males and Sexuality: Theories and Research,* edited by Kathryn Kelley, 127–39. Albany: SUNY Press, 1987.

DeMaris, Alfred, and Steven Swinford. "Female Victims of Spousal Violence: Factors Influencing Their Level of Fearfulness." *Family Relations* 45 (1996): 98–106.

Desai, Sonalde, and Linda J. Waite. "Women's Employment During Pregnancy and after the First Birth: Occupational Characteristics and Work Commitment." *American Sociological Review* 56 (1991): 551–66.

DiLeonardo, Micaela. "The Female World of Cards and Holidays: Women, Families, and the Work of Kinship." *Signs* 12 (1987): 440–53.

Dobash, Russell P., R. Emerson Dobash, Margo Wilson, and Martin Daly. "The Myth of Sexual Symmetry in Marital Violence." *Social Problems* 39, no. 1 (1992): 71–91.

Duncan, Greg J., and Bertil Holmlund. "Was Adam Smith Right After All? Another Test of the Theory of Compensating Differentials." *Journal of Labor Economics* 1 (1983): 366–79.

Durkheim, Émile. *Suicide.* 1897. New York: The Free Press, reprint, 1951.

Eisner, Jane R. "It's Perfectly Normal for Parents to Control What Their Kids Read." *Philadelphia Sun,* 20 October 1996.

Ellwood, David. *Poor Support: Poverty and the American Family.* New York: Basic Books, 1988.

Elvenstar, Diane C. *First Comes Love: Deciding Whether or Not to Get Married.* Indianapolis/New York: The Bobbs Merrill Co., 1983.

Ettlebrick, Paula. *New York Times,* 4 January 1995, Letters to the Editor.

"Experts Disagree Over Benefits, Harm Divorce Can Have for Kids." *Jackson (Miss.) Clarion Star-Ledger,* 2 September 1992.

Flewelling, Robert L., and Karl E. Bauman. "Family Structure as a Predictor of Initial Substance Use and Sexual Intercourse in Early Adolescence." *Journal of Marriage and the Family* 52 (1990): 171–81.

Forehand, Rex, Gene Brody, Nichola Long, Jerry Slotkin, and Robert Fauber. "Divorce/Divorce Potential and Interparental Conflict: The Relationship to Early Adolescent Social and Cognitive Functioning." *Journal of Adolescent Research* 1 (1986): 389–97.

Forste, Renata, and Koray Tanfer. "Sexual Exclusivity among Dating, Cohabiting, and Married Women." *Journal of Marriage and the Family* 58 (1996): 33–47.

Freedman, Vicki A. "Family Structure and the Risk of Nursing Home Admission." *Journal of Gerontology: Social Sciences* 51B, no. 2 (1996): S61–S69.

Friedan, Betty. *The Feminine Mystique.* New York: Norton, 1963.

Friedberg, Leora. "Did Unilateral Divorce Raise Divorce Rates?: Evidence from Panel Data." *American Economic Review* 88 (1998): 608–27.

Gallagher, Maggie. *The Abolition of Marriage: How We Destroy Lasting Love.* Washington, D.C.: Regnery, 1996.

Gardner, Richard A. *Psychotherapy with Children of Divorce.* New York: Jason Aronson, 1982.

Gelles, Richard J. *Intimate Violence in Families,* 3d. ed. Thousand Oaks, Calif.: Sage, 1997.

Gelles, Richard J., and Murray A. Straus. *Intimate Violence.* New York: Simon & Schuster, 1988.

Glenn, Norval D. "Values, Attitudes, and American Marriage." In *Promises to Keep: Decline and Renewal of Marriage in America,* edited by David Popenoe, Jean Bethke Elshtain, and David Blankenhorn, 15–33. Lanham, MD: Rowman and Littlefield Publishers, 1996.

———. *Closed Hearts, Closed Minds: The Textbook Story of Marriage.* New York: Institute for American Values, 1997.

Goldscheider, Frances K. "Wedded—Bliss." *The Nation,* Letters, June 26, 1995, 906.

Goldscheider, Frances K., and Linda J. Waite. "Sex Differences in Entry into Marriage." *American Journal of Sociology* 92 (1986): 91–109.

———. *New Families, No Families?: The Transformation of the American Home.* Berkeley, Calif.: University of California Press, 1991.

Goodwin, James S., William C. Hunt, Charles R. Key, and Jonathan M. Samet. "The Effect of Marital Status on Stage, Treatment, and Survival of Cancer Patients." *Journal of the American Medical Association* 258 (1987): 3125–30.

Gordon, Howard S., and Gary E. Rosenthal. "Impact of Marital Status on Hospital Outcomes: Evidence from an Academic Medical Center." *Archives of Internal Medicine* 155 (1995): 2465–71.

Gove, Walter R. "Sex, Marital Status, and Mortality." *American Journal of Sociology* 79 (1973): 45–67.

Gove, Walter R., and Michael Hughes. "Possible Causes of the Apparent Sex Differences in Physical Health: An Empirical Investigation." *American Sociological Review* 44 (1979): 126–46.

Gray, Jeffrey S. "The Fall in Men's Return to Marriage: Declining Productivity Effects or Changing Selection?" *Journal of Human Resources* 32 (1997): 481–504.

Gray, Jeffrey S., and Michael J. Vanderhart. "The Determinants of Wages: Does Marriage Matter?" In *Ties that Bind: Perspectives on Marriage and Cohabitation,* edited by Linda J. Waite, Michelle Hindin, Elizabeth Thomson, and Arland Thornton. Forthcoming.

Greeley, Andrew M. *Religious Change in America.* Cambridge, Mass.: Harvard University Press, 1989.

Grossbard-Shechtman, Amyra. "Marriage and Productivity: An Interdisciplinary Analysis." In *Handbook of Behavioral Economics.* Vol. A, *Behavioral Microeconomics,* edited by Benjamin Gilad and Stanley Kaish, 289–302. Greenwich, Conn.: JAI Press, 1986.

Grossbard-Shechtman, Shoshana. *On the Economics of Marriage: A Theory of Marriage, Labor, and Divorce.* Boulder, Colo.: Westview Press, 1993.

Grossbard-Shechtman, Shoshana A., and Shoshana Neuman. "Cross-productivity Effects of Education and Origin on Earnings: Are They Really Reflecting Productivity?" In *Handbook of Behavioral Economics.* Vol. 2A, *Behavioral Environments,* edited by Stanley Kaish, Benjamin Gilad, Roger Frantz, Harinder Singh, and James Gerber, 125–45. Greenwich, Conn.: JAI Press, 1991.

Grych, John H., and Frank D. Fincham. "Marital Conflict and Children's Adjustment: A Cognitive Contextual Framework." *Psychological Bulletin* 108 (1990): 267–90.

Hahn, Beth A. "Marital Status and Women's Health: The Effect of Economic Marital Acquisitions." *Journal of Marriage and the Family* 55 (1993): 495–504.

Hao, Lingxin. "Family Structure, Private Transfers, and the Economic Well-being of Families with Children." *Social Forces* 75 (1996): 269–92.

———. "Family Structure, Parental Input, and Child Development." Paper presented at the annual meeting of the Population Association of America, Washington, D.C., March 1997.

Harper, Cynthia, and Sara McLanahan. "Father Absence and Youth Incarceration." Paper presented at the annual meetings of the American Sociological Association, San Francisco, August 1998.

Harris, Judith Rich. *The Nurture Assumption: Why Children Turn Out the Way They Do.* New York: Free Press, 1998.

Harris, Kathleen Mullan. *Teen Mothers and the Revolving Welfare Door.* Philadelphia: Temple University Press, 1997.

Harris, Louis, and associates. "Generation 2001: A Survey of the First College Graduating Class of the New Millenium." (February 1998): 8.

Hayes, Christopher, Deborah Anderson, and Milina Blau. *Our Turn: Women Who Triumph in the Face of Divorce.* New York: Pocket Books, 1993.

Herbert, Tracy Bennet, and Sheldon Cohen. "Depression and Immunity: A Meta-analytic Review." *Psychological Bulletin* 113 (1993): 472–86.

Hernandez, Donald J., with David E. Myers. *America's Children: Resources from Family, Government and the Economy.* New York: Russell Sage, 1993.

Hersch, Joni. "Effect of Housework on Earnings of Husbands and Wives: Evidence from Full-time Piece Rate Workers." *Social Science Quarterly* 66 (1985): 210–17.

———. "Male-Female Differences in Hourly Wages: The Role of Human Capital, Working Conditions, and Housework." *Industrial and Labor Relations Review* 44 (1991): 746–59.

Heyn, Dalma. *Marriage Shock: the Transformation of Women into Wives.* New York: Villard, 1997.

Hochschild, Arlie. *The Second Shift: Working Parents and the Revolution at Home.* New York: Viking, 1989.

Hofferth, Sandra L. "Women's Employment and Care of Children in the United States." Paper presented at the Workshop on Measurement of and Research on Time Use, "National Research Council, Washington, D.C., May 1999.

Hoffman, Saul D., and Greg J. Duncan. "What are the Economic Consequences of Divorce?" *Demography* 25 (1988): 641–45.

Holden, Karen C. "The Transition from Wife to Widow: Data Issues in Measuring First-period Income Effects in SIPP and the RHS." In *Individuals and Families in Transition: Understanding Change through Longitudinal Data,* compiled by Hazel V. Benton, Debra A. Ganni, and Delma T. Frankel, 23–32. Washington, D.C.: U.S. Department of Commerce, Bureau of the Census, 1989.

Holden, Karen C., and Pamela J. Smock. "The Economic Costs of Marital Dissolution: Why Do Women Bear a Disproportionate Cost?" *Annual Review of Sociology* 17 (1991): 51–78.

Hopper, Joseph. "The Symbolic Origins of Conflict in Divorce." Paper presented at the meetings of the American Sociological Association, 1998. *Journal of Marriage and the Family* (2001 forthcoming).

Horwitz, Allan V., and Helene Raskin White. "Becoming Married, Depression, and Alcohol Problems among Young Adults." *Journal of Health and Social Behavior* 32 (1991): 221–37.

Horwitz, Allan V., Helene Raskin White, and Sandra Howell-White. "Becoming Married and Mental Health: A Longitudinal Study of a Cohort of Young Adults." *Journal of Marriage and the Family* 58 (1996): 895–907.

House, James S., Debra Umberson, and Karl Landis. "Structures and Processes of Social Support." *Annual Review of Sociology* 14 (1988): 293–318.

House of Representatives Standing Committee on Legal and Constitutional Affairs. *To Have and to Hold: Strategies to Strengthen Marriage and Relationships.* Canberra, Australia: The Parliament of the Commonwealth of Australia, 1998.

Hu, Yuanreng, and Noreen Goldman. "Mortality Differentials by Marital Status: An International Comparison." *Demography* 27 (1990): 233–50.

Jackson, Nicky Ali. "Observational Experiences of Intrapersonal Conflict and Teenage Victimization: A Comparative Study Among Spouses and Cohabitors." *Journal of Family Violence* 11 (1996): 191–203.

Jacob, Herbert. *Silent Revolution: The Transformation of Divorce Law in the United States.* Chicago: The University of Chicago Press, 1988.

Jacobson, Neil S., and John M. Gottman. *When Men Batter Women: New Insights into Ending Abusive Relationships.* New York: Simon & Schuster, 1998.

Jencks, Christopher. *The Homeless.* Cambridge, Mass.: Harvard University Press, 1994.

Johnson, Dirk. "Uncertain Future, on Their Own, Awaits." *New York Times,* 16 March 1997, 1.

Johnson, Michael P. "Patriarchal Terrorism and Common Couple Violence: Two Forms of Violence against Women," *Journal of Marriage and the Family* 57 (1995): 283–94.

Jones, Tamara. "The Commitment." *Washington Post,* 10 May 1998, Magazine section, pp. 9–13, 21–26.

Juster, Thomas F., and Frank P. Stafford, eds. *Time, Goods, and Well-being*. Ann Arbor, Mich.: Institute for Social Research, 1985.

Juster, Thomas F., and Richard Suzman. "An Overview of the Health and Retirement Survey." *Journal of Human Resources* 30 (1995): S7–S56.

Karoly, Lynn A. "Anatomy of the U.S. Income Distribution: Two Decades of Change." *Oxford Review of Economic Policy* 12 (1996): 76–95.

Kaupfer, Genevieve, Walter Clark, and Robin Room. "The Mental Health of the Unmarried." *The American Journal of Psychiatry* 122 (1966): 841–51.

Kellam, Shepard G., Rebecca G. Adams, C. Hendricks Brown, and Margaret E. Ensminger. "The Long-term Evolution of the Family Structure of Teenage and Older Mothers." *Journal of Marriage and the Family* 44 (1982): 539–54.

Kellerman, Vivien. "Long Island Q & A: Daniel O'Leary: A Researcher Looks into the Problem of Spousal Abuse." *New York Times,* 7 August 1994, Long Island Weekly, sec. 13, p. 2.

Kessler, Ronald C., and Marilyn Essex. "Marital Status and Depression: The Importance of Coping Resources." *Social Forces* 61 (1982): 2497–2507.

Kiecolt-Glaser, Janice K., Laura D. Fisher, Paula Ogrocki, Julie C. Stout, Carl E. Speicher, and Ronald Glaser. "Marital Quality, Marital Disruption, and Immune Function." *Psychosomatic Medicine* 49 (1987): 13–34.

Kiecolt-Glaser, Janice K., Ronald Glaser, John T. Cacioppo, Robert C. MacCallum, Mary Syndersmith, Cheongtag Kim, and William B. Malarkey. "Marital Conflict in Older Adults: Endocrinological and Immunological Correlates." *Psychosomatic Medicine* 59 (1997): 339–49.

Kiecolt-Glaser, Janice K., William B. Malarkey, MaryAnn Chee, Tamara Newton, John T. Cacioppo, Hsiao-Yin Mao, and Ronald Glaser. "Negative Behavior During Marital Conflict Is Associated with Immunological Down-Regulation." *Psychosomatic Medicine* 55 (1993): 395–409.

Kirshenbaum, Mira. *Too Good to Leave, Too Bad to Stay: A Step-by-Step Guide to Help You Decide Whether to Stay in or Get out of Your Relationship*. New York: Plume Books, 1996.

Kobrin, Frances E., and Gerry L. Hendershot. "Do Families Ties Reduce Mortality?: Evidence from the United States: 1966–1968." *Journal of Marriage and the Family* 39 (1977): 737–45.

Korenman, Sanders, and David Neumark. "Does Marriage Really Make Men More Productive?" *Journal of Human Resources* 26 (1991): 282–307.

Kostiuk, Peter F., and Dean A. Follman. "Learning Curves, Personal Characteristics, and Job Performance." *Journal of Labor Economics* 7 (1989): 126–49.

Kotlikoff, Lawrence J., and Avia Spivak. "The Family as an Incomplete Annuities Market." *Journal of Political Economy* 89 (1981): 372–91.

Krantzler, Mel, and Pat Krantzler. *The New Creative Divorce: How to Create a Happier, More Rewarding Life During—and After—Your Divorce*. Holbrook, Mass.: Adams Media Corp, 1998.

Lamison-White, Leatha. "Poverty in the United States: 1996." Current Population Reports series. Washington, D.C.: Bureau of the Census. September, 60–198.

Laub, John H., Daniel S. Nagin, and Robert J. Sampson. "Trajectories of Change in Criminal Offending: Good Marriages and the Desistance Process." *American Sociological Review* 63 (1998): 225–38.

Laumann, Edward O., John H. Gagnon, Robert T. Michael, and Stuart Michaels. *The Social Organization of Sexuality: Sexual Practices in the United States*. Chicago: University of Chicago Press, 1994.

Levine, Arthur, and Jeanette S. Cureton. *When Hope and Fear Collide: A Portrait of Today's College Student.* San Francisco: Jossey-Bass, 1998.

Lillard, Lee A., and Constantijn Panis. "Marital Status and Mortality: The Role of Health." *Demography* 33 (1996): 313–27.

Lillard, Lee A., and Linda J. Waite. "A Joint Model of Marital Childbearing and Marital Disruption." *Demography* 30 (1993): 653–82.

———. " 'Til Death Do Us Part: Marital Disruption and Mortality." *American Journal of Sociology* 100 (1995): 1131–56.

Lillard, Lee A., Michael J. Brien, and Linda J. Waite. "Pre-marital Cohabitation and Subsequent Marital Dissolution: Is It Self-selection?" *Demography* 32 (1995): 437–58.

Litwak, Eugene, and Peter Messeri, in collaboration with Samuel Wolfe, Sheila Gorman, Merril Silverstein, and Miguel Guilarte. "Organizational Theory, Social Supports, and Mortality Rates: A Theoretical Convergence." *American Sociological Review* 54 (1989): 49–66.

Logan, John R., and Glenna D. Spitze. *Family Ties: Enduring Relations Between Parents and Their Grown Children.* Philadelphia: Temple University Press, 1996.

Loh, Eng Seng. "Productivity Differences and the Marriage Wage Premium for White Males." *Journal of Human Resources* 31 (1996): 566–89.

Lundberg, Olle. "The Impact of Childhood Living Conditions on Illness and Mortality in Adulthood." *Social Science and Medicine* 36 (1993): 1047–52.

Lupton, Joseph and James P. Smith. "Marriage, Assets, and Savings." In Shoshana Grossbard-Schechtman (ed.), *Marriage and the Economy.* Cambridge, England: Cambridge University Press.

Lye, Diane N., Daniel H. Klepinger, Patricia Davis Hyle, and Anjanette Nelson. "Childhood Living Arrangements and Adult Children's Relations with Their Parents." *Demography* 32 (1995): 261–80.

Manton, K. G., E. Stallard, and M. A. Woodbury. "Longitudinal Models of Disability Changes and Active Life Expectancy in Elderly Populations: The Interaction of Sex, Age and Marital Status." In *Models of Noncommunicable Diseases: Health Status and Health Service Requirements,* edited by W. Morgenstern et al., 113–30. Berlin: Springer-Verlag, 1992.

Margolin, Leslie, and John L. Craft. "Child Sexual Abuse by Caretakers." *Family Relations* 38 (1989): 450–55.

Margolin, Leslie. "Child Abuse by Mother's Boyfriends: Why the Overrepresentation?" *Child Abuse and Neglect* 16 (1992): 541–52.

Marks, Nadine F., and James David Lambert. "Marital Status Continuity and Change among Young and Midlife Adults: Longitudinal Effects on Psychological Well-being." *Journal of Family Issues* 19 (1998): 652–86.

"The Marriage Warnings." *New York Times,* 30 November 1995, Metro section, p. B15.

Marwell, Gerald. "Why Ascription? Parts of a More or Less Formal Theory of the Functions and Dysfunctions of Sex Roles." *American Sociological Review* 40 (1975): 445–55.

Marwell, Nicole. "Meanings of Marriage and Cohabitation: A Qualitative Study of Puerto Rican Women." Master's thesis, The University of Chicago, 1994.

Mastekaasa, Arne. "The Subjective Well-being of the Previously Married: The Importance of Unmarried Cohabitation and Time Since Widowhood or Divorce." *Social Forces* 73 (1994): 665–92.

Matsueda, Ross L., and Karen Heimer. "Race, Family Structure, and Delinquency: A Test of Differential Association and Social Control Theories." *American Sociological Review* 52 (1987): 826–40.

Mattox, William R. Jr. "What's Marriage Got to Do With It?: Good Sex Comes to Those Who Wait." *Family Policy*. Washington, D.C.: Family Research Council, February 1994.

Mauldon, Jane. "The Effects of Marital Disruption on Children's Health." *Demography* 27 (1990): 431–46.

Mayer, Susan E. *What Money Can't Buy: Family Income and Children's Life Chances*. Cambridge, Mass.: Harvard University Press, 1997.

McKinley, James C. Jr. "Giuliani to Combat Domestic Violence with Police and Computers." *New York Times*, 26 April 1994, Metro section, p. B3.

McLanahan, Sara, and Gary D. Sandefur. *Growing Up with a Single Parent: What Hurts, What Helps*. Cambridge, Mass.: Harvard University Press, 1994.

McLeod, Jane D., and Michael J. Shanahan. "Poverty, Parenting, and Children's Mental Health." *American Sociological Review* 58 (1993): 351–66.

McManus, Michael J. *Marriage Savers: Helping Your Friends and Family Avoid Divorce*. Grand Rapids, Mich.: Zondervan Publishing House, 1995.

Miller, Naomi. *Single Parents by Choice: A Growing Trend in Family Life*. New York: Insight Books, 1992.

Miller-Tutzauer, Carol, Kenneth E. Leonard, and Michael Windle. "Marriage and Alcohol Use: A Longitudinal Study of 'Maturing Out.'" *Journal of Studies on Alcohol* 52 (1991): 434–40.

Mintz, Steven, and Susan Kellogg. *Domestic Revolutions: A Social History of American Family Life*. New York: The Free Press, 1988.

Mirowsky, John. "Age and the Gender Gap in Depression." *Journal of Health and Social Behavior* 37 (1996): 362–80.

Mirowsky, John, and Catherine E. Ross. *Social Causes of Psychological Distress*. New York: Aldine de Gruyter, 1989.

Mitchell, Susan. *The Official Guide to American Attitudes: Who Thinks What about the Issues That Shape Our Lives*. Ithaca, N.Y.: New Strategist Publications, 1996.

Mitchell, Wayne, and Tamara Mitchell. "When You Marry for a Reason Other Than Love." *Bonkers* (March/April) 20–22.

Mossey, J. M., and E. Shapiro. "Self-rated Health: A Predictor of Mortality among the Elderly." *American Journal of Public Health* 72 (1982): 800–808.

Murphy, Mike, Karen Glaser, and Emily Grundy. "Marital Status and Long-term Illness in Great Britain." *Journal of Marriage and the Family* 59 (1997): 156–64.

Musick, Judith S. *Young, Poor, and Pregnant: The Psychology of Teenage Motherhood*. New Haven: Yale University Press, 1993.

Nagin, Daniel S., and Raymond Peternoster. "Personal Capital and Social Control: The Deterrence Implications of Individual Differences in Criminal Offending." *Criminology* 32 (1994): 581–606.

National Research Council. *Measuring Poverty: A New Approach*, edited by Constance F. Citro and Robert T. Michael. Washington, D.C.: National Academy Press, 1995.

Nock, Steven L. *Marriage in Men's Lives*. New York: Oxford University Press, 1998.

———. "The Consequences of Premarital Fatherhood." *American Sociological Review* 63 (1998): 250–63.

O'Neill, Nena, and George O'Neill. *Open Marriage: A New Life Style for Couples*. New York: M. Evens and Company, 1972.

Ooms, Theodora. *Toward More Perfect Unions: Putting Marriage on the Public Agenda*. Washington D.C.: Family Impact Seminar, 1998.

Oppenheimer, Valerie Kincade. "The Role of Economic Factors in Union Formation." In *Ties That Bind: Perspectives on Marriage and Cohabitation,* edited by Linda Waite, Christine Bachrach, Michelle Hindin, Elizabeth Thomson, and Arland Thornton. Forthcoming.

Oropesa, R. S. "Normative Beliefs about Marriage and Cohabitation: A Comparison of Non-Latino Whites, Mexican Americans, and Puerto Ricans." *Journal of Marriage and the Family* 58, (1996): 668–78.

Orthner, Dennis K. "The Family in Transition." In *Rebuilding the Nest: A New Commitment to the American Family,* edited by David Blankenhorn, Steven Bayme, and Jean Bethke Elshtain, 93–118. Milwaukee, Wisc.: Family Service America, 1990.

Øyen, Nina, Trond Markestad, Rolv Skjaerven, Lorentz M. Irgens, Karin Helweg-Larsen, Bernt Alm, Gunnar Norvenius, and Goran Wennergren. "Combined Effects of Sleeping Position and Prenatal Risk Factors in Sudden Infant Death Syndrome: The Nordic Epidemiological SIDS Study." *Pediatrics* 100 (1997): 613–21.

Papanek, Hanna. "Men, Women, and Work: Reflections on the Two-person Career." *American Journal of Sociology* 78 (1973): 852–72.

Parcel, Toby L., and Elizabeth G. Menaghan. *Parents' Jobs and Children's Lives.* New York: Aldine de Gruyter, 1994.

Parkman, Alan. "Why Are Married Women Working So Hard?" *International Review of Law and Economics* 18, (1998): 41–49.

Pennebaker, James W. "Writing about Emotional Experiences as a Therapeutic Process." *Psychological Science* 8 (1997): 162–66.

Peterson, Karen S. "Does Tying the Knot Put Women in a Bind?" *USA Today,* 22 April 1997.

———. "Opinions Split over Avoiding Divorce." *USA Today,* 25 July 1998.

Peterson, Richard R. "A Re-evaluation of the Economic Consequences of Divorce." *American Sociological Review* 61 (1996): 528–36.

Petrucelli, Alan W. "Mel Harris: We Are Not the Waltons," *Working Mother,* December 1996.

Popenpoe, David. *Changes in Teen Attitudes Toward Marriage, Cohabitation, and Children, 1975–1995.* New Brunswick, N.J.: National Marriage Project, 1999.

Presser, Harriet B. "Shift Work and Child Care among Young Dual-earner American Parents." *Journal of Marriage and the Family* 50 (1988): 133–48.

Preston, Samuel H., and John McDonald. "The Incidence of Divorce within Cohorts of American Marriages Contracted Since the Civil War." *Demography* 16 (1979): 1–26.

Ray, Oakley Stern. *Drugs, Society, and Human Behavior.* St Louis: Mosby, 1972.

Regan, Milton C. Jr. "Postmodern Family Law: Toward a New Model of Status." In *Promises to Keep: Decline and Renewal of Marriage in America,* edited by David Popenoe, Jean Bethke Elshtain, and David Blankenhorn, 157–85. Lanham, MD: Rowman and Littlefield, 1996.

Rindfuss, Ronald R., and Audrey VandenHeuvel. "Cohabitation: Precursor to Marriage or Alternative to Being Single?" *Population and Development Review* 16 (1990): 703–26.

Roberts, Ian. "Sole Parenthood and the Risk of Child Pedestrian Injury." *Journal of Pediatrics and Child Health* 30 (1994): 530–32.

Robinson, John P., and Geoffrey Godbey. *Time for Life: The Surprising Ways Americans Use Their Time.* University Park, PA: Pennsylvania State University Press, 1997.

Roizen, Michael F. *RealAge: Are You as Young as You Can Be?* New York: Cliff Street Books, 1999.

Roper Center Data Review. "The Family: Marriage: Highly Valued." *The Public Perspective* 9, no. 8 (1998): 17.

————. "Why is Divorce So Common?" *The Public Perspective* 9, no. 8 (1998): 19.

————. "Americans Rate Their Society and Chart Its Values: A Roper Center Review of Findings of the General Social Survey and the 1996 Survey of American Political Culture." *The Public Perspective* 8, no. 2 (1997): 1–27.

Rosenbaum, Ron. "Staring into the Heart of the Heart of Darkness." *New York Times,* 4 June 1995, Magazine section, pp. 36–45, 50, 58, 61, 72.

Ross, Catherine E. "Reconceptualizing Marital Status as a Continuum of Social Attachment." *Journal of Marriage and the Family* 57 (1995): 129–40.

Ross, Catherine E., and John Mirowsky. "Child Care and Emotional Adjustment to Wives' Employment." *Journal of Health and Social Behavior* 29, (1988): 127–38.

Ross, Catherine E., John Mirowsky, and Karen Goldsteen. "The Impact of the Family on Health: Decade in Review." *Journal of Marriage and the Family* 52 (1990): 1059–78.

Ryff, Carol D., and Corey Lee M. Keyes. "The Structure of Psychological Well-being Revisited." *Journal of Personality and Social Psychology* 69 (1995): 719–27.

Sampson, Robert J. "Urban Black Violence: The Effect of Male Joblessness and Family Disruption." *American Journal of Sociology* 93 (1987): 348–82.

Schnarch, David M. *Constructing the Sexual Crucible: An Integration of Sexual and Marital Therapy.* New York: Norton, 1991.

Schoeni, Robert F. "Marital Status and Earnings in Developed Countries." *Journal of Population Economics* 8 (1995): 351–59.

Shaw, Kathryn L. "The Quit Propensity of Married Men." *Journal of Labor Economics* 5 (1987): 533–60.

Shelton, Beth Anne. *Women, Men, and Time: Gender Differences in Paid Work, Housework, and Leisure.* Westport, Conn.: Greenwood, 1992.

Sherman, Lawrence W., with Janell D. Schmidt, Dennis P. Rogan. *Policing Domestic Violence: Experiments and Dilemmas.* New York: The Free Press, 1992.

Sierpina, Diane. "Putting an End to a Loved One's Violence." *New York Times,* 9 June 1996, Connecticut Weekly, sec. 13, pp. 1, 12–13.

Skolnick, Arlene S. *Embattled Paradise: The American Family in an Age of Uncertainty.* New York: Basic Books, 1991.

————. *The Intimate Environment: Exploring Marriage and the Family,* 6th. ed. New York: HarperCollins, 1996.

Smith, Jack C., James A. Mercy, and Judith M. Conn. "Marital Status and the Risk of Suicide." *American Journal of Public Health* 78 (1988): 78–80.

"Sociologists Differ about Family Textbooks' Message." *Footnotes* 26, no. 1 (1998): 7, 10.

Sørenson, Annemette. "Women's Economic Risk and the Economic Position of Single Mothers." *European Sociological Review* 10 (1994): 173–88.

Sorenson, Susan B., Dawn M. Upchurch, and Haikang Shen. "Violence and Injury in Marital Arguments: Risk Patterns and Gender Differences." *American Journal of Public Health* 86, (1996): 35–40.

South, Scott J., and Glenna D. Spitze. "Housework in Marital and Nonmarital Households." *American Sociological Review* 59 (1994): 327–47.

Spruijt, Ed, and Martijn de Goede. "Transition in Family Structure and Adolescent Well-being," *Adolescence* 32 (Winter 1997): 897–911.

Stack, Steven, and James H. Gundlach. "Divorce and Sex." *Archives of Sexual Behavior* 21 (1992): 359–67.

Stack, Steven, and J. Ross Eshleman. "Marital Status and Happiness: A 17-Nation Study." *Journal of Marriage and the Family* 60 (1998): 527–36.

Stanley, Scott M., and Howard J. Markman. "Assessing Commitment in Personal Relationships." *Journal of Marriage and the Family* 54 (1992): 595–608.

Stanley, Scott M., and Howard J. Markman. *Marriage in the '90s: A Nationwide Random Phone Survey.* Denver, Colo.: PREP, Inc., 1997.

Stanton, Glenn T. *Why Marriage Matters: Reasons to Believe in Marriage in a Postmodern Society.* Colorado Springs, Colo.: Piñon, 1997.

Stark, Evan, and Lawrence Sherman. "Should Police Officers be Required to Arrest Abusive Husbands?" *Health* 8 (1994): 32.

Stets, Jan E. "Cohabiting and Marital Aggression: The Role of Social Isolation." *Journal of Marriage and the Family* 53 (1991): 669–80.

Stets, Jan E., and Murray A. Straus. "The Marriage License as a Hitting License: A Comparison of Assaults in Dating, Cohabiting, and Married Couples." In *Physical Violence in American Families: Risk Factors and Adaptations to Violence in 8,145 Families,* edited by Murray A. Straus and Richard J. Gelles, with the assistance of Christine Smith, 227–44. New Brunswick, N.J.: Transaction Publishers, 1990.

Steuerle, C. Eugene. "A Comprehensive Approach to Removing Marriage Penalties." In *Strengthening American Marriages: A Communitarian Perspective,* edited by M. K. Whyte, with contributions by D. Browning and W. Doherty. Forthcoming. Rowman and Littlefield.

———. "The Effects of Tax and Welfare Policies on Family Formation." In *Strategies for Strengthening Marriage: What Do We Know? What Do We Need to Know?* Washington, D.C.: Family Impact Seminar, 1998.

Steuerle, C. Eugene, Edward M. Gramlich, Hugh Heclo, and Demetra Smith Nightingale. *The Government We Deserve: Responsive Democracy and Changing Expectations.* Washington, D.C.: Urban Institute Press, 1998.

Stolzenberg, Ross M. "It's About Time and Gender: The Effect of Wife's and Husband's Employment on Their Own and Each Other's Health." Working Paper, Alfred P. Sloan Center on Parents, Children, and Work, University of Chicago, 2000.

———. "What is the Effect of One Spouse's Employment on the Other Spouse's Health?" Working Paper 99–15. Alfred P. Sloan Center on Parents, Children, and Work, University of Chicago, 1999.

Straus, Murray A. "Physical Assaults by Wives: A Major Social Problem." In *Current Controversies on Family Violence,* edited by Richard J. Gelles and Donileen R. Loseke, 67–87. Newbury Park, Calif.: Sage Publications, 1993.

Strong, Bryan, and Christine DeVault, eds. *The Marriage and Family Experience.* Minneapolis/St. Paul, Minn.: West Publishing, 1995.

"Studies Show Men Do Better in Marriage than Women." *Jet,* May 12, 1997, 18.

Thomson, Elizabeth, and Ugo Collela. "Cohabitation and Marital Stability: Quality or Commitment?" *Journal of Marriage and the Family* 54 (1992): 259–68.

Thornton, Arland. "Reciprocal Influences of Family and Religion in a Changing World." *Journal of Marriage and the Family* 47 (1985): 381–94.

———. "Changing Attitudes toward Family Issues in the United States." *Journal of Marriage and the Family* 51 (1989): 873–93.

Townsend, John Marshall. "Sex without Emotional Involvement: An Evolutionary Interpretation of Sex Differences." *Archives of Sexual Behavior* 24 (1995): 173–206.

Treas, Judith. "Money in the Bank: Transaction Costs and the Economic Organization of Marriage." *American Sociological Review* (1993): 723–34.

Tucker, Joan S., Howard S. Friedman, Joseph E. Schwartz, Michael H. Criqui et al. "Parental Divorce: Effects on Individual Behavior and Longevity." *Journal of Personality and Social Psychology* 73 (1997): 381–91.

U.S. Bureau of the Census. *Measuring the Effect of Benefits and Taxes on Income and Poverty: 1992.* Current Population Reports, Series P-60, Consumer Income; no. 186-RD. Washington, D.C.: U.S. Government Printing Office, 1993.

———. *Statistical Abstract of the United States: 1996* (116th ed). Washington, D.C., 1996.

———. *Statistical Abstract of the United States: 1997* (117th ed). Washington, D.C., 1997.

———. *Marital Status and Living Arrangements,* March 1997. Current Population Reports, Series P20, No. 506. Washington, D.C.: U.S. Government Printing Office, 1998.

Umberson, Debra. "Family Status and Health Behaviors: Social Control as a Dimension of Social Integration." *Journal of Health and Social Behavior* 28 (1987): 306–19.

———. "Gender, Marital Status, and the Social Control of Health Behavior." *Social Science and Medicine* 34 (1992): 907–17.

Umberson, Debra, Meichu D. Chen, James S. House, Kristine Hopkins, and Ellen Slaten. "The Effect of Social Relationships on Psychological Well-being: Are Men and Women Really So Different?" *American Sociological Review* 61 (1996): 837–57.

Ventura, Stephanie, Joyce A. Martin, Sally C. Curtin, and T. J. Matthews. "Report of Final Natality Statistics, 1996." *Monthly Vital Statistics Report* 46(11), supp. Hyattsville, MD: National Center for Health Statistics, 1998.

Verbrugge, Lois M. "Marital Status and Health." *Journal of Marriage and the Family* 41 (1979): 267–85.

Waite, Linda J. "Does Marriage Matter?" *Demography* 32 (1995): 483–507.

Waite, Linda J., Gus W. Haggstrom, and David E. Kanouse. "Changes in the Employment Activities of New Parents." *American Sociological Review* 50 (1985): 263–72.

———. "The Effects of Parenthood on the Career Orientation and Job Characteristics of Young Adults." *Social Forces* 65 (1986): 43–73.

Waite, Linda J., and Kara Joyner. "Emotional and Physical Satisfaction in Married, Cohabiting, and Dating Sexual Unions: Do Men and Women Differ?" In *Studies on Sex,* edited by E. Laumann and R. Michael. Chicago: University of Chicago Press. Forthcoming.

Waite, Linda J., and Lee A. Lillard. "Children and Marital Disruption." *American Journal of Sociology* 96 (1991): 930–53.

Waite, Linda J., and Mark R. Nielsen. "The Rise of the Dual-Career Family." In *Work and Family: Today's Realities and Tomorrow's Visions,* edited by R. Hertz and N. Marshall. University of California Press. Forthcoming.

Waite, Linda J., and Mary Elizabeth Hughes. "At Risk on the Cusp of Old Age: Living Arrangements and Functional Status among Black, White, and Hispanic Adults." *Journal of Gerontology: Social Sciences,* 54B, no. 3 (1999): S136–S144.

Waldfogel, Jane. "The Effect of Children on Women's Wages." *American Sociological Review* 62 (1997): 209–17.

Wallerstein, Judith S. Speech before the Second Annual Congress of American Family and Conciliation Courts, June 6, 1997. Text supplied by the author.

Wallerstein, Judith S., and Sandra Blakeslee. *The Good Marriage: How and Why Love Lasts.* Boston: Houghton Mifflin, 1995.

"Warning: Marriage Could Be Hazardous." *New York Times,* 19 February 1995, sec. 1, p. 40.

Webster-Stratton, Carolyn. "The Relationship of Marital Support, Conflict, and Divorce to Parent Perceptions, Behaviors, and Childhood Conduct Problems." *Journal of Marriage and the Family* 51 (1989): 417–30.

Weiss, Robert S. *Staying the Course: The Emotional and Social Lives of Men Who Do Well at Work.* New York: The Free Press, 1990.

Whitehead, Barbara Dafoe. *Promises to Keep: Decline and Renewal of Marriage in America.* Lanham, MD: Rowman and Littlefield, 1996.

———. "The Experts' Story of Marriage." Council on Families Working Paper WP14. New York: Institute for American Values, 1992.

Whitehead, Barbara Dafoe, and David Popenoe. *Why Wed?:Young Adults Talk about Sex, Love, and First Unions.* New Brunswick, N.J.: The National Marriage Project, 1999.

Wickrama, K. A. S., Frederick O. Lorenz, Rand D. Conger, and Glen H. Elder Jr. "Marital Quality and Physical Illness: A Latent Growth Curve Analysis." *Journal of Marriage and the Family* 59 (1997): 143–55.

Wilmoth, Janet. "The Timing of Marital Events over the Life Course and Pre-retirement Wealth Outcomes." Paper presented at the meetings of the Population Association of America, Chicago, April 1998.

Wilson, Margo I., and Martin Daly. "Who Kills Whom in Spouse Killings?: On the Exceptional Sex Ratio of Spousal Homicides in the United States." *Criminology* 30 (1992): 189–215.

Yamaguchi, Kazuo, and Denise B. Kandel. "Dynamic Relationships Between Premarital Cohabitation and Illicit Drug Use: An Event-History Analysis of Role Selection and Role Socialization." *American Sociological Review* 50 (1985): 530–46.

Zick, Cathleen D., and Ken R. Smith. "Immediate and Delayed Effects of Widowhood on Poverty: Patterns from the 1970s." *The Gerontologist* 26 (1986): 669–75.

Zill, Nicholas. "Understanding Why Children in Stepfamilies Have More Learning and Behavior Problems than Children in Nuclear Families." In *Stepfamilies: Who Benefits? Who Does Not?* edited by Alan Booth and Judy Dunn, 97–106. Hillsdale, N.J.: Lawrence Erlbaum Associates, 1994.

Acknowledgments

This book has been a truly collaborative project; so many people gave time, advice, comments, and especially support and encouragement that we were overwhelmed with the generosity of others.

First, this book would never have happened without Michael Aronson of Harvard University Press, who suggested the idea in the first place. I also owe intellectual debts (that we hope to repay at some later time) to my colleagues who pointed me toward recent or seminal articles, scanned the literature in their field for evidence on key arguments, read drafts of chapters, and critiqued early efforts. Nicholas Christakis did an electronic search of the literature on physiological effects of marriage when I asked him a general question on the topic. Catherine Ross answered countless e-mails on the relationship between marriage and psychological well-being and read our drafts of the chapter on marriage and emotional health. Shoshana Grossbard-Shechtman acted as our advisor and reviewer on the economics of marriage, especially marriage and earnings. Janice Kiecolt-Glaser acted as a sounding board when I pushed her research on marriage and physiological functioning way past their original focus. Nadine Marks and James Lambert reestimated their models for us so I could prepare special graphics on their results on emotional well-being of married and unmarried men and women. Theodora Ooms read the recommendations chapter and gave us sage advice on what to say and better advise on what not to say. Scott Stanley ran some estimates from his data on cohabiting, engaged, and married couples so we could couch his findings the way we wanted. Stephanie Ventura gave us an insider's view of statistics on marriage and divorce at the National Center for Health Statistics. Steven Nock read and critiqued the manuscript, pointing out where I misunderstood divorce law. Arland Thornton read and encouraged. Diane Sollee cheered us from the sidelines during the whole process. Rabbi Charley Dobrusin supplied me with the text of the *Ketubah,* the Jewish marriage contract. And Sara McLanahan suggested that a social scientist could learn a few things about writing from a writer, encouraging the collaboration that produced this book.

We also give special thanks to the students in a graduate seminar on family and household demography that I taught in the winter of 1998. After some arm-twisting, the students agreed to critique an early manuscript of this book. They did a wonderful job, with lots of ideas of new directions, places where the argument didn't work, and infectious excitement about the whole effort. Thanks to Katy Puckett, Jack Iwashyna, Elaine Marchena, Yoosik Youm, Yun-Suk Lee, Joaquim Vieira, M. Delia Ramirez, Jeff Reynolds, Jibum Kim, and Mark Nielsen. I hope your students can do something as nice for all of you sometime.

This whole project started when I was elected president of the Population Association of America, the professional association of demographers, and had to write a presidential address. That address, "Does Marriage Matter?" lays out the key argument that we make here. I am grateful to the PAA for giving me the opportunity to think broadly about a topic—marriage—at the heart of population studies.

None of this work would have been done without the coauthors who shared in the research that laid the foundation of this book. Lee Lillard had the original idea to look closely at the relationship between marital status and risk of dying. Trying to explain our findings started me thinking about the social institution of marriage and exactly how it worked. Kara Joyner and I started our work on sexual activity and sexual satisfaction *because* I was thinking about what marriage did for people. Marin Clarkberg, Rafe Stolzenberg, and I looked at why people pick cohabitation rather than marriage for their first union, giving me some insights into what, exactly, cohabitation is and what it offers. Mary Elizabeth Hughes and I compared the functioning of older men and women, married and single, and found some striking—and disturbing—differences that we report here. Michael Brien and Lee Lillard let me join a study they were doing on the links between cohabitation, marriage, and child-bearing. And Rafe Stolzenberg, Mary Blair-Loy, and I looked at the ways that marriage, cohabitation, and parenthood drew people or pushed them toward religious institutions. I thank them for the intellectual exchanges and for their ideas.

I want to give special thanks to both the National Institute on Aging and the National Institute on Child Health and Human Development for their support of my research on marriage. Richard Suzman of NIA and Christine Bachrach of NICHD both supported and encouraged my research efforts. I can't thank them enough.

And a team of University of Chicago students helped get this project done. Becky Sandefur put together data on trends in marriage. Nate Radley spent the summer after graduation listening to music on his headphones while he checked all the references in the bibliography for accuracy. Christine Li and Jennifer Barba looked up journal articles, tracked down quotes, and got involved with and excited about the ideas. Susan Lee struggled with the index. And Nick Dempsey put the manuscript into final form, located all the impossible-to-find cites, and pointed out where things didn't fit.

One person gave far more than anyone except a coauthor should. Fran Goldscheider read the first draft of the manuscript and made notes on every page. She argued with our reasoning and pushed us to be more evenhanded. She told us where we needed to give another perspective and pointed us toward the authors and articles to do it. She read the revised text to let us know if we had gotten it right. This is true friendship.

We need to thank the institutions that supported us while we wrote this book, the University of Chicago and the Institute for American Values. Both gave us the freedom to speak our minds, and the time to put our thoughts into words.

And, finally, I want to thank my husband, who, early in my career, believed in me when no one else did. He often put his own goals aside to help me reach mine.

Thank you all.

—Linda Waite

Two people made my participation in this book possible: David Blankenhorn, president of the Institute for American Values, who knows a good idea when he sees one; and Linda Waite, whose intellectual courage conceived this book in the first place, whose painstaking years of original research made it possible, and whose brilliance, intellectual generosity, and kindness of heart made the process of working on it a rare privilege and a delight.

—Maggie Gallagher

Index

130–132, 183; and children's psychological health, 124, 125, 128–129, 132, 146–147, 183; and children's relationships with fathers, 128; vs. conflict, as damaging to children, 132, 138, 139, 143, 144, 147; educational effects on children, 133–134; family professionals' views of, 4, 7, 143–148, 176–178, 188–189; fear of, 180; financial impact on women and children, 99, 106, 108, 118–120, 126, 196–197; government statistics on, 191–194; and happiness/ psychological well-being, 57, 67, 68, 70, 73–74; and illegitimacy in next generation, 136–137, 184; and immune function, 57; and income, 99, 101, 106, 107, 108; and net worth, 112, 113, 120; no-fault, 101, 178–180, 182, 195–196; probability of, and husbands' wage premium, 180; required waiting periods for, 196; risk of, for single mothers who marry, 184; and sex, 78, 79, 82; staying together for sake of children, 4, 7, 142–148, 177; and suicide, 67; support/counseling for couples considering, 189, 191, 196, 198. *See also* adult children of divorce

divorced men, and health-compromising behaviors, 53, 55

divorced women: and health-compromising behaviors, 59; mental health deterioration, 70

divorce law, 108, 109, 178–180, 195–196; Americans for Divorce Reform, 206

divorce rates, 143, 179, 187, 188, 195; of cohabitors who marry, 46

domestic partnership legislation, 10, 200, 201

domestic violence, 5–6, 150–160; child abuse, 135, 159; and cohabitation, 155–156, 157, 158; dating couples, 150, 151; and family ties, 158–159; killings, 154, 155; mandatory arrest policies, 158; rates of physical violence and injury, 152–154, 155–156; two types of, 153; warning labels on marriage licenses, 152; women as initiators of, 153

drug use, 54–55, 131, 134. *See also* substance abuse

Durkheim, Émile, 75

Earned Income Tax Credit, 194–195

earnings. See income

economic partnership, marriage as, 25–31, 40, 174–175

economic specialization of spouses, 25–30, 102–103, 114, 187

education: advantages to children of married parents, 133–134, 136; effects of divorce on, 147; and income, 122, 147; and single parenthood, 199–200; of wives, and husbands' earning power, 104, 105. *See also* school performance

elderly people: and depression, 166–167; health benefits of marriage for, 60–61

Ellwood, David, 122, 202

emotional health. *See* psychological health

emotional support, spouses as providers of, 31–33, 56–58, 68–70, 77

employment benefits, 9–10, 15, 21. *See also* domestic partnership legislation

environmental mastery, 70

Essex, Marilyn, 165

Ettlebrick, Paula, 9–10

extramarital sex. *See* infidelity

fairness issues in marriage, 171, 172, 181

family professionals: responsibility to support marriage, 188–190; views of divorce, 4, 7, 143–148, 176–178, 188–189

Family Relations, 151

family relationships: children of single/divorced parents, 125, 128–129; cohabitors and, 42–43; and domestic violence, 158–159; and financial support, 117–118

Family Research Council, 95

family structure: changes in, 171–172, 202; and children's well-being, 11, 138; and juvenile delinquency, 134–135; and net worth, 111–114

family violence. *See* domestic violence

father-child relationships, 128, 129, 139

fathers: sharing of income with children, 119, 126; single fathers, 126

federal government: marriage/divorce data collection by, 191–194. *See also* public policy

Feminine Mystique, The (Friedan), 163

feminist critiques of marriage, 1, 163

fidelity, 19, 39, 90–94. *See also* infidelity

finances, 18–19, 21, 30–31; and cohabitation, 39–41; effects of marriage on income, 97–109; effects of marriage on wealth

jealousy, and violence, 157
Jencks, Christopher, 121
Jewish marriage contract, 95
Johnson, Michael, 153
Journal of Marriage and the Family, 47
Joyner, Kara, 84, 86, 93
juvenile crime/delinquency, 129, 134–135

Karoly, Lynn, 118
Kellogg, Susan, 1
Kessler, Ronald C., 165
ketubah, 95
Kiecolt-Glaser, Janice, 56–57
Kiernan, Kathleen, 132
killings, 154, 155
Kirshenbaum, Mira, 177
Korenman, Sanders, 101
Kotlikoff, Laurence, 115
Krantzler, Mel, 4
Krantzler, Pat, 4
Kurz, Demie, 143

Lambert, James, 69–70, 167
Laumann, Edward, 79
lawyers, and no-fault divorce, 178
Lee, Gary, 161
Lee, I-Sing, 48
leisure time, 44
lesbian marriage, 20, 200–201
life expectancy, 50–51, 131. *See also* death rates
Lillard, Lee, 50, 59, 184
loneliness, 76, 77
Louisiana Covenant Marriage Act, 196
love, sex as expression of, 84–85, 89–90
Lupton, Joseph, 112

McLanahan, Sara, 121, 125, 126–127, 133, 136, 139
McRae, Christine, 125
Margolin, Leslie, 159
Markman, Howard, 79, 82, 85, 168–169
Marks, Nadine, 69–70, 167
marriage: attitudes about, 1–3, 7–9, 174, 183; changes in use of term, 8–9, 177–178; as damaging to women, 5, 161–168; as economic partnership, 25–31, 40, 174–175; eroding support for, 174–185; fairness issues, 171, 172, 181; feminist critiques of, 1, 163; as financial union,

40–41; government statistics on, 191–194; myths about, 4–7; privatization of, 6, 8, 11–12, 16–17; proposals to support, 188–201; as public contract, 17, 18–23; as public good, 186; as sexual union, 94–95; as threat to individual fulfillment, 1, 66; traditional models of, 14–15, 171–172, 181
marriage contract: enforceability of, 178; public nature of, 17, 18–23
"Marriage License as a Hitting License, The," 150
marriage licenses, warning labels on, 152
marriage penalties, in public policy, 175, 194–195
marriage preparation/education, 189–190, 197–199, 205
marriage quality: and attitudes toward divorce, 181–182; and children's well-being, 141–149; health effects of, 56–57, 74; surveys of, 74–75, 168–169. *See also* unhappy marriages
Marriage Savers, 205
Marriage Savers (McManus), 198
Marriage Shock (Heyn), 78
marriage vow, 23–24, 34
masculinity, and husband role, 29
Matsueda, Ross, 134–135
Mayer, Susan, 127
meaning, shared sense of, 62–63, 75–76
Medicaid, 199
medical benefits of marriage. *See* health effects of marriage
men: father-child relationships, 128, 129, 139; financial benefits of marriage for, 60, 99–105; health effects of marriage for, 53–56, 62, 164, 166, 171–172; health risks of single men, 51, 53–55; income sharing with children, 119, 126; life expectancy, 50; roles of, 14, 29, 76; single fathers, 126
mental health. *See* psychological health
Mintz, Steven, 1
Mirowsky, John, 166
money. *See* finances; income; wealth
Monitoring the Future survey, 63–64
monogamy: and sexual satisfaction, 90–94. *See also* fidelity
Morowitz, Harold, 47
mortality rates. *See* death rates
mother-child relationships, 128
motherhood: and earning power, 107–109; and household duties, 106–107; as

Gerald Peskin

Charles Bork

LINDA J. WAITE is a professor of sociology at the University of Chicago and the author of *New Families, No Families*. She lives in Glencoe, Illinois.

MAGGIE GALLAGHER is a director of the Marriage Program at the Institute of American Values, a nationally syndicated columnist, and the author of *Enemies of Eros*. She lives in New York City.